CW00690822

SONS OF VULCAN

ROBERT DUNCAN
SONS OF VULCAN
IRONWORKERS AND STEELMEN IN SCOTLAND

BIRLINN

To all industrial workers who wrestle with metal and fire

First published in 2009 by
Birlinn Limited
West Newington House
10 Newington Road
Edinburgh
EH9 1QS

www.birlinn.co.uk

Copyright © Robert Duncan 2008

The moral right of Robert Duncan to be
identified as the author of this work has been
asserted by him in accordance with the
Copyright, Designs and Patents Act 1988.

All rights reserved. No part of this
publication may be reproduced, stored or
transmitted in any form without the express
written permission of the publisher.

ISBN: 978 1 84158 769 1

British Library Cataloguing-in-Publication Data
A catalogue record for this book is available
from the British Library

Designed and typeset by Mark Blackadder

Printed and bound by Bell & Bain Ltd, Glasgow

CONTENTS

ACKNOWLEDGEMENTS

Although writing this historical survey of industrial work in Scotland was an individual task, I want to acknowledge the professional and voluntary assistance of many people during its three years of research and preparation. I am grateful to other historians and writers whose published and unpublished work contributed in any way to this book, and trust that my use of such sources is duly recorded. In this regard, there are too many fellow historians to thank by name, but I wish to record special thanks to Neil Ballantyne, whose excellent doctoral thesis provided many important insights, fresh sources and useful points of comparison with my own findings and conclusions on work processes and industrial relations in the iron and steel heartland of late nineteenth-century Lanarkshire.

I spent many hours in the Local History Room at Motherwell Heritage Centre, where Margaret, Steven and Brian were courteous and patient in responding to my seemingly endless orders for materials. I thank Brian Hall for computerised screening of illustrations from photographs and prints in North Lanarkshire Council's Museums and Heritage collections, and for reproducing some other images for the book. Museums and Heritage staff at Summerlee, Airdrie Library and Lenziemill were also helpful and resourceful, as were their Ayrshire colleagues at Dick Institute, Kilmarnock, for census and other sources. The indefatigable Audrey Canning at Research Collections, Glasgow Caledonian University, tracked down some rare trade union items on foundry work.

Yet again, I am indebted to staff at the National Library, Edinburgh, and Mitchell Library, Glasgow, for their expertise and effort, and to local library staff in Strathaven for dealing with many requests for inter-library loans. I am also grateful to North Ayrshire Council archive staff at Ardrossan and to the School of Scottish Studies, Edinburgh, for access to photocopies of transcripts from the oral history project on Glengarnock; and to my former employers at the Workers Educational Association for access to recordings and transcripts from part of its extensive Salt of the Earth project. Here, I wish to pay tribute to the late Neil Rafeek, a diligent and skilled oral historian, who worked closely with me on this project nearly ten years ago. He did most to create a valuable primary source from recorded testimonies of Lanarkshire steelmen, and I hope that he would have applauded my selection of this testimony in the final chapters.

Finally, I wish to thank my wife, Anne, for compiling yet another index; for rescuing me from computer problems; and for her unfailing encouragement and support.

Robert Duncan
Strathaven
January 2009

CHAPTER 1
FURNACE, FOUNDRY AND FORGE:
THE IRON INDUSTRY AND IRON WORKERS
BEFORE THE INDUSTRIAL REVOLUTION

PROLOGUE

On Boxing Day, 1760, at the Carron Iron Works near Falkirk, four miles upriver on the Firth of Forth, a crew of furnace-fillers worked a long shift, supervised by skilled furnace-keepers from Coalbrookdale, in distant Shropshire. Their principal task throughout the day was phased manual loading of numerous charges of heavy raw materials – a mix of coking coal, ironstone and limestone – from a raised platform into the mouth of a forty foot high, open-topped, new model blast furnace. Carron Company had been formed a year earlier, the foundations of the works constructed on a greenfield site, and the first of its four planned blast furnaces 'blown in' and made ready for production. For everyone with a stake in the enterprise, a strong sense of occasion and anticipation attended this event as, for several hours, they awaited the conclusion of the carefully regulated, coke-fired smelting process. After the slag had been drawn off, the moment arrived with the final tapping or pouring of the molten metal from the furnace into the channels of the cooling sand bed, and the expectation of a successful outcome in the form of good-quality pig iron for the foundry.

For the owner partners, English industrialists Dr John Roebuck and Samuel Garbett and the Edinburgh merchant capitalist William Cadell, it was a test of their investment and enterprise, and of their trust in the superior capacity and productivity of the coke-fired process over the traditional charcoal-fired furnace. For the master smelters from Coalbrookdale, it was yet another demonstration of their expertise as skilled workers, proud of their craft and their proven ability to wrestle and transform to a productive end the highly volatile, and physically dangerous, cauldron of roasting raw minerals. For the crew of incoming, already experienced, English furnacemen now employed at Carron, it was a virtual baptism of fire in a strange country. Moreover, if this latest trial proved positive, while no long-term employment could ever be guaranteed, there were at least some prospects of work at relatively high wages for this class of worker, as long as he remained capable, industrious and sober.

On the first day of production and for some time thereafter, the smelting process and quality of iron did not work out entirely as expected. Consequently, furnace-keepers were ordered to experiment further with other grades of coking coal, regulation and intensity of the heats, composition of the layers of coke, ore and limestone flux, timing of the loading of this charge, and tapping operations. Yet, despite the need for such pragmatic trial and error, owners and workers alike were on the verge of achieving an important milestone in the industrial history of Scotland. Carron was the first ironworks in the country to pioneer and adopt the techniques of coke-fired smelting that had been developed successfully by the Darby family of iron masters at Coalbrookdale. It was also the first ironworks to exploit ore and coal from the carboniferous measures of central Scotland, and to employ its own ironstone miners and colliers.

Carron was conceived and built as an integrated ironworks, accessing neighbouring resources of iron ore and coal, and consuming its own furnace iron in several extensive foundry workshops and forges. However, although it can be argued that the new Carron complex marked the birth of large-scale heavy industry in Scotland, it did not provide the catalyst for an immediate take-off into the industrial revolution in that sector. As a prototype modern ironworks, Carron stood alone for over twenty years. Its example was followed elsewhere in the Central Lowlands between 1779 and 1801, when a coke-fired smelting industry was established at various locations across the coal and iron fields. Until then, and despite various financial, technical and labour problems during the troubled 1760s, Carron built a reputation in Britain and abroad for an impressive range of cast-iron goods designed by versatile pattern makers, and made by teams of iron founders and moulders. One of the largest foundries in Europe, it was also a munitions factory, and from the 1770s until the end of the wars with France in 1815, a major producer of cannon for the British state.[1]

INTRODUCTORY SURVEY

Before Carron, the iron industry in Scotland existed on a small scale. Although on the verge of fundamental change in country and town by the middle of the eighteenth century, Scotland was still an economically backward country, the great bulk of its population a poverty stricken agrarian, rural society. In those adverse conditions of life, there was no domestic mass market for iron goods and no mass production technique available to service that demand, had it existed. Moreover, making and refining iron was dependent on traditional charcoal-fired processes which were relatively slow and expensive, and thus costly to customers.

Charcoal is a product of partly seasoned and charred wood, and its carbon content was the vital agent of fuel in making and refining iron. As the result of smelting and beating, iron ore was converted into usable, commercial iron and sold on in the form of rectangular bars. This malleable or wrought iron, produced by the long-established direct reduction process, was prevalent in Scotland until the eighteenth century. Although we know very little about the numbers, composition, organisation and skills of the smelters who made iron by customary methods, the main tasks can be outlined. A heap of iron ore was heated for a few hours in a partially enclosed charcoal-fired hearth. Working in turn, smelters expended much energy in operating hand-held bellows. Aided when possible by natural draughts of wind, they blew air into the fire, thereby aiming to help generate sufficient heat to work up the ore into a spongy mass called a bloom. When judged ready, the emerging bloom was then lifted from the hearth with tongs, hammered to remove the slag, and cooled. Then, as a rough ingot, it was reheated and hammered to reduce impurities in order to render it less brittle and more workable.

The primitive smelting sites were called bloomeries and were located all over the country wherever supplies of iron ore, woodland and water could be readily exploited by an enterprising landowner or venture capitalist.. Bloomeries used local ore, much of it high grade. It was mined from outcrops or dug from bog land and, although the smelted iron ingot was often good quality, the smelting team could produce only small batches of marketable iron at any one time. Further processing was necessary to convert this crude iron into a more refined bar iron, and this was carried out elsewhere by blacksmiths and forgemen. Using coal or charcoal for the fire, the blacksmith in a local workshop then worked this iron by hand-held hammer on an anvil. Most often, he added scrap metal, and with this mix of re-worked iron, he made horseshoes and forged small quantities of common nails and other simple implements such as pokers and shovels. By the early eighteenth century, good quality bloomery iron was drawn out into longer bars in the few forges that were equipped with a tilt hammer, activated by a water-powered wheel.

Another wheel would also have driven the bellows at the re-heating furnace. In the first water-powered rolling mills, the forgemen in this, as yet, small specialist sector, were able to produce iron plates and sheets. An important customer of the millmen in Central Scotland was the salt industry in many of the coastal communities of the Firth of Forth. Iron plate formed the body of the large evaporating pans, some 6 metres long and 3 metres broad, in which sea-water was boiled and distilled.

The addition of a slit mill to the forge allowed iron to be cut into strips, and production of rods for cutting and shaping into nails. Before and around the formation of Carron several important malleable iron firms, all using water power for hammer and rolls, turned out a limited, but growing, range of finished products in their forges and mills. Among the early large concerns was the Glasgow-based Smithfield forge, where the slit mill was pioneered in 1738. Its workers turned out regular orders of nails, axes, hoes and spades for the domestic market and the American colonies. From the 1760s, the Dalnotter Iron Company, near Dumbarton, produced the same range of items for both markets, also chain links and hoops for barrels. The Cramond Iron Works, founded in 1752, and owned by the Carron Iron Company between 1760 and 1770, had a rolling and slitting mill, and specialised in making rods for its nail-making business. Later, it was also well known for hoops, spades, shovels and ploughs. Edge tools such as files were made at Rutherglen and Strathbungo, with initial help from Sheffield cutlers and steel workers. The Monkland Forge, at Calderbank, also made a range of steel tools. Its forgemen used charcoal in the finery process to harden the iron. After 1805, it became the Monkland Iron and Steel Company, diversifying into wrought iron boiler plates for some of the first iron-hull sailing vessels.

However, none of those secondary and finishing works made their own bar iron and forgemen and finers continued to use charcoal. Instead, until the later eighteenth century, the forges and mills preferred to rework the more refined high grade bar iron imported from Sweden and Russia. Indeed, for nearly 300 years, the amount of imported iron from the Baltic countries was consistently greater than the output of the Scottish bloomeries. This dependence on imported bar iron, and the high costs of traditional bloomery iron and finished forge iron goods, would not be redressed until two developments had become firmly established in both branches of the iron industry. The first was the introduction of the coke-fired blast furnace, with its greater capacity as a mass primary producer of pig iron for foundry use. The second was improved methods of making malleable iron from pig iron, and rolling it out into a greater variety of shapes and sizes. The breakthrough in making wrought iron was to be achieved by the puddling process, introduced into Scotland to a limited extent from the 1790s. As will be explained in the next chapter, iron puddling involved severe manual labour, and a high degree of manipulative skill and judgement. However, until the advent of the coke-fired blast furnace, and the puddling furnace thereafter, the qualities of charcoal-fired processes could not be superseded for making basic pig iron or for refining cast iron and wrought iron.[2]

THE CHARCOAL-FIRED IRON INDUSTRY

According to scholarly evidence, the laborious processes of the bloomery began to be replaced by the more productive blast-furnace technology shortly after 1600. The new method was introduced to Scotland by skilled English smelters and forgemen who, over the years, transferred their exclusive expertise ever northwards from the original iron industries of the Sussex Weald to the Midlands, and later to Furness in the Lake District. However, this transition was gradual and, in Scotland during the seventeenth and early eighteenth century, the more significant bloomery sites co-existed with, and easily outnumbered, the early blast-furnace operations.[3]

Location of blast-furnace plants was determined, above all, by the availability of extensive acres of woodland, which could be leased or purchased and exploited for making charcoal on an industrial scale. Such swathes of woodland existed mainly in the Highlands of Scotland. In Lowland and southern areas most of the traditional forests had long been cut down and cleared for settlement and farmland while, for hundreds of years, the insatiable demands of the shipbuilding yards for supplies of timber had removed millions of oak trees. In the north of England, iron masters faced a desperate shortage of charcoal fuel, as their local sources of hardwood had become denuded or too expensive to lease, forcing them to search further northwards for this essential supply. Thus, for incoming English iron companies who chose to locate expensive blast-furnace plants in the Scottish Highlands, it made economic sense to transport iron ore and a skilled workforce to the site, even over long distances, instead of incurring the greater expense and trouble of carrying endless supplies of very bulky and fragile charcoal to smelting plants in Cumbria or Lancashire. For such reasons, the few charcoal-fired, blast-furnace operations in eighteenth-century Scotland

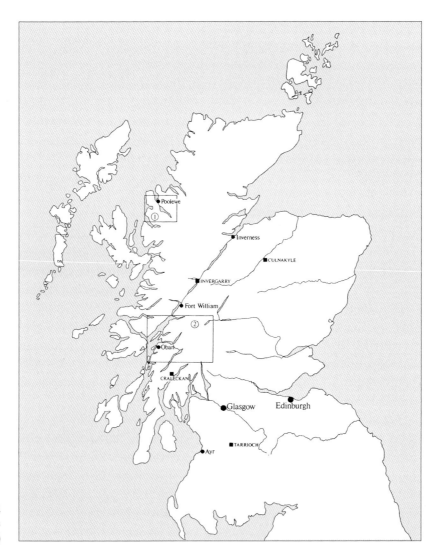

Charcoal
blast furnaces
(J.H. Lewis, 1984)

were located in the Highlands rather than in the Central Lowlands, where the iron industry was later to take root and concentrate amidst abundant local resources of coal, ironstone and limestone.

The charcoal-fired iron industry was put on a more productive and commercial footing by companies willing to invest capital on a large scale. This commitment meant equipping blast-furnace and other industrial plants, an infrastructure of landing stages for ships, road transport access for horses and carts and accommodation for incoming workers. It also involved taking long leases of extensive woodland areas for making charcoal; carrying in

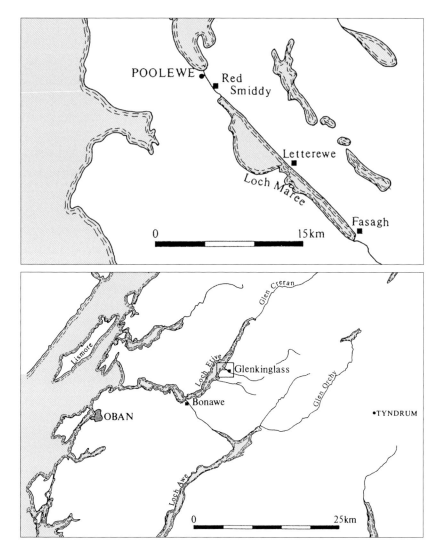

higher-grade iron ore from a distance, including England and recruiting and organising a varied workforce, especially skilled labour at furnace and forge.

During the pre-Carron era, there is recorded evidence of ten charcoal-fired, blast-furnace operations in the Highlands, in fitful production between 1610 and 1754. The earliest ones were at three separate sites on the eastern shore of Loch Maree in Gairloch parish. In 1610, Sir George Hay, a minister of state, landowner and entrepreneur, combined the interests of commercial enterprise and political duty in the latest of several attempts to impose central government law and order on the dissident clans of northwest Scotland. This initiative, situated in and around Letterewe, included construction of ironworks, essentially as weapons factories to make heavy guns. Production of cannon and shot, and iron bars for sale elsewhere in Scotland, continued intermittently until at least the 1630s. Blast-furnace smelting is also reckoned to have taken place for a short time during the late seventeenth century at Lochaber, on the Breadalbane estates; and a linked forge turned out articles such as window bars and hammers.

Attracted by commercial opportunities following the Treaty of Union in 1707, and the availability of cheap and abundant woodland for charcoal, Scottish, English and Irish industrialists and speculators formed companies to produce blast-furnace iron in the Highlands. Between 1718 and 1729, four ironworks, albeit with relatively brief productive lives, were established in quick succession: at Achray near Aberfoyle (1718–24); Glenkinglass (c.1722–c.1738); Invergarry (1727–36) and Coulnakyle (Abernethy), south of Grantown-on-Spey (1729–c.1734). The two largest, most enduring, and successful ironworks were established later, at Bonawe (1753–1876), and the Argyle or Craleckan, at Furnace (1754–1813). Before 1760, the cumulative total output of pig and forge iron from the Highlands was quite modest. During that time, it formed only a tiny part of the iron industry within Britain, where over 160 blast-furnace sites were in use in Ireland, and over 100 in England and Wales, of which a few were already coke-fired. However, some features of this phase of the iron industry in Highland Scotland, especially the recruitment and deployment of a labour force in remote and rural settings, are of peculiar interest and deserve some attention.

A common feature of all the charcoal-fired blast-furnace and refining plants was the need to recruit skilled labour from England, particularly smelters, founders and forgemen. Those classifications of workers alone possessed the practical knowledge of the sophisticated techniques of iron production and refining. A forge in this charcoal phase of the industry functioned with the following processes and division of labour. Pig iron from the blast furnace was melted down by the smelter in a hearth known as a finery. This first part of the refining process was identical to that undertaken in the traditional bloomery, whereby a cold blast of air was directed onto the metal to reduce its carbon content. The mass of metal and slag was then removed from the hearth and beaten into a roughly shaped lump (bloom). This task was carried out by the finer. From the finery, the wrought-iron bloom was taken to a second hearth, called a chafery, where hammermen shaped the bloom into a block under a tilt hammer. Further reheating, without

Remains of Craleckan furnace, at Furnace village (J.Butt, *Industrial Archaeology of Scotland,* 1967)

blast, and more hammer pressure to draw out the block shape into the desired gauge of bar, completed a skilled, sophisticated process. Before the modern era of chemical knowledge, scientific measurement and precision technology, it was entirely appropriate that the art and craft of making and refining iron was often termed a 'mystery'.

Smelters and founders were among the first colony of English iron-working craftsmen, most probably from the Furness area, employed at Letterewe. Cannon and their mountings were furnished from cast iron in the first foundry workshops in the country. A boring mill, one of the earliest machine tools to be devised for working cast iron, was used for the intricate task of hollowing out the gun barrels. At Letterewe, bar iron was also produced by forgemen. Unusual working conditions prevailed at the time in this beautiful but wild part of Wester Ross. It is not known whether the crews of English iron workers were subject to military discipline, or were engaged as contract labour, but we are told that they carried weapons to defend the works and themselves against attack by hostile natives, who regarded them as intruders.

Among the eighteenth-century Highland ironworks, Achray and Coulnakyle (with its two forges, water-powered tilt hammers, fineries and chafery) had to recruit their various forgemen from England. The other four works possessed neither forges nor mills, concentrating on production of pig iron. Three of the blast-furnace works, Invergarry, Bonawe and Argyle, were

Remains of Bonawe blast furnace (J. Butt et. al., *Industrial History in Pictures; Scotland*, 1968)

owned by different Furness iron masters, and the pig iron produced in the Highland furnaces was destined for casting in their English foundries, or sold on directly to iron-trade customers, again mostly in England.

For their Highland operations, the Furness masters preferred obviously to recruit furnacemen and founders from among their own specialist workmen and send them to the company's northern outpost. Experienced men from Yorkshire were also recruited initially for Invergarry, where founders were paid the (then) huge wage of 12 shillings a week, such was the inducement which had to be offered to men who were most reluctant to move to this remote part of the western Highlands. At Glenkinglass, owned by Irish charcoal and iron interests, it proved difficult to find and retain skilled English smelters and founders. It was both necessary and advisable to train up some local men, and one of them, a Macdonald, was eventually promoted to leading founder during the short productive existence of this firm.

At Achray and Glenkinglass, the consortium of Irish owners brought in their own trusted gang of coalers (charcoal burners) from Ireland. The Furness-owned works at Invergarry also employed gangs of Irish coalers although, at most of the Highland ironworks, it was normal practice to contract local woodsmen and burners, sometimes on a seasonal basis, to supply the enormous quantity of charcoal required for the blast furnace, and smaller amounts for reheating and refining use in the forge. At Bonawe, in peak times, up to 600 local people were employed in the manufacture and transport of charcoal. At Furnace, it was thought that the ironworks was an advantage to the local population, 'in giving employment and bread to a considerable number of hands, both male and female, in cutting and peeling the woods and in making charcoal'.[4] In this rural phase of iron smelting the greatest part of the labour force always consisted of those workers involved in the vital tasks of fuel supply – limestone quarriers and breakers, woodsmen, cutters, charcoal burners – and in other ancillary jobs such as carting. The Highland blast furnaces owned by the Furness masters were usually supplied with quality iron ore shipped from the English home base to the west coast and then inland. However, at other works, ore supply involved an additional preliminary task, as it was quarried either locally or some distance away and carried across country by pack horse. The ore had then to be broken down and prepared before loading into the blast furnace. Compared to the numbers of workers involved in all such preparatory tasks, production and maintenance workers at furnace, foundry, or forge formed only a small minority at any ironworks. As a typical example of a production unit, in the 1780s, at Bonawe, the master smelter had a team of six or seven assistant founders at and around the single furnace and casting shop.

The skilled craft workforce in charcoal-based iron smelting and refining in Scotland was numerically small and essentially self-contained. From studies of identical groups of iron workers in England and Wales, it may be assumed that they were jealous guardians of the mysteries and arts of iron working. As far as possible, they kept recruitment within the family and kin group, or at least within the network of recognised occupations within their own sector of the iron trade. Master smelters and master forgemen from England were engaged as subcontractors and they in turn asserted their independent outlook by choosing, supervising and paying their own crews of assistants and labourers. The iron masters or owners had little or no choice but to concede authority to the craftsman on such exclusive and restrictive practices, as the constant scarcity of skilled, experienced labour was a vital source of bargaining advantage to the key worker.[5]

Nevertheless, through no fault of the workers, adverse circumstances often led to the premature end of contracts, summary dismissal and further migration in the search for work at their trade. In Scotland, their fate was to be no different. With the exceptions of Bonawe and Furnace, mismanagement, long distances from markets and supplies of quality ore, high overall costs, and eventual business failure, ended the short lives of the blast-furnace ventures in the Highlands, and dispersed the workforce. While contracts lasted, payment of wages was based on tonnage and piecework, and high wages were possible for assistant smelters and forgemen. Other inducements had to be offered to persuade the incomers to work and settle in this new, often hostile, environment, and the workers themselves set preconditions for creature comforts. For instance, at Invergarry, while housing accommodation was included in the contract, the issue of basic domestic amenities and provisions had to be resolved at the very start of the venture. As there was no guarantee of local availability of household utensils, items such as bedding, iron pans and girdles, and other preferred goods such as brewing vessels and a malt kiln, had to be brought up from Furness.[6] Working and sweating for long hours in the fierce heats of furnace and forge induced a raging thirst that was not satisfactorily quenched by tepid water from a pitcher. Hence the ready demand for ale, while consumption of native whisky also contributed to the prevalent drinking culture at other occasions.

At these sites, the pattern of productive work at furnace and forge was often irregular, and periods of idleness and underemployment were not uncommon. Broken or weakened water wheels and tilt hammers, and problems with furnace flues and hearths, all interrupted the flow of production, and repair time often resulted in enforced delays. Low water levels also stopped or halted the wheels that provided connecting power to the furnace bellows. This could happen for weeks on end, during which time the furnace was out of blast, and production of iron had ceased. In slack periods, or during lengthy stoppages, repair and maintenance tasks occupied some of the spare labour time.

There are few hints in the surviving record of outright labour troubles, but long delays in payment of wages and shortage of basic provisions such as oatmeal could provoke restiveness and conflict. For example, in 1723, at Achray, an aggrieved and worried manager, John Wilson, in fear of his life, wrote to the partners, 'I am hopeful that you will relieve me out of this thraldom by speedy sending up some money, for this unhappy crew are like to tear me in pieces.'[7] English iron workers, hit by privation, fraternised with fellow-countrymen who were soldiers at nearby Fort Augustus, and were apparently tempted to enlist as an alternative means of earning a living.

Non-work and leisure time pursuits in those frontier areas included opportunities for fishing, hunting, poaching and drinking sessions and sprees. The owners and agent at Bonawe could not prevent consumption of alcohol in the workplace and drunken behaviour outside it, although such practices interfered with productivity, work discipline and their concern for orderly and responsible behaviour. In 1782, George Knott, one of the owner partners, wrote an angry instruction to his local agent manager, 'to put a stop, if possible, to that confounded drinking in general, and by showing the example it may be more easily done, for I believe there is not such another drunken hole in the Kingdom.'[8] He reprimanded the agent for selling bottled whisky on his own account, but later had to concede the opening of a licensed public house at Taynuilt. Opportunities for illicit distilling and smuggling compounded the problem, and Knott had been informed that the furnace quay at Bonawe had earned an unsavoury reputation as 'principal smuggling harbour' in the Oban excise area. Again, he demanded that measures be taken to stop the smuggling, probably to no avail.

Company rule also encouraged rational pursuits and self-sufficiency among the workforce at Bonawe, and additional payment-in-kind privileges were granted to key workers. Whereas the poorly paid charcoal gangs and the labourers around the ironworks in these outposts were usually accommodated in makeshift cabins of wood, turf, and some of stone, at Bonawe, the 'real

Houses of workers at Bonawe (J. Butt et. al., *Industrial History in Pictures; Scotland*, 1968)

good and necessary families' were rewarded with the best housing, solidly built dwellings of stone and slate. The two-roomed houses had living and kitchen space on the ground floor, and a stair loft as sleeping quarters. Bothies provided basic accommodation for single skilled workmen, if they were not boarded with families. Crofts and allotments accompanied the houses, and the workmen were expected to apply themselves to cultivate their land, grow vegetables and keep animals, for which they could obtain a lease of grazing rights. The company initiated a subsidiary cottage industry among the workmen's wives and widows, whereby wool was spun into yarn and transported for sale in the Kendal district. It was conceived as a source of gainful employment to make up the family wage when iron production was slack or at a standstill, and 'as a step necessary to prevent the workmen running into debt', or into poverty. However, grievances persisted over infrequent wage payment, sometimes for a month or more; being in debt and having to use the company store to purchase basic provisions. Imported oatmeal, a vital part of the diet, was often in short supply and of poor quality, and wages were at times partly in cash and in food. Life and the rewards of work were undoubtedly harsh and many English incomers found it difficult to adapt and thrive. While the Lorn Iron Company provided the civilising and disciplinary agencies of church and school for the Bonawe workers and their families, amenities and welfare continued to be rudimentary into the early nineteenth century in this, the longest lasting smelting settlement in the Highlands.

IRONWORKS IN THE SCOTTISH LOWLANDS:
THE FIRST GENERATION 1760–1830

In 1784, a notable foreign visitor to the industrial giant, Carron Iron Works, was surprised and amazed by the sights, sounds, technology and work processes in this most unusual of places, where war munitions were made as well as ploughshares and a range of appliances and articles for home and hearth:

> Above one hundred acres of land have been converted into reservoirs and pools, for water directed from the river, by magnificent dams built about two miles above the works, which after turning eighteen large wheels for the several purposes of the manufacture, fall into a tidal navigation that conveys their castings to the sea. These works are the greatest of their kind in Europe; there are sixteen hundred men employed.
>
> A man attended us at the gate, who said that he was ordered to conduct us everywhere, with the exception of the place where the cannons were bored, which no stranger was permitted to see. He conducted us first into an immense court, surrounded with high walls and vast sheds. This place was covered with cannons, mortars, bombs, balls, and large pieces which bear the name Carronades. Amid these machines of war, these terrible instruments of death, gigantic cranes, capstans of every kind, levers and assemblies of pulleys, serving to move so many articles of enormous weight, are erected in situations convenient for that purpose. The various movements, the shrill creaking of pulleys, the continuous noise of hammers, the activity of those arms which give impulsion to so many machines; everything here presents a spectacle as new and interesting.
>
> He conducted us to the works for smelting the ore; where four furnaces, of forty five feet in height, devoured both night and day enormous masses of coals and metal. One may from this judge the quantity of air necessary to feed these burning gulphs, which disgorged, every six hours, whole floods of liquid iron. Each furnace is supplied by four air pumps, of a great width, where the air, compressed into iron cylinders, uniting into one tunnel, and directed towards the flame, produces a sharp rustling noise, and so violent a tremor, that one not previously informed of it would find it difficult to avoid a sensation

of terror. These wind machines, this species of gigantic bellows, are put in motion by the action of water. Such a torrent of air is indispensably necessary to support, in the highest state of ignition, a column of coal and ore forty-five feet high; and it is so rapid and active, that it projects a vivid and brisk flame more than ten feet above the top of the furnace. Everything is placed in regular order, within reach of the workmen. The baskets for each charge are always counted; a time piece, which strikes the hour beside the large furnaces, determines the precise moment for putting in the charge. It is the same with the outflow of the melted iron; the clock announces when they should proceed to that operation; and each workman then flies to his post.

We visited the place where the crude iron is refined in reverberatory furnaces, to be afterwards cast into mortars, etc. We saw also where the moulds are prepared, and another place where they are dried. We were also conducted into a vast workshop which suggested the most pleasant of ideas, for its productions consisted of the various implements of agriculture, the arts and domestic use. Labour and workmanship are, in this place, assisted by so many machines and ingenious processes, that its commodities are executed, both in a shorter time, and with greater perfection, than in other establishments of the same kind.[9]

James Nasmyth, inventor of the steam hammer, visited Carron in 1823 as a 16 year-old, and later recorded a sense of its industrial scene and toil:

When seen partially lit up by the glowing masses of white hot iron, with only the rays of bright sunshine gleaming through a few holes in the roof, and the dark, black, smoky vaults in which the cumbrous machinery was heard mumbling away – while the moving parts were dimly seen through the murky atmosphere, mixed with the sounds of escaping steam and rushes of water; with the half-naked men darting about with masses of red hot iron and ladles of molten cast iron – it made a powerful impression on the mind.[10]

Another visitor to Carron, physician Jacob Pattison in 1780, was even more revealing in his verdict about the condition of foundry workers: 'The appearances of those within are truly diabolical, most of them very naked and as black as the region they live in – they are said not to be very long lived – this

is little to be wondered at, as most of them seem half parched.' He described
one assistant furnaceman, whose tasks included entering the partially cooled
chamber to regulate it, but still in 'insufferably hot' conditions: 'For 13
shillings a week, most of which money he is obliged to expend in liquor to
keep any fluids at all in his body . . . his visage and appearance is that of a
skeleton, his eyes are sunk, his voice hollow . . . he is very near dried up, and
I think it is not difficult to foretell his fate – the heat will certainly one day
catch him like tinder or touchpaper and crackling, he will disappear.'[11]

Compared to their charcoal-bound predecessors in the Highlands, Carron
and most of the nine coke-fired smelting works established in the Lowlands
by 1802 operated on a different and larger scale: in size and capacity of
furnace and industrial plant; in extent of productive power and in the concentration of hundreds of workers employed on a widening range of skills and
tasks at each location. The smallest ironworks – the single blast-furnace
Balgonie works in Fife – and the giant Carron, with its elaborate pools, dams
and lades to feed a rush and depth of water to several large wheels, retained
the driving force of water power. At other ironworks, water-power levels were
often unreliable, and the new, more regular and efficient power of the steam
engine was introduced to generate cold air blast for the main smelting
furnaces and reheating furnaces inside the foundry. The larger smelting works
with forge departments, at Wilsontown and Muirkirk, also used steam power
to activate hammers and rolling mills. Working the water-powered tilt
hammer in the forge was a highly skilled job and we are informed that, when
this vital worker fell ill for a long period at Calder Iron Works, there was not
a competent tilter in the whole of Scotland to replace him.[12]

Millwrights, expert makers and repairers of water wheels and pumping
apparatus, adapted their skills from wood to iron. They joined a new breed of
practical specialist workmen – the engineers and mechanics – who were
masters of the applied workings of shafts and gears, and the intricacies of
cylinders and propulsion in steam-power technology. The expertise of this
craft élite of engineers and mechanics in wood and iron ensured transmission
of machine power for the ironworks: blasting air into the furnaces, driving the
hammer and the rolling mill and directing the movement of cranes and
pulleys for heavy hoisting. However, at this stage of development, the direct
labour processes in the actual making, casting and refining of iron at furnace,
foundry and forge, and a host of servicing operations, were hardly penetrated
by mechanical aids and technical advance. Despite the harnessing of power as
observed by the Carron visitor in 1784, until well into the nineteenth century,

sheer manual labour and muscular effort by individuals and teams, exercise of skill and judgement and dexterity with hand tools, would continue to predominate in the myriad of charging, loading, heating, hammering, dressing, cutting, lifting and moving operations within an ironworks.

Before 1830, Carron always headed the list of ironworks for size of plant and numbers of workers. In November 1761, the company already employed over 700 workers, including colliers and ironstone miners. Although, at this early stage, only two blast furnaces were in production, and extensive foundry workshops and forge areas were gradually being built and utilised, around three hundred workers were directly involved in iron manufacture, casting and other finishing operations. While it is not possible to enumerate and differentiate precisely the workers employed at the industrial plant in its growth period, by 1800 the total company workforce had risen to around 2,000, of which at least one-third encompassed all grades of iron workers within the industrial site itself. The giant works and its varied labour force of miners, iron workers and armies of support workers spawned a large resident population grouped in several irregularly laid out company villages at Larbert, Stenhousemuir, West Carron and Carronshore. Organised as outworkers, nailers were housed at Carron and Camelon, with a small workshop forge attached to the rows.

Although not on the same scale as Carron, Wilsontown, Muirkirk and Clyde ironworks were all substantial enterprises, and more significant than the other contemporary smelting plants . Wilsontown was an integrated and modern works, fitted with Boulton and Watt steam engines, puddling furnaces for making bar iron, and extensive forge sections for finishing rods, sheet iron and boiler plate. Its foundry workers made a wide range of castings, including cannon during the long war with France. Wilsontown employed around 500 workers at its peak in the early 1800s, and housed an industrial community of nearly 2,000 people who depended on the works for a living. Most of its skilled workers came from England. Forgemen were accustomed to movement, pursuing fresh opportunities of higher wages in boom years. There is an interesting example of a William Lambert who moved to three different forges in the north of England between 1797 and 1802, finally arriving at Wilsontown, after leaving Newland in Furness.[13] At that time, the industrial plant, and its associated mining activities, was a busy, diverse place: 'The coal and ironstone miners, the furnaces, the forges, the rolling mill, the shops of smiths, carpenters, engineers, and millwrights, all were crowded with workmen.'[14]

Muirkirk, like Wilsontown, was an integrated ironworks created in a remote inland location amid infinite workable reserves of coal, ironstone and other minerals. In the 1790s, around 500 workers provided the raw materials and labour for three blast furnaces, a puddling plant and forge, and formed an industrial community of over 2,000 inhabitants by 1800.[15]

By the 1800s, the Clyde Iron Works, with three modern blast furnaces, had the largest foundry in Scotland next to Carron, and also specialised in production of cannon and shot for the war effort. While descriptions of the process are available from Carron, in 1803 a foreign industrial spy observed the tasks of cutting and boring cannon at the Clyde foundry:

> The boring of the cannon is done here, as everywhere in England, in the horizontal position. The boring and turning machine was driven by a steam engine, and four cannon could be turned and bored at once. The turning was done by hand, often by boys, and just as easily as turning a piece of wood. The cast iron was unusually strong and dense, but on the other hand so soft that it could almost be filed like wrought iron.[16]

Sketch of Muirkirk
Iron Works, c. 1840
(J. Butt et. al.,
*Industrial History in
Pictures; Scotland,*
1968)

KEY
1. Furnace
2. Furnace
3. Furnace
4. Furnace
5. Forges
6. Rolling mill
7. Ironstone kilns
8. Coking ovens
9. Canal
10. Railway

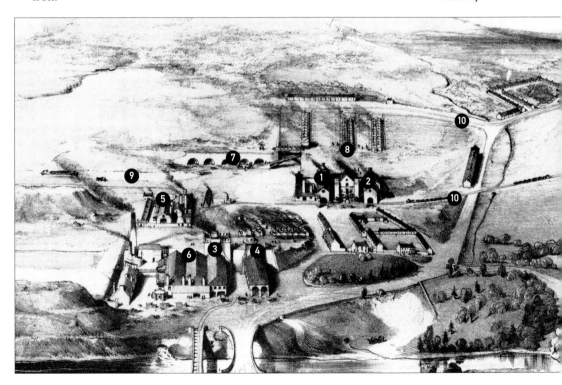

The size of the workforce at Clyde Iron Works and its associated coal and ironstone mines fluctuated into the early nineteenth century, but it numbered upwards of 300 in the mid 1790s. By 1830 the combined workforce had risen considerably and formed an identifiable and permanent mining and industrial community in company houses at Tollcross, to the east of Glasgow.

In this review it is worth mentioning that the eighteenth-century malleable-iron works at Dalnotter and Cramond, though smaller concerns than the smelting and integrated plants, employed a considerable labour force and contributed to the formation of new communities. Dalnotter, the bigger of the two firms, employed over two hundred workers at its substantial forge, nail and chain-making workshops and large warehouse in nearby Glasgow. It also housed its workers locally and financed a school.[17] The workforce profile at Cramond is also interesting. During the 1760s, when the mill was part of Carron Company, production was concentrated on nail rods and barrel hoops. In 1762, the operative labour force at forge and mill was remarkably small, comprising a master forgeman, his apprentice, a furnace heater, two millmen, a cutter, a carpenter and two boy labourers. By the 1790s, under new ownership, and having expanded its range of products and volume of sales, its regular workforce had risen to around 80 men and boys. The inventory of workers included 2 slitters, 12 millmen and rollers, 6 forgemen and hammermen, 12 spade and handle makers, 11 nailers, 22 boys (12 working at nails, 7 drawing and straightening hoops, an apprentice slitter and 2 forge assistants), 3 masons, 2 carpenters, 2 carters, and 6 assorted labourers. The workers all lived in and around the ironworks village and elsewhere in Cramond parish, and made up the largest distinctive group of workers and families within its overall population.[18] Also noteworthy is the considerable number of English names among the skilled labour force at Cramond. As shown below, this example was a close reflection of the origins and composition of skilled labour at furnaces, foundries and forges throughout the industry in Scotland during this formative period.

RECRUITMENT OF LABOUR, WORKING CONDITIONS AND LABOUR RELATIONS IN THE IRON INDUSTRY 1760–1830

We have been expecting to hear from you about one or two good founders which we imagined you would be able to get from

Rotherham, and we can't help thinking from the information about them that if you would exert yourself one or two of Walker's hands could be procured. What we principally want is a man for axle bushes and if he has been used to pots and sad irons and loam work would be the more valuable. We would either have them work by the day or piece. If the former 10s. a week or 12 for a very good man with any more moderate encouragement as you see proper. Travelling charge you know must be granted with a house and firing free.

We are afraid you won't succeed in getting a finery man for the forge, but if you hear of a good hand that is not under article we think he might be bribed to come to as good a forge perhaps as any in Britain where he would have good work and civil usage. You might venture to give him £10 in hand, £20 more when he arrived in Scotland and if he should not like his situation when he arrived here we will pay his charges back again and risk the £10.[19]

First on the scene, the experience of the Carron Company and of its iron workers makes a useful case study during the first decades of this major firm, illustrating the problems of coming to terms with the new world of competitive industrial capitalism. For the employers, one of the most pressing concerns was to recruit a workforce, and especially to attract highly skilled iron workers of proven character.

In the early years, the Carron owners had to recruit all departmental managers and iron-related skilled tradesmen from outside Scotland. Principal recruiting grounds were the established iron-working areas of the Midlands and north of England. Keeping abreast of developments in the labour market, and ever alert to pursuit of expert workers in the initial stages, enterprising owners exploited their network of contacts within the established iron industry in England. For example, despite the doubts revealed in the above extract from Carron records, the owners did get their 'finery man' and a few others with expertise in the use of charcoal fire to cleanse pig iron of impurities before conversion into bar or malleable iron in the forge. Specialist iron founders were also procured, such as Robert Hawkins, trained at Coalbrookdale and a relation of the Darby dynasty of iron masters. He was considered a most valuable acquisition, contracted at the top salary of £100 a year, with a particular remit to instruct workmen in the arts and crafts of cylinder boring and grinding processes. He was one of the leading craftsmen brought to Scotland at high cost to teach native workers, especially in the expanding foundry work trades. Almost from the start, the Carron Company began to cast heavy guns, and had to engage two or more teams of specialist moulders and founders from Sussex, the home of gunfounding. The emphasis on procuring a craft iron founder for 'bushes', as specified in the extract above, declared the intention of the Carron owners to go into production of wheel and machine parts. They also hoped that their iron founders would be versatile, and display expertise in fashioning large pots and containers, for which there was an expanding domestic market.

At the outset in 1759–60, other select groups of key workers – masons, bricklayers, bellows makers, millwrights, smelters, charcoal and coke burners – had all been secured from England to build essential furnace plants, to commence operations and to become foremen and instructors of emerging teams of workmen. Such leading men were also uniquely placed to know and engage capable assistants within their trade, and to persuade them to come to Scotland. An example of the sensitivity attached to securing and retaining key men is revealed in a company letter from 1760. Garbett counselled his partners to be careful not to offend the resident master slitter, the Englishman Richard Lees, at the newly acquired Cramond mill. He feared losing him and his co-workers, endangering production and profit at this crucial interim stage before development of the main forge and nail business at and around Carron: 'He may in many respects be of great use to us. He hath acquaintance amongst forgemen which we shall find it difficult to obtain.'[20]

An Englishman, John Raybould, was appointed on a subcontracting basis to bring six experienced nailers, all 'sober and industrious', to Scotland, to take charge of nailmaking operations at Carron. His task was to supply rod to outworking nailers, give out orders for different brands of nails, collect in the finished products, pay out wages on piecework rates and expand the business. Raybould and his immediate co-workers were each provided with free house and garden near Falkirk, and their conditions of contract were reputedly equal to any offered by competing firms in England.

Among the skilled élite, master smelters or furnace-keepers were vital appointments. They were in short supply throughout the industry and every effort was made to secure the best calibre of this category of skilled man for Carron. Thomas Cranage, a master furnace-keeper, trained at Coalbrookdale, was placed in charge of smelting operations at the first blast furnace. Fellow countrymen were appointed for the second furnace, and the planned arrival of two additional blast furnaces in the mid 1760s prompted more anxious raids into the Midlands for reputable furnace-keepers.

In their attempts to entice English expertise, the Carron iron masters usually kept within the bounds of master and servant law, engaging men who were already out of contract, or due for completion. However, on occasion, they were not averse to underhand and illegal dealing, tapping vital personnel such as two firemen or heaters who broke contract in Shropshire to start with enhanced conditions at the foundry furnaces.

Where feasible, the Carron policy was to dispense with the privileged highly paid English craftsmen as soon as sufficient numbers of capable, but lower paid, skilled workers had been trained. To retain the supply of workers who had been trained up at the company's expense, and to prevent or restrict them from leaving on their own terms, the employer sought to encourage them to enter into legally binding written contracts or articles. The contract bond at Carron, containing details of hours, wages and other conditions and obligations, could be for ten or even fourteen years. An important condition of contract insisted that each skilled journeyman, such as moulder or founder, train up a number of apprentices or assistants, including sons, thus attempting to establish an effective and loyal vital section of the workforce, and maintain continuity of approved standards of work habits and performance.

Carron especially, but also the other smelting works thereafter, had not only to contend with difficulties of initial recruitment and retention of key workers who were often in short supply. They had also to recruit and install an adequate labour force, including many unskilled workers and labouring poor from traditional, often land-related, casual and seasonal employment, who were not easily and readily used to the work discipline and regular consistent effort which was demanded by industrial capitalism.

In an extreme case of finding workers, desperate to expand the potentially lucrative market for nails, the Carron Company resorted to child labour to overcome shortage of willing recruits. Nailmaking was a miserable, poorly paid, sweated trade that few adult males or boys could be persuaded to enter for a living, and pauper children from an Edinburgh poorhouse were procured as conscript labour. This is not to condemn Carron in the context of the time, as recruiting orphans from institutions and poorhouses and indenturing them as child labour in workshops, factories and mills was a common practice in the eighteenth and early nineteenth centuries. Moreover, according to the Carron spokesman, it was reckoned a good prospect for each of the interested parties: for the boys, the guardians and benefactors of the poorhouse and the employer:

We do not think the Poorhouse boys can ever enter into a more certain business than the Nail Trade. A diligent person with a pair of tolerable hands can always make ten shillings a week and there is no danger of it ever turning out of fashion . . . we agree to take lads at above twelve years to bind for seven years. The Carron Coy. agree to keep them in meat, drink and cloaths for that time. To learn them the art of making nails by good workmen and sober, decent characters. If the boys behave well the Company will probably give them some gratuity beside meat and cloath, but this article must be left entirely to the Coy's generosity.[21]

The pauper apprentice arrangement did not work out successfully. Several consignments of boys were delivered from Edinburgh and farmed out to nailmaking tradesmen. More than twenty boys, around half of the total conscripts, absconded whenever they could, complaining of overwork and ill-treatment, and by the end of the 1760s Carron had abandoned the practice as being more troublesome than it was worth. However, as described in the following chapter, until the middle of the nineteenth century, pauper children were still being conscripted into nail manufacture. Within a few years, sufficient numbers of nailers in various locations, such as Bannockburn, Kilsyth, Kirkcaldy and at Carron, were working for the company. Much later, in 1820, Carron engaged a colony of Irish nailers who had been made redundant at Wilsontown ironworks. The incoming nailers exchanged unemployment and grinding poverty for work at low wages. They were settled at Nailer Row, Carron, which had been built for this section of workers nearly fifty years before, and were apparently subjected to discriminatory treatment from some of the local workers.[22]

In the early years, instilling and maintaining work discipline and achieving quality control in standards of production and workmanship were major headaches for the Carron owners and managers. Even the most prized skilled men from England were frequently found lacking. Allowing for the possibility that demands and expectations of work performance were unrealistically high, as early as February 1761 the furnace-keepers were accused of carelessness and gross misconduct. Apparently, the operation of tapping slag from the furnace was repeatedly mismanaged. The young owner manager, William Cadell junior, asserted that trouble tended to arise only when the keepers were 'self-conceited, drunken, foolish and careless'. Conversely, good iron was produced so long as they were 'sober and sorry for their behaviour'.

In particular, Thomas Cranage, mentioned earlier as a first-class acquisition, was reputedly the leading culprit, and was dismissed for drunkenness and ineptitude. Again, after production trials, Cadell also dismissed the next batch of keepers on the second furnace for failing to achieve expected tonnage output. He had to admit defeat when another new team could do little better and were not at fault while experiments were still being conducted with furnace operations. The master slitters at Cramond in the 1760s also proved a great disappointment and had to be replaced at great expense and effort. Christopher Bell was warned twice against selling ale at the mill. He defied company policy, which explicitly banned any employee from selling or dispensing alcohol in or adjacent to the workplace, and was eventually dismissed for ruining a new set of rollers.[23]

The Carron Works was an open premises until 1764, when it was decided to erect high walls and an entrance gate with porters to guard the movement of workers and visitors. This measure was intended to improve work discipline by clocking in and out, preventing distractions from unwanted visitors, including industrial spies, and restricting opportunities to embezzle goods and materials. During the 1770s, systematic penalties ranging from fines to dismissal were posted for theft, defective workmanship and bad time-keeping, and the force of the law was invoked to punish and deter severe crimes such as embezzlement. Already, in 1769, the company had adopted a harsh attitude to yet another frustrating case of theft of rod iron, demanding that the worker 'be whip't thro' Falkirk as soon as possible in terrorum to others'.[24]

During the 1760s and 1770s Carron experienced a few episodes of industrial unrest, with strike action and disturbances among miners, and military intervention to quell disorder. However, there is no such record of turbulence and revolt among the iron workers, although in 1773 a group of furnace-keepers acted together to ask for an increase in wages and were disciplined for disloyalty and combining against the masters.[25] In common with iron masters everywhere, the Carron company would not tolerate combination and solidarity among the workers to improve wages and conditions. Yet, they fully supported combination with other masters to fix wages and impose other restrictions on their workers. The interlinked owner partners of ironworks at Muirkirk, Glenbuck and Clyde, combined to discipline the workforce. While the linked firms assisted each other with recruitment of skilled men, they made a pact not to poach each other's workers, and agreed not to employ incoming workers unless they produced a written line of recommendation from the previous employer. Sometimes they used crude means to enforce industrial discipline, setting a pattern of coercion that would become only too familiar during the next century and beyond. For example, in the 1780s–90s, the Muirkirk employers broke up labour demands among limestone breakers and carpenters by imposing wage cuts and staging lockouts until the men submitted and returned to work on the master's terms.[26]

Virulently opposed to any incipient trade unionism among its workers, Carron was nevertheless unlike most other coal and iron masters, by being progressive in some respects of its labour relations. For example, the company was unusual in that it paid its workers on a frequent and regular basis. As already mentioned at Bonawe, long pays, sometimes up to a month or five weeks, deprived workers and their families of ready cash and increased the likelihood of their falling into permanent debt and poverty. Instead, until the 1780s at Carron, pays were usually fortnightly, and weekly payments there-after became common practice. Carron was also unlike other companies in refusing to own company stores or to contract them out. It thus kept its workers free from the evil clutches of the truck system, which thrived on the

Blast furnace, Carron
Iron Works, late
nineteenth century

long pay system. It was a virtual licence to defraud workers and their families who, short of ready money, were obliged to use tokens in the company store, and were charged exorbitant rates of interest for credit in the form of goods or cash. Lastly, Carron was also unusual in refusing to arrest money from the men's wages to pay outside debtors. In pursuing all those measures, company motives were undoubtedly mixed. On one hand, they could be seen to act fairly in the eyes of the workers, and encourage loyalty, commitment and gratitude; but were also a means to discourage expectations of wage rises and keep the total wages bill as low as possible.

At Carron, a tradition of family employment had become established by the early nineteenth century. Parents and others introduced their dependants into company labour and, while this reproduction of generations of workers was a sign of progress and stability for the company, as will be seen in later chapters, it was not necessarily a sign of wellbeing and contentment among its varied workforce. At Carron, as elsewhere, the first generations of iron workers, many at an early age, had been inducted into a new regime, often harshly and forcibly, to endure seemingly endless hours of toil in a hostile and punishing environment of scorching heat, fumes, dust and industrial disease.

CONCLUSION: BEFORE THE HOT-BLAST REVOLUTION

Between 1760 and 1830, several coke-fired iron smelting works, their foundries and forges, had appeared on the industrial landscape of central Scotland. After the first burst of expansion between the 1780s and 1802, no further expansion occurred until the boom year of 1825, when a smelting plant was established at Chapelhall. For prolonged periods, lasting years, ironworks were vulnerable to economic slump, downturn and closure, and consequent loss of livelihood for hundreds of workers. Omoa, Glenbuck, Balgonie and Wilsontown all failed, hit by bankruptcy and market depression, whereas Carron, Clyde and Muirkirk profited from production of munitions during war years and never had to close. Although Wilsontown ironworks was partially revived in 1820 and survived until 1840 with a much reduced workforce, the impact of closure after 1813 was particularly disastrous for its large working population. Its skilled ironworkers could leave and hope to find similar employment elsewhere, but the fate of many other workers was dire. In the words of a local minister writing in the 1830s, 'a whole population was turned adrift upon the world', and many families had to be sustained for years as parish paupers.[27] When Glenbuck also closed in 1813, its workers lost tenancy of their houses, and they were abandoned without being repaid the value of tokens issued in lieu of wages.[28]

While most smelting plants had mixed fortunes, a much larger number of independent foundries had nevertheless been stimulated into existence by availability of home-produced pig iron and by increasing demand for cast-iron wares and machinery, especially for textile mills and collieries. By 1813, there were over 50 foundries, widely dispersed, but concentrated in the Clyde and Forth valleys. By 1825, more than 70 foundries were scattered throughout Scottish towns, including 18 in Glasgow. Finished metal goods from Carron, Shotts and Clyde were quality products, and the Scottish foundries were manned by highly skilled labour. There is some evidence to suggest that Scotland could not easily retain its skilled foundry labour, as top men were always in demand south of the border. For instance, in 1822, after widespread advertising, the Welsh giant ironworks, Dowlais, recruited its foundry manager from an engineering foundry in Aberdeen.

By 1830, several thousand foundry men and boys were already the most numerous and most versatile section of labour in smelting plants. In contrast, the forge and malleable iron sectors and their workforce were not as prominent. Production of malleable iron by the puddling process had been insignificant and, in any case, cast iron rather than wrought iron was preferred for finished products ranging from lamp-posts to gas and water pipes, components for steam engines and drive shafts for mills. The efforts of puddlers had not yet been successful in overcoming production problems. They were thwarted by inferior quality forge iron supplied from blast furnaces, while the interaction of roasting metal and the usual lining of sand in the bottom of the puddling furnace created a lot of slag and wasted much of the iron. These difficulties would not be overcome until the late 1820s, when forge iron was roasted along with other iron, including scrap. The additional metal replaced the sand lining in the reinforced furnace hearth and contributed to an efficient boiling process. In 1830, still hampered by high costs and poor quality output, puddling as a means of producing wrought-iron was almost non-existent in Scotland, except at Muirkirk. Elsewhere, wrought iron ware was produced from pig iron bars by conventional processes of hammering, rolling and refining.[29]

Before 1830, iron manufacture and finishing was yet a minor, though growing, sector of industrial capitalism in Scotland. Textile industries, especially production of cotton goods, using water and steam power, and a large workforce, had dominated since the 1760s. However, in the second stage of the industrial revolution in Scotland, from the 1830s until the 1870s, the leading sector was the iron industry. This was the greatest ever period of its expansion and influence at home and abroad. Before this period, all constituent parts of the iron industry – from the giant Carron to the smallest foundry, their various owners and managers, the host of smelters, foundry workers, forgemen, craft and unskilled support workers – were essentially the forerunners of the coming revolution in heavy industry. Between 1760 and 1830, the iron industry was dwarfed by the large textile sector and its predominantly female 150,000 workers. However, the number of men and boys in the textile sector was still higher than in the entire iron industry, where fewer than 10,000 were employed in a peak year. In coal and ironstone mining, the workforce had also risen to an estimated 10,000 by 1830. Outside the textile mills, in handloom weaving alone in 1830, the majority of its 80,000 workers in Scotland were male, providing another comparative measure of the lesser significance of the iron industry as a source of male employment. However, within the next 20 years, the decline of hand loom weaving and the unprecedented expansion of the iron industry ensured that the respective numbers and employment prospects of weavers and iron workers would undergo a dramatic reversal.

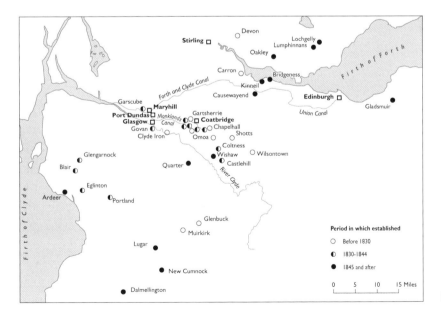

Blast furnace plants

CHAPTER 2
IRON WORKERS IN THE AGE OF THE INDUSTRIAL REVOLUTION:
WORK PROFILES AND CONDITIONS

At night, ascending to the hill on which the Established Church stands, the groups of blast furnaces on all sides might be imagined to be blazing volcanoes, at most of which the smelting is continued Sundays and week days, by day and night, without intermission. By day, a perpetual steam arises from the whole length of the canal where it receives the waste water from the blast-engines on both sides of it; and railroads, traversed by long trains of waggons drawn by locomotive engines, intersect the country in all directions.

A description of Coatbridge, 1841.[1]

Iron smelters, moulders and smiths are generally short-lived, and considered old men at 45 to 50 years of age.[2]

From the 1830s, the hot-blast and accompanying exploitation of massive resources of quality blackband ironstone and splint coal, particularly in North Lanarkshire, laid the foundations for the revolutionary transformation of iron smelting in Scotland. Those improvements, initiated by enterprising iron and coal masters, and implemented by many thousands of iron workers and colliers, resulted in dramatic savings in fuel, materials and costs for Scottish smelting firms, and enabled production of top grade foundry iron. Above all, Gartsherrie iron, made in Coatbridge, dominated the British market and some foreign markets for over 40 years, and brought untold wealth to the Baird family of iron masters. As will be explained later, the enterprise and immense personal fortunes of large Scottish iron masters were based on a cheap labour regime, imposed ruthlessly on skilled and unskilled workers alike.

The principal locations of this extraordinary expansion of plant,

Gartsherrie blast furnaces, 'old side', built in the 1830s (North Lanarkshire Council)

production and labour were the mineral-rich parishes of Old Monkland and New Monkland, in North Lanarkshire. Since 1800, all pioneering groundwork for the new era of expansion in smelting had been carried out within the bounds of Old Monkland parish. It was here that David Mushet, then manager of Calder Iron Works, discovered the potential of blackband ironstone. Between 1828 and 1832, the main experiments of J.B. Neilson with hot-blast in full-size furnaces were conducted at Calder and Clyde Iron Works. At Calder, in 1831, raw splint coal was first substituted for the usual poorer quality coking coal in the furnace. In 1830 the new smelting plant at Gartsherrie and its first circular shaped blast furnace led the way with the hot-blast technique. During the 1830s and 1840s, the rising capital of Old Monkland, the 'iron burgh' of Coatbridge, with six smelting plants, 50 blast furnaces, an emerging train of malleable iron firms, and its huge influx of workers engaged in heavy industry, coal and ironstone mining, was the nerve-centre of the new developments. From the late 1830s, Monklands iron masters pursued fresh leases of iron ore elsewhere, expanding their blast-furnace empire into Ayrshire and other parts of Lanarkshire. By the 1870s, with 40 blast furnaces in several locations, William Baird and Co. was possibly the world's largest single producer of foundry pig iron.

Smelting plants produced quality pig iron to serve an increasing number of light and heavy casting foundries throughout central Scotland, although the bulk of foundry iron was destined for export. The Scottish iron foundry of the nineteenth century varied in size, classification of moulding work and range of finished articles. Many foundries, as in the Falkirk area, specialised in light casting work, producing hollow-ware goods such as cooking pots, large pans and containers, domestic stoves and grates and various pipes and guttering. Others, as in the engineering foundries of Glasgow, the lower Clyde, and Motherwell, increasingly served the massive requirements of the shipbuilding industry, and specialised in large, heavy castings for the likes of boilers and tanks, engines, machinery and machine parts, hoisting and winding gear, bridge girders and locomotives.

In contrast to the basic smelting and iron founding sectors, production of wrought iron by the improved puddling process made a slow start, breaking through eventually in the 1840s and 1850s. Initially, this renewed malleable iron sector was located mainly in the Monklands and Glasgow. Rapid railway construction from the late 1840s encouraged further production of bar iron, while the Clyde shipyards became a major customer for wrought-iron hull and boiler plate, until steel superseded iron from the 1880s. The Glasgow-based and Monklands iron masters also extended operations further into North Lanarkshire, setting up additional malleable ironworks and blast-furnace capacity. With twenty ironworks of various descriptions, Old Monkland, and Coatbridge at its centre, was the most heavily industrialised parish in mid-Victorian Scotland. However, by the 1860s and 1870s, the burgeoning industrial communities of the Motherwell and Wishaw area had grown to rival Coatbridge and its satellite villages for the foremost concentration of puddling furnaces and rolling mills in Scotland. The North Lanarkshire industrial belt was among the largest producers of iron in Britain, and already called the 'Staffordshire of Scotland'. The Glasgow contribution in malleable-iron works was also significant, including: Blochairn, and Glasgow Iron Company's large works at St Rollox, both in the north of the city; Dixon's 'Blazes' at Govanhill and Parkhead Forge. Despite the growing advance of the steel industry in North Lanarkshire from the 1870s until the First World War, iron manufacture, and particularly the malleable-iron sector, was still ahead in numbers of firms and workers.[3]

The expanding iron industry from the 1830s onwards was dependent on a huge and increased influx of labour. Scottish, English, Irish and Welsh workers were crowded into hastily-built company towns and settlements around ironworks and coal pits. While the character and culture of ironwork settlements and master–worker relations in this extended industrial frontier are considered in later chapters, the following section focuses on the structure, conditions and tasks of this diverse labour force during the mature phase of iron manufacture.

SMELTING: BLAST-FURNACEMEN

As already indicated at Carron, furnace-keepers were the leading, skilled men at smelting furnaces, and remained so from the onset of the hot-blast process in the 1830s. The furnace-keeper was manager of operations, with responsibility for overseeing the amount, proportions and frequency of the charge of materials; regulating the pressure and temperature of the hot blast; supervising the removal of slag and the final tapping and disposal of the molten iron. He managed the team of workers at his furnace. They included an assistant keeper, an engineman and a boilerman who attended the blast apparatus; a hoist operator; charge fillers and other underhands; boys who prepared sand moulds in pig beds and lifters who removed the cast-iron bars from the beds. Until direct payment of workers became the norm in the 1870s, the head furnace-keeper contracted and paid the whole team and was ultimately responsible for quality of the finished product.

Smelting took place in the bowels of the furnace, hidden from view, and was not open to human interference until samples were taken towards the end of the process. The keeper's skill at managing the conglomeration of coal, ironstone and limestone charge through the processes from initial heating and loading to tapping required a number of careful judgements and adjustments, based entirely on experience and observation. For instance, at the concluding stage, when the slag was being sampled, if this waste was too fluid he, or his main assistant, could decide to take remedial action and order another charge of iron ore. Similarly, if the slag appeared to be too thick, more limestone could be added to assist final tapping of the molten iron. The whole process took around twelve hours, and constituted a work shift. Normal times for tapping the furnaces were at 6 a.m. and 6 p.m. Extra hands were needed at casting time, and this operation usually required support from arrivals on the relieving shift.

A team of furnace-fillers loaded the charge at various intervals throughout the shift. In a large-capacity 60 foot-high furnace, as at Gartsherrie in the late

Overleaf. Bottom of elevator: furnace charging at Coltness Iron Works (North Lanarkshire Council)

1860s, as many as sixty charges were loaded during a 12-hour period. The weight of each charge per ton was given as follows: coal, about 0.5; roasted ore, about 0.3; limestone, about 0.15:

> Two men are employed to feed each furnace. One fills half a charge of coal into a large iron barrow, and the other half a charge of the other materials into a second barrow. The men and the barrows reach the staging communicating with the mouth of the furnace by means of a hydraulic lift. The coal is thrown in first, and the other materials immediately afterwards.[4]

The hand charging work of the fillers was brutal and unskilled. They wheeled heavy iron barrows loaded with an average weight of 0.25 tons of minerals. At times, heaving the load finally into place at or near the furnace top was a most difficult and dangerous task as, struggling for breath and eyes smarting, fillers had little or no protection from a swirl of smoke, gas fumes and shooting flame. Furnace tops were not capped with cone shaped appliances until the 1870s, a measure which did help to reduce danger and discomfort for charge hands. Labourers who emptied and wheeled away roasting slag and cinders from the furnace hearth worked in hazardous, scorching conditions. Likewise, in the casting pit, workers struggled to control and channel the surge of molten metal that streamed from the tap hole into the sand beds. The melting point of iron is approximately 1500° C, and pouring and casting were carried out in an atmosphere of suffocating heat. Such tasks were described as 'very severe labour, and the faces of the men have a half-roasted appearance.' According to a contemporary Coatbridge writer, 'blast-furnace men have always been easily distinguished from the rest of the community, by the peculiar red and scorched appearance of their faces.'[5]

In this chain of work processes, lifting and piling scores of cast-iron pigs after they had solidified in the sand beds was among the most physically punishing labour around furnaces. Cast-iron pigs each weighed over 1 cwt. While still hot, they had to be manoeuvred from the sand beds with the aid of a heavy hammer, before being lifted by hand, and put into piles for weighing. Further lifting was involved when loading pig bars for the works foundry or forge, or into wagons for use elsewhere. In similar bouts of hard manual labour, solidified slag had also to be broken up with hammers and carted away to the waste heap. Of course, no record was kept of strained and broken bodies resulting from such crushing manual lifting done six days every week,

or of the burns, respiratory disease and debility which were a by-product of furnace labour.

Blast-furnace tasks of filling and casting were the preserve of adult males, as qualities of physical strength and endurance were at a premium. However, boys were employed as labourers to make sand moulds in the pig beds. This was a fairly simple operation, carried out during a short shift each day or night, and involved use of sand, rectangular spars of wood as templates and tools such as a mallet, a rake and a shovel. This description of their tasks belongs to Clyde Iron Works in 1842, and is probably typical of such employment in smelting plants in the west of Scotland:

Hand charging at top of blast furnace, Coltness Iron Works (North Lanarkshire Council)

Pig lifters at the 'breaker', Coltness Iron Works (North Lanarkshire Council)

With regard to the nature of the employment in iron works, the making moulds into which the molten iron is run from the furnace into pigs, is the only employment connected with blast furnaces in which children are employed. Each furnace requires one moulder for the morning and another for the evening casting, each of which takes place at six o'clock, and the moulds take about three hours to make. In front of each furnace is a space covered with sand, sometimes under a shed and sometimes in the open air. The boy who makes the moulds arranges on the ground a number of wooden bars at equal intervals side by side, resting at one end against a long bar which forms the matrix for the 'sow' as it is called, and to which all the iron pigs are attached when first cast. Seven or eight bars now being arranged at proper intervals, and tapped with a wooden mallet to make them lie even, sand is thrown upon them with a shovel. The bars being then again tapped to loosen them are neatly taken out, and leave the impressions or moulds for the pigs. The process is then repeated until the necessary number of moulds is made. There are usually about six beds with from 28 to 30 pigs in each to a furnace. Excepting the night work and the labouring on Sundays, there seems nothing injurious about this employment.[6]

Furnace-keepers contracted the boy sand moulders, who were often their own children. Boys were employed at this work from a very young age. For example, at Glengarnock Iron Works, William Blue began at the pig beds in 1868 at age nine, and John Kane was ten when he started in 1877. Blue recalled that sand in pig beds was trampled barefoot, and daily wages were a pittance. As he grew older and stronger, he became a furnace-filler, which required very vigorous barrow work in 12-hour shifts.[7] In contrast to the apparently easier work of the sand moulders, it will be seen later how many more boys were employed at dangerous and heavy tasks, often for long hours, in foundries and forges.

An informant in the late 1860s claimed that 'one furnace gives employment, directly and indirectly, to fully 200 men and boys.'[8] Although he did not specify how this total was divided up, it is not difficult to endorse his calculation. His figure was based on the experience of the giant Gartsherrie smelting plant, dedicated entirely to pig iron production, when its 16 furnaces, working at full capacity, were serviced by around 3,000 workers.

Considering how labour was deployed in and around a blast furnace, each furnace was worked by two teams on twelve-hour shifts, and many auxiliary workers were also involved. Labourers broke down ironstone lumps with hand hammers to no more than the size of a fist. Other workmen attended kilns where ironstone was cleaned of surface dirt and given a preparatory roasting before being fed into the furnace. Another squad crushed limestone into small lumps and prepared it in heaps. Although the work of coke oven-keepers and minders had been made obsolete by substitution of raw coal in furnaces, coal supplies had still to be sorted, stacked and carried to the loading stage. Gartsherrie and its two banks of furnaces consumed a thousand tons of coal every twenty-four hours, indicating a voracious appetite for fuel and labour-intensive effort from many workers. Apart from the core-smelting crew of keepers, fillers and casting-pit labourers, engine men furnished and directed the blast and the injection of water, and looked after the steam-powered machinery. Among the auxiliary workers were the boy sand moulders, the slag and cinder barrow men, the pig lifters, wheelers and weighers, carters and hauliers and drivers of small steam locomotives (puggies) on rails around the furnaces. Finally, brickmakers and bricklayers

Boys making pig iron beds, Coltness Iron Works (North Lanarkshire Council)

also merit inclusion in this incomplete inventory, as large quantities of brick were needed for furnace repair and relining.

Blast-furnace operations were continuous, and around the clock. Keeping the furnaces in blast meant an alternate six- and seven-day week for essential furnace teams. Until 1914–18, they worked on twelve-hour shifts. Day and night shifts rotated on alternate weeks, and the weekly changeover from day- to night-shift teams entailed a gruelling double shift of 24 hours every second Sunday for the day-shift workers. In 1842, while it was reported that blast-furnace plants in the west of Scotland continued to work through Sunday, only Gartsherrie and its neighbour, Summerlee, had decided to stop production for 12 hours on Sunday, without any harm to business. Workmen had a day off, and the furnaces had a rest from the blast, allowing any emergency maintenance before resumption of production on the Monday.[9] However, this arrangement was shortlived, and smelting was resumed as a normal practice on Sundays. There was the occasional exception, to allow time for furnace repair. On account of the prohibitive costs of being 'out of blast', it was considered that furnaces should not stand idle for long, in case they cooled too much, thereby cracking the brick lining, causing a shutdown and requiring extensive repair. Fettling crews of bricklayers had the dirty, dusty, hot and noxious job of relining furnace interiors. This essential repair and maintenance was usually carried out several times a year, normally on Sundays. A 72-hour working week was the norm for smelting teams throughout the nineteenth century, although pig-bed boys and lifters worked fewer hours. It will be seen later that from the early 1890s smelters challenged their punishing schedule, aiming at shorter hours and abolition of Sunday working.

FOUNDRY WORKERS

Among skilled workers, the cupola keeper was heating specialist and principal founder, responsible for one or more furnaces He supervised the process whereby the particular grade of pig-iron bars was reheated and boiled to a molten state, ready for pouring into moulds. The skilled founder in nineteenth-century Scotland had a practical knowledge of the uses of different grades of pig iron for casting and, when melting and re-melting, knew how to mix and apportion them according to the character and require-

ments of the intended mould. The skill of mixing pig irons to give the appropriate casting remained the product of experience rather than theoretical, or
book-based, scientific knowledge. However, it was usual to mix No. 1 and No.
3 pig irons for general foundry needs, while No. 3 and No. 4 (the strongest
grade of foundry iron) were used for heavy castings, such as machine parts,
girders and columns.[10]

Next in line, journeymen moulders and trained boy assistants were
essential skilled workers on the foundry floor. Before mass-production
techniques and machine moulding were introduced towards the end of the
nineteenth century, the specialist hand moulder was a craftsman, capable of
the most complex intricate work for customer orders in light or heavy casting.
However, he depended on the élite pattern-maker, who worked outside the
confines of the moulding workshop, for the design or model for the mould,
which was usually made of wood. During the 1860s, at a prominent Scottish
foundry, the art of the hollow-ware moulders, preparing common, three-
legged, cast iron cooking pots which could be suspended over a fire, was
described in the following way:

> The patterns for a pot consist of nine pieces – two for the body, three
> for the feet, and two for each of the ears. The body pieces have been
> formed by taking a completed pot, denuding it of feet and ears, and
> cutting it vertically into two pieces. These pieces the moulder takes
> and, placing the severed edges together, lays them down on his bench
> with the bottom upward. He then encloses the pattern in a circular
> casing, which he fills up with sand. The sand is rammed down all
> round and over the pattern, care being taken during this process to
> insert the feet pieces, and also a wooden plug to form a 'gate' through
> which to pour the metal. The moulder then turns the box over, and fills
> the inside of the pot with sand. The next part of the operation is to
> take out the pattern and leave open and entire the space it occupies.
> The advantage of having the casing and the pattern in sections now
> becomes manifest.
>
> The upper section of the casing is unfastened and taken off, when
> it is seen that the sand bears an impression of the bottom of the pot.
> The side pieces are in like manner removed, leaving the body pattern
> clear. The latter is carefully lifted off, one half at a time, exposing the
> 'core', or globular mass of sand which represents the interior of the
> pot. The surface of the sand is next thickly dusted with ground

charcoal, and rubbed quite smooth – a process which makes the iron take a finer skin than it would otherwise do. The feet and ear pieces having been withdrawn, all that is now necessary is to put the casing together again, fasten it tight up, and prepare the 'gate' by pulling out the plug and rounding off the edges of the hole. So compact does the sand become that the completed mould may be moved about freely without sustaining injury. An expert hand can mould a pot of the largest size in from fifteen to twenty minutes.

The next stage, casting the molten metal from the foundry furnace into the moulds, and the subsequent processes of dressing and finishing, are also observed:

> After a certain number of moulds have been prepared, the workmen proceed to 'cast' them. The molten metal is carried from the furnaces in huge ladles, and appears to be as fluid as water. When it is poured into the mould, gas is at once generated, which finds its way through the sand and, issuing from the joints of the casing, becomes ignited. Were the gas not allowed to escape, the mould would burst, and the consequences to the workmen would be most disastrous. It is a curious fact that, while a few drops of water would ruin a mould, the boiling metal may be poured in from a height of a couple of feet without disturbing a particle of the sand. When the metal has cooled sufficiently, it is dug out of the sand and taken to the dressing shops, where roughnesses are removed. Articles cast in several pieces are then carried to the fitting shops, where they are put together. Kettles and stew pans, which are to be tinned, are first annealed, and then passed to turners, who put a smooth and bright surface on the inside. The tinning is then done, the handles are put on, the outsides japanned, and the completed goods removed to the warehouse.[11]

The moulder at times worked on products which required only basic, simple patterns or measurements but, as the above description of his work suggests, expertise with materials used for moulding was always crucial for the success of each operation. Loam – a mixture of water, sand, clay and a fibrous material such as horse dung, straw or sawdust – was normally used for moulding hollow and circular objects of any size, including pots, cylinders and pipes. Loam was an easily worked material which, even in large objects, allowed the mould to be shaped and rounded off with hand tools such as a trowel and a shaped wooden board. When coated over a brick foundation, which provided a bulky core for heavy castings, loam could be applied to the required shape, without moulders needing an exact pattern to guide them.[12] However, the all-round moulder was experienced in making cores from sand and other solid materials.

Our description, above, of the expertise of the pot moulder included his use of green sand (meaning that it was soft and unbaked, rather than green in colour), the most common material for making moulds during the nineteenth century. This mixture of sand, coal or charcoal dust and water, had to be carefully pressed and packed in the moulding box, and required much skill, in order to produce a smooth interaction with the movement of molten metal and gases produced during the casting process. Failure to ram (pack) sand in the appropriate way ruined the cast and resulted in wasted work, for which the moulder was blamed and fined.

In the hollow ware and light castings sector of foundry work, boys and trainee moulders and dressers were nearly as numerous as journeymen. It was in this class of foundry work, according to reports on child labour in ironworks in central Scotland in 1842, that the greatest number of boys was employed:

> as most of the articles manufactured being of a light description, they can be moulded and cast by boys. The chief work of boys in iron foundries is the making of moulds for casting small articles, such as cast iron pots, cleaning and dressing the above. In the greensand shops, each boy has a bench with ground charcoal, sand, etc, on the floor beside him, and a few simple tools. A space is allotted to each, extending from the wall towards the centre of the shop, where he places his moulds in a row when made. The cupolas or furnaces are in a state to cast twice a day: one in the morning and the other in the afternoon. The smaller boys doing the lighter articles are at one end of the building, and they rise in size and strength progressively. At the time of casting, two boys from adjoining rows convey the molten metal from the furnace in a pot suspended from a long handle, which they carry by each end. A third boy, or a man on purpose, ladles out the metal from this pot, and pours it into the moulds. When sufficiently cool, a boy takes off the outer cast-iron boxes in which the mould is formed and takes off

from the article the 'gate' or excrescence at the part where the metal
was poured into the mould. The pots are then dressed with
sandstone and water to take off the rough parts, the sand which
adheres to them etc. The lads are generally apprentices, beginning
about thirteen years old, and earning from 3 shillings to 4 shillings a
week, paid by the piece.[13]

Some foundry boys were apprenticed or indentured from the age of 12, as at
Carron. Earlier, in 1803, an observer at Clyde Iron Works foundry had
indicated that 'several 10 to 12 year old boys were employed, who moulded
small pans and other fine castings in sand with admirable skill. One of the lads
pushed his daily wages higher than one of the older moulders was able to
do.'[14] At the nearby Falkirk Iron Company, which employed four hundred
workers, boys started work on the foundry floor as early as age seven and
eight, for example, as water carriers and messengers. Most foundry boys were
the cheapest labour, exploited by employers and subcontracting workmen,
who were often their close kin. Few boys had contracts and were engaged,
wherever possible, instead of adult males. The following testimonies of boy
moulders and dressers at Falkirk Iron Company illustrate working conditions
in the early 1840s.

Donald Elder, a nine-year-old pot moulder, worked 'on James Anderson's
account; he pays me 2 shillings a week; will give me more when I can work
more'. Robert Fotheringham, a 12-year-old moulder, 'began to work three
years ago; does not mind it now, did when first at it, as the metal sore burned
me, and threw me idle. I get 3/6d a week from my master, Richard Glen, to
whom I was bound a year since by Father. We work very long hours, while 14
and 15.' Andrew Laing, another 12-year-old moulder, had already 'wrought 4
years at pot moulding; works every day, 12 to 14 hours; rests 20 minutes at
each meal; master gives me 3/6d a week. Father was a moulder but has been
discharged for hard drinking; mother gets my wages.' William Morrison, an
11-year-old dresser, 'works from 5 in morning until 6 and 7 at night; do not
like such long hours, as have only two rests of 20 minutes each during day.
Can earn 2/6d a week. William Granger is my master; he has four other
laddies in his employ, some men have seven. We get our licks occasionally'.
This remark raises the issue of punishment and abuse at the hands of subcontracting journeymen who were in charge of the youngsters, but there is no
way of knowing the extent of enforced discipline. Managers giving evidence
to the 1842 Employment Commission were guarded in their comments. At

Carron, it was claimed that boy foundry workers were 'fairly treated by their parents or masters', while the managing partner at Falkirk Iron Company was more forthcoming, although still evasive:

> The contractors sometimes certainly chastise the boys lightly when necessary, but there is no system of punishment in the works, and I have very seldom had complaints of corporal punishments. The parents generally tell the contractors to whip them and keep them in order; no instructions whatever are given to the overlookers to punish the children.

At Carron, works manager Joseph Dawson reported that 'our processes do not require necessarily very young children; when employed it is to assist parents, who always work by the piece in the moulding shops. The dressers and other young boys work much after the same way'. John Sutherland, a 14-year-old moulder, informed that 'Father brought me to the foundry when I was eight years of age; was first at the dressing; am bound to the company for twelve years; am turned over to Father for five years'. He and his brother, William, a nine-year-old moulder, 'start together at 5, sometimes 6, in the morning, and lay by at 5 and 6 at night, whiles later'. William worked 'at the wee boxes [small moulds]; can't say I dislike it, though I often get burned'.

Twelve-year-old Michael Hurley, 'works for Father as dresser. Dressing is cleaning the casts from the loam, and knocking off the overcastings'. His brother Alexander, age 14, also a dresser, had already worked there for four years; 'am apprenticed, and turned over to my father's cousin; he pays my wages to Father'. John Hoskin, a 13-year-old assistant smith and fitter, had already worked in that section for four years. 'I fit and file the grates on Father's account; can't say what he gets for me, as he works by the piece'.[15]

In the mid nineteenth century, usual working hours for all manual grades in foundries was no less than twelve a day for five days a week, including a customary arrangement of two short meal breaks, around 8 a.m. for breakfast, and around 1 p.m. for lunch. The regular working week was Monday to Saturday, stopping earlier on Saturday. Unlike blast-furnace and forge workers, foundry workers were not required to do nightshifts although, as related above, founders in engineering shops were known to work overtime and do evening work to complete an important order or do emergency repairs for machines. In the 1860s, the prominent Glasgow cast-iron pipe makers, Stewart and Co., worked variable hours into the evening. Its casting shop foreman reported that, 'we never work by shifts, have no regular time for giving over', but 'very seldom work after nine o'clock'. Their boy workers were also caught up in this long hours arrangement.[16]

Total meal and rest times varied, amounting to one and a half to two hours in the day. According to reports, the diet of foundry workers was at least nutritious, if monotonous, consisting of porridge for breakfast and broth, or potatoes or kail with herring for the midday meal. A family member brought in the food, or the worker went home for a meal break if he lived close by.

Foundry workers toiled in the most foul, polluted and hazardous conditions. The 'black squad' in the shipyard and engineering foundries was given that nickname because of the filthy nature of their work. Yet, there is little sense or understanding of this grim reality in early official reports of foundry work. Thomas Tancred, who investigated conditions of boy labour in foundries in the west of Scotland in 1842, displayed ignorance, prejudice and under-statement. For example, he concluded, 'I cannot learn that there is anything deleterious to health in the foundries, excepting that the brightness in the melted metal occasionally affects the eyes, and as they [the boys] are generally barefooted, they are liable to get burns in the feet by stepping upon the iron'. He went on to report that the foundry, as 'the place of work, is an open shed, plentifully ventilated, and if occasionally exposed to great heat, the atmos-phere at least is cool'. Moreover, he was convinced that industrial disease and debility did not figure prominently as reasons for the poor health and early demise of foundry workers. Instead, he claimed that self-inflicted drunk-enness and bad housing were mostly to blame: 'The principal causes of ill health amongst founders, moulders etc, are their intemperate habits, and the filthy habitations in which too many of them reside.'[17] If moulders had a reputation for heavy drinking and alcohol abuse that damaged their health, the effects of pervasive work-related lung and heart disease were undoubtedly lethal.

According to Carron's principal historian, the company's accident record for the early nineteenth century was 'good'. While fatal accidents were few, 'minor accidents there were in plenty, burns of course predominating in the foundry'.[18] However, frequent exposure to burns from molten metal was unavoidable, especially during casting operations, carried out twice a day, in morning and afternoon bursts. They were a melee of hectic, dangerous activity for founders and moulders, conducted in blistering heat, smoke and fumes. Moreover, in the moulding shop, after casting operations were completed, the worker had to contend with the insidious, potentially fatal, damage to lungs occasioned by long-term exposure to clouds of spent charcoal, sand and metal dust that were released at the 'knockout' stage, when moulding boxes were emptied. Dressers and sandstone grinders were also susceptible to debility from long-term inhalation of grit and particles raised by constant chipping, filing and turning operations. Eye injuries were a frequent occurrence among foundry workers, and temporary loss of the use of an eye was a normal hazard. From the 1860s, Glasgow Eye Infirmary treated many cases each year.

The Scottish Iron Moulders' Union claimed that unhealthy foundries and, in particular, inhalation of all kinds of dust, combined with the exhausting demands of piece-work earning, ruined prospects of life into and beyond middle age. The rules of the Scottish trade union in 1858 referred to the 'aged members' between 40 and 50. Each year, a third to half of the deaths of members were attributed to industrial and respiratory diseases that we now know as pneumonia, silicosis and fibrosis.[19] Occupational deafness among founders and moulders was a common debility, and was especially so among plate and boiler makers and riveters, as all were exposed to long periods of high decibel hammering and clashing metal.

Into the early twentieth century, foundries continued to be workplace hell-holes, as an experienced Clydeside moulder testified:

The conditions under which the moulder worked were vile, filthy, and insanitary. The approach to the foundry resembled that of a rag and bone shop, or marine store. The entrance was usually strewn with all kinds of scrap iron and rubbish. The inside was in keeping with the outside. Smoke would make the eyes water. The nose and throat would clog with dust. Drinking water came from the same tap as was used by the hosepipe to water the sand. An iron tumbler or tin can served as drinking vessel until it was filthy or broken, before being replaced. The lavatory was usually placed near a drying stove, and consisted of open cans that were emptied once a week – a veritable hotbed of disease.

Every night pandemonium reigned while the moulds were being cast. The yelling and cursing of foremen; the rattle of overhead cranes; the smoke and dust illuminated by sparks and flames from the molten metal made the place a perfect inferno. Glad we were, when it was all over, to creep into some corner alive with vermin of all kinds, to close our eyes for a few minutes.[20]

MALLEABLE-IRON WORKERS

In a malleable iron works, the sequence of essential production processes and division of labour was as follows. Puddlers produced balls of raw wrought iron in a furnace. Next, shinglers hammered the still roasting iron lumps into rectangular-shaped blooms. The blooms were then sent to the forge mill for initial rolling into rough bars. At the refining stages, the bars were re-heated, and passed several times through the main set of rolls, being compressed gradually into the required grade and shape; for example, into bars, plates, sheets, angles, or rails. They were then sheared to exact size and length, straightened and carefully stored/piled. The malleable articles were then ready for sale, or passed on for reworking at the firm's own engineering workshops as, for instance, at Beardmore's Parkhead Forge in the 1860s and 1870s, then a leading example of an integrated malleable-iron producer and specialist finishing works.[21] Alternatively, the rolled products were destined for an engineering workshop elsewhere, where they were further forged, fitted and welded, with other shapes, into heavy, large and complex products such as machines, locomotive engines, boilers and ship parts.

Puddlers

In a malleable-iron works, puddlers were primary production workers, converting pig iron into the rudiments of wrought iron. Puddling furnaces

Puddling at Waverley Works, Coatbridge, the last malleable-iron works in Scotland

were made of brick, encased in cast iron and situated in the forge at the beginning of the manufacturing process. They were usually spaced in a row or bank inside a large roofed building with open sides. Compared to its blast-furnace big brother, the much smaller puddling furnace required more constant attention and meticulous care from key workers. Each puddling furnace required a two-man team of operators: the forehand puddler and his assistant, or underhand. One or more ancillary workers, usually young lads, also helped at a puddling furnace, sometimes on a shared basis.[22]

It is reckoned that puddlers had one of the most physically demanding jobs in heavy industry. After observing the work processes at Parkhead Forge in the late 1860s, the industrial journalist David Bremner wrote: 'The work of the puddler is probably the severest kind of labour voluntarily undertaken by men.'[23] Moreover, puddling was widely acknowledged as the most difficult of the metallurgical crafts, requiring great skill and a high level of decision-making and responsibility. The puddler had no instruments to gauge temperature or to measure chemical reactions, and had to rely on careful eye judgement and accumulated practical experience to time key operations. For example, he had to decide when the mass of iron had 'come to nature' or, in other words, was ready for dividing up into several lumps, and when to separate and run out the slag. The forehand puddler planned and directed all furnace operations, including the following tasks. He prepared and repaired the lining of the hearth (fettling); supervised loading and heating of the charge of pig iron, scrap and fuel; worked and agitated the charge until balls of iron were formed; tapped the slag; lifted the wrought-iron balls from the furnace and saw to their transfer to the shingling hammer.

The various stages of the puddling process constituted one 'heat', and lasted for two hours or so. The puddler worked several 'heats' in long shifts of 12 or more hours, in a dangerous environment of roasting metal and torrid heat arising from peak furnace temperatures of 1300° C.

Bremner's graphic description of the series of tasks to produce a 'heat' does not include tapping of the slag following removal of the iron lumps, but his account of the puddler's work appears otherwise comprehensive. His description starts with insertion of a furnace charge of 4 cwts of pig iron and scrap:

> The pig iron, which has previously been broken into pieces of convenient size, is thrown in, and the doors of the furnace are closed and sealed up with cinders. Intense heat is then generated; and so

fiercely does the fire burn that the flame issues from the top of the chimney, which is upwards of forty feet high. In about a quarter of an hour after the furnace has been sealed, the iron shows signs of melting, and an aperture in the hearth door, about six inches square, is opened. The puddler, whose eyes seem to be proof against a light as dazzling as the sun at noon, looks in at the opening, and determines whether it is time to disturb the iron. As soon as he sees the finer angles of the iron begin to melt, he thrusts in a stout rod of malleable iron, and moves the lumps of metal about, so that the entire mass may be equally heated. If this were not done, the parts which melted first would be burned up and lost, and the quality of what remained deteriorated.

The puddler's assistant takes a turn at this part of the work; and during its progress the heat is occasionally moderated by means of the damper, or by dashing small quantities of water upon the iron. At frequent intervals, the puddling bar is withdrawn, and cooled by being dipped into water. The iron dissolves gradually on the hearth, and after a time begins to heave and bubble, innumerable jets of flame bursting forth all over its surface. The desired chemical change is now going on. The hot air from the furnace sweeps over the iron and carries off a great part of the carbon, sulphur, phosphorus, and silicon contained in the pig iron. Care must be taken to prevent the metal from becoming too fluid; and as soon as it attains a pasty consistency, the heat is moderated. Meantime the puddler uses his rod vigorously, and as the metal begins to 'dry', the labour of moving it about is increased. The metal at length seems to curdle and become granular. The heat of the furnace is again raised, and the particles of metal begin to adhere together.

From this point the chief puddler undertakes and completes the operation. As the metal agglutinates, it becomes very difficult to move. The puddler has to exert himself to the utmost; and he dare not relax his efforts for a single minute, else all the previous labour would be worse than lost. Though the perspiration pours from his face and arms, and oozes through his scanty clothing, he must toil on. His eye is never removed from watching the contents of the furnace; and the expression of anxiety on his face indicates that the operation has reached a critical point. When the metal has attained a certain degree of consistency, the puddler divides it into five or six heaps. He then works each heap into a 'ball' or 'bloom'. The door of the hearth is opened and one after the other the balls are drawn out with a large pair of tongs, and dragged over the floor to the shingling hammer. As the balls are dragged from the furnace they have a spongy appearance, and slag and other impurities trickle from them. The various occupations described occupy, on the average, about two hours.

It is the puddler's duty to convey the 'balls' from the furnace, and to place them one by one on the anvil of the shingling hammer. Before the invention of the steam hammer, a somewhat clumsy contrivance was used for squeezing the slag out of the puddled iron and beating it into shape. Now the steam hammer is everywhere employed for those purposes. When the puddler lays a 'ball' on the anvil, he waits to see the result of the first blow, and from it he is enabled to judge of the quality of his work.[24]

In England, it was not the responsibility of the puddler and his team to transport the fireballs of puddled iron to the shingling hammer. No reason is offered as to why the customary practice was different in Scotland, although puddlers resented having to take the time and trouble of this responsibility. Earlier reports state that the underhand puddler used tongs to drag and manoeuvre the heavy fireballs of iron along the plated floor of the forge to the hammer. In another version of this whole operation, a long-serving iron heater, Bernard McAuley, who witnessed Motherwell puddlers in the early 1900s, recalled the hard toil of the principal tasks:

You flung in pig iron and maybe a barrow of turnings [scrap] until you'd six or seven hundredweight in the wee furnace, and when it melted you rabbled it. A rabble was a long bar, about eight feet long, with a paddle or a hook at the end, and it passed through a wee hole in the furnace door. You pushed it into the molten iron, and turned it, and twisted it, and pushed it about for an hour or an hour and a half; and while you were doing that, the heat was gradually withdrawn. You could feel the iron thickening – it was like pushing your rabble into putty, terrible hard work – and all the time you were forming it into big lumps or balls, each of them weighing maybe a hundredweight or so. That was the hard bit of the job, forming those balls. It was heavy work and terribly hot. When they were ready you whipped one ball out with a pair of tongs and ran it on a bogey along to the steam hammer. You hear a lot from old fellows like myself about how hard the work was at the steel-making, but making iron was harder still. It was so hard that often only a certain type of man would do it. There is no job in any industry in the country today that is anything like so strenuous, and even in the old days it attracted a special class of man.[25]

The tasks of preparing a 'heat' were repeated several times in the course of a working shift. According to various sources, in late nineteenth-century Scotland, puddlers would normally work until five or six heats had been completed, taking between eleven and fifteen hours. However, the workload and duration of a shift varied, depending on furnace size and capacity; quality of pig iron and fuel; the ability, strength and resolve of the leading puddler and his team; and ready access to the hammer. Puddling furnaces worked night and day, only being closed down on Saturday afternoons and on Sundays, or for exceptional repairs during the week.

A remarkable first-hand account of such conditions at puddling furnaces is revealed in the diary of a 'special class of man', a puddler called David Willox, while working at Parkhead Forge in the 1870s. In a separate personal history of his native Parkhead area of Glasgow, he tells of his early life, including how he became a forehand puddler after a succession of jobs as boy and youth.[26]

Born in 1845, David Willox was brought up in a family of hand loom weavers. He trained as a hand-loom weaver before he was ten, but worked briefly with his unsettled father at coal pits in Armadale before returning to Parkhead village to resume working life as a weaver. The trade was in decline, and the growing presence of Parkhead Forge was an alternative source of employment. Not yet fourteen, Willox started in the 'Old Forge':

> I got on very well in the Forge, and went to work underhand at a scrap furnace with Michael Young . . . oh, it was fearfully hard and hot work but Young was a good gaffer and bore me wonderfully well. I was terribly troubled with growing pains and I was tired, tired at nights, but the money was considered good, some 3s 6d or 4s a shift, and I braced myself to it as best as I could . . . but it was killing me, and was advised to take an easier job at the steam hammer, which I did at a much lower wage.[27]

After assisting at the hammer, he was promoted to furnace heater but left after a dispute about his wages. Now sixteen, he found an opportunity as trainee underhand puddler in the new part of the Forge, and 'resolved to learn the iron puddling'. A forehand puddler agreed to induct him into the world of puddling while the lad worked for next to nothing in wages. Then, another forehand took him on as underhand, at 3 shillings a shift. He 'gradually improved' as a learner puddler and for a short period worked as an underhand at the large Mossend Iron Works. He became a fully fledged forehand puddler when he 'got a furnace' at Parkhead, and remained there in that capacity until 1873 when, aged 28, he was promoted to forge foreman.

Willox commenced his diary in June 1872, providing details of his working hours, shift pattern, and conditions. He worked a punishing pattern of alternate weeks on day and night shift. For week beginning 3 June, he recorded six shifts, totalling seventy-three working hours:

Monday: 'started work at 3.30 am, left work at 5 pm'
Tuesday: "   'after 6 pm'
Wednesday: "   6 am, 'finished 7.30 pm'
Thursday: "   7 am,   7 pm'
Friday: "   8 am,   7 pm'
Saturday: "   7 am,   'done at 4 pm'

Although working long hours, he commented favourably on his experience that week, with entries such as 'got on very well with my work'. He had started unusually early on Monday morning to prepare the furnace lining for production; to load and set the charge of pig iron, scrap and coal fuel, and fire up for the first heat.

He then had Sunday and Monday off, before starting the nightshift rota that evening. Hours are not given for that particular week, but five shifts were worked (Monday–Friday), with Saturday off. However, he had to work several hours on Sunday morning, as it was his turn to fettle the furnace, which was 'under repairs'.

Having to acclimatise themselves to working in conditions of ferocious heat was already debilitating for puddlers. However, during summer, from the middle of June until early August, the additional effect of working through heat waves on dayshifts was at times unbearable, as revealed in the following diary entries for June 1872:

Tuesday 18: 'This has been a terrible day with heat – nearly all the puddlers knocked off. Only five of us finished on the shift, and little wonder!'
Wednesday 19: 'This has been another terrible day with heat'

Friday 21: 'Another hot day for working – a poor day's work, very tired all day'

Tuesday 25: 'Terribly hot at work, don't know when I sweated as much'

Then, for Monday, 1 July, Willox recorded, 'went to work before 5 this morning, had a very hard shift, after 7pm when I got done, weather keeping warm, very tired tonight.'

On Friday, 16 August, despite the oppressive weather and no opportunities for a breather in cool air, he allowed himself a brief word of congratulation: 'hot day, had to work pretty hard for my heats, but got them nevertheless.' Later, an entry for August 1876 recorded, 'it has been fearfully hot in the works today; some of the men have cramped and had to stop work.' On such occasions, when excessive heat threatened the ability and will to work, Willox exerted self-discipline, resisting the temptation to drink copious amounts of beer. He saw that many fellow puddlers succumbed to the conditions. In efforts to slake their raging thirst and beat dehydration, they drank too much, lowered their efficiency even further and weakened their powers to finish a shift, resulting in a proportionate loss of earnings.

Occasionally, other adverse material conditions also conspired against winning a successful shift and satisfactory earnings. For instance, on Friday, 26 September 1873, he complained, 'We have been getting on very poorly this week, a great many of the puddlers getting hung every shift.' 'Hung' was the term used for loss of a heat, as in this case 'chiefly owing to one of the hammers being under repairs'. In such circumstances, puddlers had to wait overlong for an available shingling hammer, affecting the quality of the iron. At other times, as in November 1876, he recorded, 'the iron is hard to work' and 'the iron is very grey, consequently the puddlers are losing heats.' In March 1876, 'the puddlers are getting very bad dross to fire with just now.' In those cases, puddlers were taking a longer time to complete the heats, having to wrestle with a problematic pig-iron mix or poor quality fuel.

By 1900, the puddling process in Scotland remained the same, but certain improvements in furnace efficiency and working practices had the effect of reducing protracted shifts and overall working hours. Firstly, steam jets now blew hot air into the furnace, reducing melting time and the length of heats. Secondly, instead of having to break up and prepare scrap and roasted cinder to fettle the furnace lining, those materials were brought to the puddler.

Moreover, by arranging a fee with the shingler, he no longer had to leave his furnace to go to the hammer and place his puddled ball on the anvil. Although the actual work was no less arduous, with dedicated focus on craft tasks and no enforced interruptions, he could now produce five heats on a regular basis and an occasional maximum of six heats, within a twelve-hour shift.[28] From his experience as a young puddler at the Stenton Iron Works, Wishaw, around the 1914–18 period, William Millsop confirmed that the forehand who had the 'energy and the eye to make the furnace travel' could work up five heats and make decent tonnage in a single shift.[29]

Puddling was an occupation best suited for fit young men, and many who stayed at the furnace could not last the pace of such exhausting toil into middle age. In Lanarkshire by 1900, some forehands in their 30s and 40s whose physical powers were deserting them 'could maintain their income and extend their careers by paying extra in order to secure the services of an able underhand who would shoulder more of the burden.'[30] The underhand who agreed to take on this additional responsibility and share of the strenuous work could also profit in the sense that he practised the main skills much earlier than usual and hastened the day when he could be promoted to forehand. Other puddlers no longer fit for heavy work had to settle for lighter and generally more menial tasks around an ironworks or elsewhere. One such example was Elliot Fraser, age 71, the oldest serving worker at Dalzell Iron and Steel Works in 1920. He had begun there as a puddler in 1872 but after a few years became 'incapacitated for such strenuous work by severe sciatica' and had spent the rest of his long working life there as a general labourer.[31] Others left prematurely, stricken by severe injury and declining health arising from the rigours of their occupation. Puddlers were prone to failing sight and even blindness from long-term exposure to peering into the intensive bright light of the furnace bowl. There was also a high incidence of debility and death from pneumonia, brought on by physical exhaustion and chest infections from exposure to extreme changes of temperature and chills. David Willox was more fortunate, although he suffered a couple of bad injuries between 1872 and 1878. A foot was severely bruised and painful for several months after a piece of iron fell on it, and he was informed that he narrowly escaped amputation. Less serious was scorching on one side of his face from a sudden blast of escaping boiler steam in the forge. We can understand why he was an ardent supporter of the Glasgow Royal Infirmary, raising workplace subscriptions to help finance treatment for injured workers like him.[32] He was also among the minority of puddlers who managed to save enough money to leave the forge and go into business, in his case as co-owner of a small chemical works, while still in his thirties.

Forgemen and Millmen

From the 1840s, the shingler hammered and shaped the puddled iron, while at white heat, with the aid of a Nasmyth steam hammer. Using long experience and eye judgement, his objective was to expel remaining slag and impurities from the balled iron before pressing the metal into a thick, flat block, and making it ready for the rollers. The shingler's work was skilled, heavy and dangerous, for which he wore protective gear:

> His feet and legs are encased in iron armour, his body is covered by a stout leather apron, and he wears a mask of the same material. One stroke of the hammer makes apparent the use for this warlike attire, for it sends out in every direction jets of liquid fire, which patter against the legs of the workman, and would inflict fearful injuries were they to come in contact with the skin. The manipulation of the ball under the hammer is severe work, and requires great expertness. The shingler uses a pair of tongs about four feet in length, and with these seizes the ball and turns it on the anvil each time the hammer ascends. He so

Shingling at Waverley Works. Note the visor and leg armour worn by the shingler manages that the iron assumes the shape of a brick, and the operation occupies only two or three minutes.[33]

The forge team at the hammer comprised the forehand shingler, an assistant and a hammer driver, who worked under his direction. The assistant also worked the tongs and manipulated the puddled iron. He also did other jobs, such as clean down the hammer. The shingler subcontracted his team, and paid them a basic shift wage from his tonnage rates.

Forehand rollers were the most skilled and most highly paid craftsmen among forge and mill teams. Like master puddlers and shinglers, the roller was paid on the basis of tonnage achieved, while he subcontracted his team on a shift wage. By the middle of the nineteenth century, rolling mill plants were far more sophisticated than the simple pair of rolls used in earlier malleable-iron works. With the three-high mill, a third roll was introduced, allowing the iron piece to be passed between the bottom and middle rolls, and back again between the top and middle rolls. The other early nineteenth-century invention to improve quality and save time on rolling was the guide mill. This consisted of a metal box fixture at the front of the finishing rolls, allowing the piece of iron to be correctly levered into the rolls. However, while rolls were steam powered, rolling operations were manual activities and very labour intensive. Productivity on regular working days was high, as in this example from Glasgow Iron Company's works at St Rollox in 1862. James Bissuld, roller, stated that, 'we work from 6 to 6. We have 14 to 15 heats in the day. Each heat takes three quarters of an hour. There are 40 or 50 bars rolled out of each heat.'[34] Assuming the accuracy of this evidence, and organised for efficient throughput, the team handled around six hundred passes of iron bar through a set of rolls in one busy shift.

After the shingling stage, and at the start of the mill process, forge rollers worked in small teams, using sturdy tongs to lift, position, turn and feed the still-hot iron block into and through a two-high rolling mill. At first, they continued to press out slag residue while forming a rough elongated bar. Appropriately, forge rollers were known in the trade as 'roughers'. Wrestling the heavy iron blocks into emerging bar through the forge rolls was among the most strenuous labour in the malleable-iron industry, and depended on brawn rather than skill. A fellow worker remarked ruefully that it was 'a job for a horse and not for a man'.[35] In the following stages, where the bar iron was processed through refining sets of rolls, the forehand craft rollers used their expertise, hand and eye judgement to manipulate and reduce the lengths of metal to the required thickness (including tinplate sheets almost as thin as paper), shape, strength and quality. Reworking the iron several times, they adjusted the screws and grooves for each set of passes, and experienced rollers were capable of producing all grades of iron to customer specification, from the common, merchant iron through to crown 'best', and the highest calibre 'best, best, best.'.

YOUNG WORKERS IN MALLEABLE IRON

In forges and rolling mills, boys from the age of eight to lads of seventeen were employed as assistant labour in a variety of jobs, including some skilled work.

In 1842, boys were observed at work in the three existing modern malleable-iron works in the west of Scotland, namely Dixon's Govanhill Iron Works; Dundyvan, Coatbridge and the Monkland Iron Company at Calderbank. There, the age of underhand puddlers was reported to be between 14 and 17. 'Door-drawer' boys who assisted at the reheating furnaces and stoves were between ten and fifteen years old. At the rolls, 'catchers', 'heavers-up' and 'straighteners' were between 12 and 16 years old.

> The boys called door drawers are attached one to each heating furnace. The boy's duty is to pull a rod, which raises the door of the furnace, whenever the heater requires it. The iron then goes to the forge rolls, through which it is passed several times in a red-hot state. Each time the bar passes through the roller it is supported by the catchers, who pass it back over the top of the roller to the heavers-up, who insert it again between the rollers. This is done by means of hooked iron rods, suspended from a beam overhead, so that the boy, holding the longer end of the lever and catching the red-hot bar in the crooked end, hoists the bar up and passes it back to the heavers-up. This is hot work, and not very light for young boys, the glowing iron sending out a powerful radiation as it approaches them. The bar being now rolled out to its proper dimensions, is dragged on one side, and beaten straight by men or boys, according to its thickness. There are also young persons assisting the shearers who cut the boiler plates, and at the mills for rolling these out.
>
> It cannot be denied that the forge work continued by one set of

hands all day, and by another set at night, without leaving the work for meals, and occasionally causing exposure to great heat, though with frequent intervals of rest, is a sort of labour at which no child under 14 or so should be employed.[36]

Twenty years later, an enquiry revealed that, although the workforce was mainly grown men, small numbers of boys aged between ten and fourteen were still employed at dangerous tasks at malleable-iron works in central Scotland. For example at Parkhead Forge, which employed eight hundred workers, including over twenty boys, one boy worked at every two mill furnaces, lighting and firing, as well as operating the doors. At Dixon's, several boys were interviewed, and their evidence contained the following passages:

I am past 13. I have worked here about eight months. I pull up and fire at a mill furnace. I never went to school. I can't read. Father is a labourer. He works here.

I am past 13. I have worked here between two and three years. I run down with the iron from the roll. It is small bar iron. I have never been burnt very sore. I was burnt, but no much. I have seen a boy badly burnt here.

I am past 11. I have worked here two years and a half. When I first came I worked in the small mill. I straightened iron. I now work at the big mill. I run down with the iron. I was burnt once, It is all right now. I was burnt when I was at the little mill.

I am going 10. I have worked six months. Father is a puddler. I draw the door of a mill furnace.[37]

At Colville and Grey's Clifton Iron Works, Coatbridge, a manager reported:

We have only one small guide mill. There are five boys employed at this mill. We only work it during the day. Some of these boys are as young as 9. The boys sometimes get burnt at the small mill. I do not think we have more than one bad case during the last year. There are six more boys employed in scrap picking and piling. They are older, about 12 or 14 years old. At the big mill, where we make angle iron, there are 12 boys on each shift, all above 14 years of age. We have no boys under 17 employed as underhand puddler. The underhands are generally men.[38]

Clearly, a youth had to be fit and strong before being taken on as underhand. However, at a lower, starting level, on the eve of the First World War, William Millsop was already a bogey boy at the age of 14, attending puddling furnaces at the Stenton Iron Works. After each heat, it was his job to hurry loads of roasting iron to the steam hammer. He and other lads of his age doing the same job then worked a twelve-hour shift, five days a week, for a total weekly wage of 12/6d. He was one of the conscientious, resilient lads to earn promotion to underhand puddler and, when a young man, to be selected on merit as a forehand puddler.[39]

Piling and reheating malleable iron at Coats Iron Works, Coatbridge, in 1927

For boys in iron-rolling mills in the pre-1914 era, the workload and hours were equally hard. James Watt, born in Calderbank in the early 1890s, started work at the age of 13 at Globe Works, Motherwell. He piled iron for the reheating furnaces: 'The cutter-down cut the plates of puddled iron into bits about 20 or 25 lbs each, and I piled them six high for charging. It was heavy work for 2/6d a day. You can calculate for yourself. You'd two furnaces with six heats a day each, that's twelve heats. And there were forty piles a heat. It was 24 or 25 tons a day you were shifting.'[40]

William Kelly started as a general labourer, aged 14, at Etna Iron Works, Motherwell, getting 'the enormous sum of 1/2d for a 12-hour day. My next job was at the rolls, into the hard and hot work. You had to hook the bars by hand over the roughing rolls, and that wasn't easy. Then my brother wanted me as a pilerunner on his 9-inch mill. Of all these jobs, this was the hardest. You had to run them out of the furnace, and then get the charge and heat up. You did all the stoking yourself . . . 4/2d a day for it, and a shilling from the heater, and you had to work for it, the sweat dripping off you.'[41]

NAIL-MAKERS

As discussed in Chapter 1, nail-making was a product of malleable-iron working. Nails were cut from iron rods and working conditions continued to be an atrocious case of sweated labour for men and boys. In particular, it involved gross exploitation of boys. Some worked with their nailer fathers, but most other boys were still being farmed out from charity poorhouses in Edinburgh and Glasgow. Into the 1840s, nail-making was centred principally in two localities – at Camelon (Falkirk) and at St Ninians (Stirling). Four firms dominated this small workshop industry, and most of the orders were subcontracted to journeymen nailers. The nailers and their assistants were caught up in a vicious cycle of exploitation. At a time of economic depression, when the market price for nails had been declining for several years, the firms reduced contract piece-work rates paid to local nailers who, in turn, drove themselves and their assistants to longer hours and increased production. As a Camelon nailer put it: 'The lowness of wages keeps men perpetually at the anvil.'[42]

Employment of around 200 boys in atrocious conditions came under scrutiny in the extensive parliamentary enquiry of 1841–2. R.H. Franks, who investigated child labour in mines and ironworks in central and eastern

Scotland, was outraged at what he witnessed, especially at Camelon, where most of the poorhouse boys had been placed and boarded with nailers. The nailers worked in squalid, insanitary conditions, amidst the heat, fumes and dust of confined brick outhouses equipped with a small forge. An experienced and thorough investigator, Franks concluded that the desperate plight of the boy nail-makers was one of the worst examples he had encountered, and he had already reported on the scandalous conditions of girls employed in coal pits.[43] His report is full of damning evidence, and is worth reproducing at some length here. He describes the primitive nature of the work done, almost entirely with simple hand tools:

> The child in the first place squares the rod of heated iron of which the nails are formed, i.e. flattens the rod equally on four sides; the hammer in striking off the required length of rod by a little ingenuity at the same time points the nail which, being received into, and firmly held by a small pair of iron block pincers, is shanked or headed to the required form by repeated blows of the hammer on a small portion of the rod left exposed for that purpose. This process is executed with great rapidity, and I was informed by several of the nail masters that three months' teaching was sufficient to enable an infant to accomplish the manufacture of 1,000 nails a day – provided they were (as it is termed) tasked – of which 'tasking' it may be necessary here to give some explanation. The first task is up to 'porridge' time, during which time they have to complete never less than 250, frequently 350 nails. The second task is up to 'potatoes and herring', from 300 to 500 nails; and the third task up to broth or tea-time, to complete the entire 1,000 or 1,250 nails, as is required of boys who have been two or three years at the work. But even this last meal does not put a close to their labours, as the men frequently work till 10 or 11 o'clock, assisted by their infant apprentices, who recommence their toil at five or six the next morning.
>
> Such is a plain and unexaggerated statement of the exhausting labour of these infant slaves. These boys rarely exceed seven or eight years of age; and it may fairly be said that they are starved into quickness at their work, as their meals depend on the quality of work done.[44]

Franks took evidence from several boy nailers at workshops belonging to George Fairbairn, Camelon Park and Stark and Gunn, Camelon Town, and was convinced that his enquiry was hampered by intimidation – 'I have reason to believe the boys were restricted from speaking the whole truth.'[45] For example, George Erskine, age nine, who had been a nail-worker for a year, stated, 'it is very sore work', but, 'I like it fine.' Franks recorded, 'Upon the question being repeated as to how he liked the work, and whether he told the truth about his liking for it, he said his master, Andrew Pott, told him to say he *liked the work fine*'. This boy's testimony included the following revelations, which were typical evidence on hours and workload at the Camelon brick-sheds: 'We start at six in the morning and lay by at half past nine and half past ten at night. Task is 1500 some days; but my usual quantity is 7500 a-week of nails.'[46]

Another orphan nailer at Camelon informed that, 'the hours of work are overlong; I should like them shorter if I were not driven to make the same quantity of nails; I don't care about work, but I do not like so much of it, and it has made me run away twice, but they got me again. The sore work causes boys to run off'.[47]

Boys who fled were pursued and punished, as one nail-maker explained: 'Some years since the punishment for runaways was chaining down and flogging for days together: this has been abolished, and strapping only when necessary introduced.'[48]

In St Ninians parish it was no longer common practice to take in poorhouse and orphan boys. There, within the colony of 40 nailshops at Whins of Milton, the journeymen generally employed their sons, who apparently were not 'tasked' and ill-treated in the same way as the other unfortunate boys.[49] However, in Scotland sweated labour conditions for production workers in the nail trade remained miserable and unregulated for many years. Such conditions were changed, if not wholly improved, when machine manufacture of nails replaced traditional hand labour as, for example, at the Excelsior Iron Works, Wishaw, from the late 1860s. Yet, for many years to come, it was more profitable, and practicable, for firms to employ sweated hand labour to produce short runs for a huge range of specific shapes and sizes of nail, while investing in mechanised capacity for production of the larger, and more popular, bulky orders.

CHAPTER 3
MASTERS AND IRON WORKERS:
RECRUITMENT, SETTLEMENT AND
COMPANY POLICIES c.1830–1870s

LAYING DOWN COMPANY LAW

James Baird, boss at Gartsherrie during its first 20 years, boasted of his ability to master the workforce at what was, at the time, Scotland's largest iron smelting plant. Without need for a layer of managers or foremen above the sub-contracting production men, he exercised a personal divide-and-rule policy among several hundred workers. Apart from obvious power to hire and fire, his hold over the men and successful working at the furnaces was based on the following claim:

> I may say every man was the overseer of his neighbour. They were all engaged by the piece, and if the Keeper did not do his duty, the Filler and the Engineman suffered by it; and they were not slow in complaining. Again, if the Filler or Engineman was remiss, it was to the loss of the Keeper. Thus every man was an overseer, and his own interest kept him sharp.[1]

Piece-work contracting, the tonnage payment system and differential earnings certainly had a divisive effect on the workers. However, Baird's explanation of the control and discipline he exerted over the workforce was disingenuous and incomplete. Relying on members of furnace teams to regulate the performance of each other's work was one measure. He also exercised direct supervision, giving out orders to the skilled men. When necessary, he was capable of using other means, some coercive, to impose his authority as employer. For instance, during construction and early production stages at Gartsherrie, Baird had to overcome the problem of a shortage of skilled and able labour, in particular, competent furnace-keepers, enginemen and cokers. In the initial recruitment drive, 'We had to look out for men, but it was not easy to get the best, as the most experienced workmen were under engagements. We had accordingly to take what turned up, and I can't say they were all of the best sort.'[2]

As discussed in previous chapters, furnace-keepers were key appointments. They considered themselves a special breed of skilled worker, and Baird found that they 'were disposed to claim some mystic knowledge that no one else possessed' concerning the processes of iron smelting. They had taken care to maintain their traditional status as a hereditary occupation, passed on from father to son or to some other trusted male worker. However, especially at the pioneering Gartsherrie plant, the development of the hot-blast revolution put prospective furnace-keepers at a disadvantage. Any claims to possession of exclusive expertise were exposed when they failed to cope with the unfamiliar, technical difficulties of the new hot-blast apparatus, the cooling pipes and the precise conditions of smelting operations at improved, larger furnaces. From the start, Baird sought to resolve such difficulties by becoming a 'hands-on' employer, taking personal charge of the furnace department, and learning the practicalities of smelting operations as well as any keeper or engineman. Yet, while he showed undoubted leadership example as both owner and works manager, it should be pointed out that James Baird also relied in the long term on the technical advice of his chief furnaceman, Archibald Smith.[3] Nevertheless, this hard-headed, ruthless iron master had determined that furnace keeping, and smelting operations generally, were no longer to be regarded as a mystery and a restrictive practice, but as rational applied activities which could be taught and learned by capable workers, and subject to the direction of owners or managers. From then, at Gartsherrie and elsewhere, furnace-keepers lost their status as a privileged class of worker, although they still had to be fairly intelligent, tough, diligent, practical men, and able to command a squad, in order to retain their key positions within the workforce.

James Baird's treatment of furnace-keepers during a dispute in 1843 signalled the authoritarian anti-trade union stance of pig-iron masters for the remainder of the nineteenth century. He had already dismissed, evicted and blacklisted mineworkers who had dared to take strike action on wages in 1837 and 1842. The Gartsherrie furnace-keepers reacted to a sudden reduction of piece rates, struck work and resorted to the law court to charge the employer with breach of contract. The employer retaliated, claiming that the keepers had failed to lodge the contracted month's notice of intention to stop work. Although the workers insisted that no such contractual conditions existed, they were arrested and tried behind closed doors at Airdrie sheriff court. The

James Baird,
iron master

strike leaders who had brought the action were sentenced to 60 days in prison. The severity of the conviction, and the collusion of the magistrates among the local iron masters, revealed the arbitrary application of Master and Servant law. This case also served as a savage, salutary lesson to any workers in the Monklands district who sought to challenge the authority of a principal employer.[4] For many years to come, it appeared to have the desired deterrent effect, to intimidate blast-furnacemen from taking any collective action to redress grievances.

RECRUITMENT AND SETTLEMENT

As the Gartsherrie scene indicates, in the hot-blast era from 1830 onwards, it was no longer necessary or feasible to attract and recruit specialist furnace-keepers and other skilled blast furnacemen from England or elsewhere beyond Scotland. Instead, unlike the previous period of pig-iron manufacture, when skilled labour had to be transferred north, resources of expertise and practical training in blast and smelting technique were generated from workers within companies in Scotland, where the new developments had been pioneered. Among smelting plants in west and central Scotland, there was possibly one exception to this general situation. The Nithsdale Iron Company, an English partnership, built a plant with three furnaces near New Cumnock in the early 1840s. The partners had experience in the iron trade in Durham and Yorkshire, and preferred to import skilled labour, including keepers and enginemen from Shotley Bridge and Consett.[5]

In comparison, within the malleable-iron sector, the sources and pattern of recruitment of skilled labour remained very different, as expertise was not readily available and had to be imported from south of the border. This position can be shown from documentary evidence of incoming workers, and of housing provision and allocation in various iron company towns and villages within Lanarkshire. In the following survey of skilled and unskilled labour across the smelting and malleable sectors, several ironwork communities have been selected as case studies. As no new malleable-iron works were established in Ayrshire in the early and mid nineteenth century, the focus of enquiry in this county is confined to characteristics of companies and labour at its various smelting plant locations. The intention of the overall survey is to illustrate the range of evidence; to test some points of enquiry; to explore the identity, mobility, destination and nationality of iron workers and examine company practices towards their workforce in particular locations.

The Lanarkshire Scene

In 1839–40, the first malleable-iron works to use the improved puddling process established in England and Wales were laid down in Scotland at three locations. In each case, the malleable plant was set up alongside existing smelting plants: at Govan Iron Works, in Glasgow; Dundyvan Works, Coatbridge and the Monkland Iron Company's works at Calderbank (near Airdrie and Coatbridge). While the Govan plant was equipped with 40 puddling furnaces, Dundyvan and Calderbank each had over 50 puddling furnaces, and considerable forge and rolling capacity. On their respective sites, they formed the biggest malleable plants in Scotland until the late 1850s.

Some characteristics of incoming skilled labour and housing provision at the large Lanarkshire plants are featured in the following accounts, from an outside observer in 1841, and from a manager at Dundyvan in the early 1860s:

> Two ironworks, the Dundyvan and the Monkland, where malleable iron is made, have drawn a great number of their men, amounting with their families to about 1,000 persons between the two works, from Wales, Staffordshire, and other parts of England. They are provided with a superior class of houses, erected expressly for them, consisting of two storeys, and with about twice the accommodation required for the Scotch, they form a society among themselves, not mingling with the natives, and expend their high wages in good cheer of every kind, occasionally entertaining each other with wine, turkeys, and other sorts of poultry.[6]

> When the manufacture of malleable iron commenced at Dundyvan and Calderbank Iron Works in 1839, the skilled workers required were brought chiefly from the iron manufacturing districts of England and Wales, the greatest numbers being from Staffordshire. These workmen were designated refiners, puddlers, shinglers and rollers, and like those employed at blast furnaces, were paid in proportion to the weight of iron produced. The wages earned by these men for some years were enormous, compared with present rates. The majority were very illiterate, purse proud and arrogant, quarrelsome and overbearing towards the other working classes, which led to frequent brawls and fighting.
>
> The dwellings of the English workmen were invariably patterns of cleanliness and order. The houses were built for their accommodation after the same style to which they had been accustomed to reside in, when in their native place. They consisted of long ranges of two-storeyed tenements, each family having four apartments.[7]

Among the company houses built at Dundyvan, English Row and English Square were prime examples of the better class of accommodation for incoming skilled iron workers. According to census data in 1841, the heads of families in the two-storey dwellings above were predominantly English, alongside a small number of Welsh. In 1851, while the number of English heads of household had halved, the other houses being occupied by Scots, all houses were still inhabited by malleable-iron workers. Although specific job titles are not provided by the enumerator, it can be assumed that his general entry of 'malleable iron maker' encompassed the skilled grades of puddler, shingler and roller as inhabitants of those particular houses.

The company village of Calderbank, with 1,000 inhabitants in 1841, also had an English Row, and a Welsh Row. They were among around 250 houses erected during two bouts of malleable and blast-furnace expansion, initially in 1840, and in the 1844–5 boom. Welsh Row was composed of low, single-storey dwellings, without a damp course, and was by no means quality provision for the incoming puddlers. However, the 20 houses in English Row were the best of the whole stock, befitting their intended class of occupants. They were built with red brick, in the southern style, and were roomy, two-storey dwellings, occupied by the skilled élite, particularly by rollers from England. In 1851, every head of household in English Row belonged to the labour aristocracy among iron workers and gaffers. Boiler-plate rollers from England, and a few from Wales, formed the majority of household heads. The general manager of the ironworks, a 47-year-old Welshman, and foreman of the malleable-iron works, a 33-year-old Welshman, also lived there. Ten years later, the occupational profile of this row remained relatively unchanged. The works manager, William Marshall, occupied the biggest house, which had 12 windowed rooms. His neighbours were the headmaster of the ironworks school and the Methodist minister, an Englishman who lived alongside the rollers, puddlers and heaters who were his fellow countrymen. In 1851, New Square, a tenement property built in the mid 1840s, was also regarded as decent provision, with two roomed houses. It was then occupied exclusively by malleable-iron workers, mainly of English and Welsh extraction. The two-storey South Square contained English and Welsh puddlers and rollers, but they already lived alongside less skilled Scots and Irish iron workers.[8]

This pattern of recruitment and settlement of skilled labour in the opening phase of malleable-iron production was continued and repeated in other industrial locations from the 1840s until the 1860s. For example, in 1866, when John Williams, who came from a family of iron masters in Wolverhampton, set up the Excelsior Iron Works on the Wishaw estate at Shieldmuir, he arranged to bring skilled malleable-iron workers from Staffordshire. The company built two-storey houses, with several apartments, in the English style. Consequently, according to the 1871 census, the appropriately named English Row and Buildings housed the workforce of 117 males, from the age of 12 upwards, of whom no fewer than 105 were identified as English-born.[9]

However, one of the most conspicuous examples of this related theme of skilled-labour recruitment and settlement belongs to the start of industrial development in Motherwell, during the 1840s and 1850s, many years before the town became the 'Steelopolis' of Scotland. When a consortium of Lanarkshire pig-iron masters established the first malleable-iron works at the north end of Motherwell village in 1846, an undisclosed number of imported Welsh puddlers and millmen were recruited among the principal contingent of skilled men. They were accommodated in 110 new company houses at Milton Street and Kirk Street, adjacent to the industrial site. After closure in the depression of the late 1840s, plant and houses lay empty until 1853, when the Glasgow Iron Company bought the whole site. Thomas Morton, a South Staffordshire man who had come to Scotland in 1851 to manage the company's ironworks at St Rollox, was transferred to take charge at Motherwell. He engaged the essential core of experienced skilled labour from Staffordshire and elsewhere in the Midlands. By 1861, Motherwell Malleable Iron Works had expanded its puddling capacity to 46 furnaces, and its rolling and finishing departments were fast becoming the biggest in Scotland. It employed nearly 600 workers, rising to 800 by the end of the 1860s. This total included a colony of English-born workers and families (nearly 400 people) living in the best of a newly enlarged stock of nearly 400 company houses in and around the Milton district. The company houses had 1,700 occupants in 1871, most living in single-storey dwellings, set out in rows, squares and streets. Most English rollers, and several puddlers, were concentrated in the more roomy houses in Milton Street, as also were leading staff such as Josiah Evans, forge manager, and Francis Pile, rolling mill boss. The majority of iron workers, comprising Scots and Irish, inhabited the other rows and squares.[10]

In the iron-work communities of Victorian Scotland, occupational and, to some extent, social segregation were practised in house allocation. The leading skilled and highest paid workers continued to reside in the best houses, while lesser grades and labourers were dispersed throughout the other rows. In malleable-iron company houses, for peculiar reasons of skilled worker recruitment, the bulk of better housing stock was allocated in the early years to incoming English and Welsh labour, rather than to native Scots or to immigrant Irish labour. However, iron masters reckoned it was only necessary, short-term interest which had prompted them to offer attractive and preferential terms of employment and housing to skilled labour from outside

Scotland. As the original core of imported skilled men was gradually depleted, either from having moved on, incapacity or death, it was regular company policy to find less costly replacements. They were readily available from reserves of cheaper Scots and Irish labour who could be trained up or promoted to skilled production workers such as puddlers. This changing balance of recruitment towards Scots and Irish labour is reflected in allocation of work and houses at local level. Within the malleable-iron district in

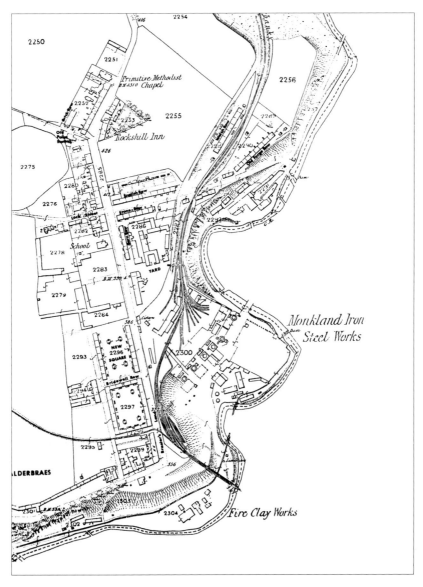

Calderbank, c. 1860. Names of rows inserted

Motherwell in 1861 there was a growing Irish presence among puddlers, underhands and labourers. In the mixed-sector iron communities of Calderbank and Dundyvan, Irish workers were increasingly numerous by the 1850s, but more so among the ranks of blast-furnacemen and general unskilled labour in and around the pig-iron works. In Calderbank, a community of 2,500 inhabitants in 1861, Scots and Irish blast-furnacemen and ironworks labourers occupied the meaner houses. For instance, the occupants of Welsh Row and Old Forge Row had become distinctively Irish, and the heavily populated Squares contained Irish and Scots families whose livelihoods depended upon most grades of work in forge and mill, and coal and ironstone pit labour.

Unlike forges and rolling mills, smelting plants had a large and predominantly unskilled labour force. From the late 1840s, having fled from the horrors of famine, land hunger and landlord oppression, the continuing influx of Irish immigrant males formed a significant component of this sector of unskilled industrial labour throughout western and central Scotland and, most conspicuously, in particular areas of Lanarkshire and Ayrshire. In the 'iron burgh' of Coatbridge, whose six industrial villages had a significant and concentrated Irish presence, most Irish males in 1861 were unskilled iron workers, followed by labourers in ironstone and coal mining.[11] The Irish profile in the town's pig-iron smelting sector is confirmed by Andrew Miller, writing in the mid 1860s: 'At many of the works the great majority of the men now employed at the blast furnaces are Irish.'[12] He could also have informed us that the overwhelming majority of unskilled Irish iron workers were Catholics, who were subject to all sorts of discrimination and commonly exploited as cheap labour. Among the Irish immigrants were a minority of Ulster Protestants, who, like native Scots, but unlike their Catholic brethren, were already skilled workers in engineering and metal trades, or had access to apprenticeships and journeymen status. However, as there was no formal apprenticeship in puddling, it was possible for some able and favoured Catholic Irish workers to progress from underhands to forehands in that occupation.

The Ayrshire Scene

Irish prominence is confirmed even more strongly within the profile of smelting workers in the iron-working communities of Ayrshire during the heyday of the industry from the 1840s until the 1870s. The majority of Irish workers were in the unskilled class of furnace-fillers and labourers, and many more found work in the county's extensive ironstone pits and coal mines. However, at one specific location, the large smelting plant at Glengarnock, Irishmen were also conspicuous in holding the responsible posts of furnace-keepers and assistant keepers. Their religious affiliation is not known, but it is likely that they were Protestants from the north of Ireland, who had gained experience in smelting either within Ayrshire or elsewhere in western and central Scotland.

The iron-working frontier of Ayrshire during this formative period was less of a melting pot of nationalities than the Lanarkshire communities examined above. In mid nineteenth-century Calderbank or Motherwell, voices and accents would include English and Welsh alongside various Scots and Irish dialects. Apart from the notable exception of the English partnership and workforce at Nithsdale, the same mingling of voices was not apparent in the blast-furnace villages of Ayrshire, where the evidence of census data points overwhelmingly to solid recruitment of Scots and Irish among all grades of worker in smelting plants, and a near complete absence of English-born labour. From Glengarnock in the north to Dalmellington in the south, smelting plants were the property of Lanarkshire iron masters who tended to transfer and promote key production workers and managers from their existing staff, or recruit from other companies in Scotland, to fill responsible positions in Ayrshire. For example, at Lugar, the owner partners, John Wilson (Dundyvan) and the Dunlop brothers (Clyde Iron Works) employed several furnace-keepers in 1851. Only one was English, with no obvious background of previous employment in Scotland, but all the others had this continuity of work experience. An Inverness-born keeper, aged 29, had worked recently in the Monklands and at Kilbirnie (Glengarnock). An Irish-born keeper had been at Lochgelly, the site of a smelting plant. Carnwath-born Daniel Girdwood, aged 33, had lived in Old Monkland during the late 1830s, and may have worked at Dundyvan. James Campbell, an Irishman, had been at Clyde and Dalry within the previous ten years, and the Clyde connection suggests earlier employment with the company. The Dalry connection suggests employment at the Blair or Kilwinning Iron Works. James Dorman, then a 36-year-old keeper, gave 'Clyde, Lanarkshire' as his birthplace. The ages and birthplaces of his children indicate recent workplace movements. His older daughter, aged nine, had been born at Gartsherrie, and another daughter at Dalry two years later. Most recently, an infant son was born in Auchinleck parish, where Lugar is located.[13]

At the same time, in the Doon valley at Dunaskin, Dalmellington Iron

Company contracted experienced men from Lanarkshire, As mentioned earlier, the owners, the Houldsworths, had operated the Coltness smelting plant at Newmains, near Wishaw, since 1837. The formidable Hunter brothers, Muirkirk-born, were managers at each ironworks: John at Dalmellington, and James at Coltness. Matthew Percy, aged 40 in 1851, and 'foreman of furnaces', had also been born at Muirkirk. His name suggests English extraction, and he may have come from a skilled family background at Muirkirk Iron Works. It is fairly obvious that he had been transferred from Newmains, as several of his children had been born in Cambusnethan parish. Thomas Morton, furnace-keeper, aged 38, also from Wishaw and Cambusnethan, was most likely an ex-Coltness worker. Two other keepers had been recruited from ironworks in the Coatbridge and Falkirk areas. However, the 'foreman over furnace-fillers' was an Irishman, aged 45, who managed an Irish-born majority among this large section of unskilled workers. In 1871, there were apparently no English-born workers among the iron workers and miners at or in the vicinity of Waterside village, where the Dalmellington Iron Company houses were concentrated. The ironworks had recently expanded from five to eight furnaces, and had increased its numbers of young Irishmen, who did the heaviest jobs alongside other young men, notably from Ayrshire and Kirkcudbright.[14]

Housing standards in the Ayrshire iron-working communities, as in pit villages and isolated miners' rows, were similar to those in Lanarkshire. Insanitary living conditions, shared dry closets for outside toilets, no indoor water supply and gross overcrowding of families and lodgers in small, single- and two-room houses with earth or stone floors, were typical of company provision. More roomy accommodation was available for key workers, but apparently not to the same extent as the company housing that was reserved initially for top grades of malleable ironworkers in Lanarkshire. For instance, in Glengarnock, houses were sandwiched between furnaces, slag heaps and railway lines. In 1861, Front Row, part of 'the square', was the best accommodation. Managers, pay clerks, furnace-keepers and enginemen occupied its two-room houses. The tenants of other single- and two-apartment houses in the Square were a mix of skilled and unskilled workers, including many Irish. Monkey Row consisted of small houses occupied by Irish furnace-fillers and textile workers employed nearby at the Kilbirnie thread mills. In 1861, the occupants of Long Row – the first back to back houses built locally for incoming iron workers in the 1840s – were distinctly Irish, composed of furnace-fillers and labourers.[15]

COMPANY REGIMES AND VICTORIAN VALUES

Worker settlements around major ironworks were either company towns, districts or villages where, for the most part, property and people were owned and controlled by the iron masters, their managers and agents. Those settlements, located in the industrial frontier of nineteenth-century Scotland, were rough and turbulent places which, especially in the early years, were adorned with few amenities of civilised life and welfare provision. Disorderly behaviour, as expressed in drunkenness and brawling, was prevalent. Sectarian incidents between Protestant and Orange elements on one side, and Catholic Irish on the other, were frequent occurrences in the company settlements of Victorian Scotland, and were symbols of a troubled, divided and unequal society. Confronted by a diverse, shifting, often unruly mass of workers, some prominent iron masters increasingly chose to exert discipline, not only in the workplace, but also in the immediate community, where they sought to dictate the behaviour of workers' lives.

The priority for all masters was to ensure profitable production, and ironworks – smelting plants in particular – were a large capital investment. Continuous production and regular output were the order of the day, requiring long hours and work discipline. Costly blast furnaces were usually kept in operation, even in periods of downturn, when the market price of iron had fallen. In those circumstances, the masters continued to stockpile and cut back on costs, principally by reducing wages. Pressures to enforce wage cuts were intensified from the 1860s onwards in the face of growing competition, especially from smelting firms in the north of England. As will be discussed later, industrial strife was an inevitable consequence of such attacks on wages and conditions, inasmuch as iron workers were provoked by a strong sense of grievance and were prepared to resist by taking collective action.

During industrial disputes, iron masters threatened and used the familiar battery of crude coercive weapons, such as lockouts, organised strike-breaking, blacklisting, dismissal and eviction from company houses. However, at other times, and over a long period of years, some leading iron masters also exerted additional measures of control and persuasion to win respect, corporate loyalty and obedience. This minority of employers made conscious efforts to impose their own set of declared values at the workplace and within company territory. At their most consistent level, such efforts amounted to a civilising mission to influence behaviour and raise the moral and cultural level of workers and their families, while ensuring that workers deferred to the authority of the employer and patron.

Employer-sponsored initiatives usually included a range of work and community-based activities and facilities aimed at promoting positive behaviour and loyalty to the firm. This gospel of improvement, linked with discipline, emphasised the material and moral rewards of hard work, good living and self-reliance. Those virtues were demonstrated by sobriety or complete abstinence from alcohol consumption; habits of thrift and good management in spending and saving; being a practising Christian and showing evidence of godliness and cleanliness; being family orientated and pursuing approved recreational and educational activities.

The Baird family of iron masters, at Gartsherrie and the adjoining company town at the top of Coatbridge, embodied this highly prescriptive approach towards their local workforce. They dominated public life at all levels. William Baird, in 1841–6, and his brother James, in 1851–7, were members of parliament for Falkirk Burghs constituency, which included Airdrie. Staunch Tories, and fervently committed to the Church of Scotland, they recognised the value of organised religion, bible teaching and schooling of the young as instruments of industrial and social discipline. Over several decades, the multi-millionaire iron masters endowed several churches and manses within the locality, and were enthusiastic builders of works schools. In addition, the Bairds founded Gartsherrie Academy for the children of the district. In 1872, mainly in Lanarkshire and Ayrshire, there were 5,000 children in 'Baird schools'. Their patronage also included institutes, reading rooms and parks.[16] They barely tolerated other Christian denominations, but their sense of obligation extended to granting land in Coatbridge to the Catholic Church for St Patrick's chapel (to accommodate many Irish workers), and to the Episcopalians for St John's church. James Baird and some later company partners were virulently anti-Catholic in public and political life. However, although this stance represented, and probably encouraged, popular anti-Catholic sympathies among their Scottish workers, it did not prevent them from employing a minority of Irish Catholic workers as cheap labour when it most suited. Nevertheless, discrimination was widely practised against this class of worker as, at Gartsherrie and elsewhere, entry to skilled jobs and apprenticeships was guarded by Protestant foremen. While Orange, Protestant or masonic allegiance did not guarantee preference, it undoubtedly helped in any search to obtain regular work. More controversially, despite the Baird connections with militant Protestantism, there is no clear evidence that they deliberately and crudely promoted religious sectari-

anism in the workplace to provoke further rivalry and division. There were
other means of reducing the workforce to subservience, without adopting
practices likely to inflame disorder and disrupt regular production. Certainly,
for years, they employed a full-time Church of Scotland missionary at
Gartsherrie, who visited workers' homes, and held Sunday services in the
company's schools. Popular lectures of a moral and uplifting outlook were also
sponsored there, alongside temperance societies for young and old. Intrusive
interventionism, bordering on surveillance of workers' lives, was also explicit
in regular inspection of company houses for tidiness and cleanliness, with
prizes for the best-kept houses and a system of fines for negligence. In later
years, a company policeman was employed for this purpose, while he also
made it his business to collect and supply information on the conduct of
workers and their families.[17]

The Houldsworth family of iron masters, at the company villages of
Newmains and neighbouring Cambusnethan, also demonstrated an
aggressive paternalism and pursued a controlling influence. In the same vein
as the Bairds at Gartsherrie, the Houldsworths ruled over the company
domain as a strict, conscientious Victorian father ruled over his family and
household, encouraging and enforcing approved behaviour and obedience.
Also Church of Scotland and Tory, they sponsored and encouraged participation in works schools, missions and churches, temperance and teetotal
societies, adult education classes, musical bands and recreational facilities.
Determined to stamp out drunken behaviour at the workplace and in the
immediate community, Henry Houldsworth, his managers and their
successors used their authority to ban licensed premises within their
properties and estates. Prohibition of the sale of alcohol drinks was enforced
from 1849 and, although workers showed initial resentment, the regulation
had to be accepted, apparently leading to a local decline in liquor
consumption and attendant disorder. The anti-drink crusade was strongly
represented in Good Templar societies, and in Band of Hope clubs for
children. As a young man, Robert Russell, future manager of Coltness Iron
Company, conducted Newmains Band of Hope for many years. As well as
enjoying its social activities, the growing generation of workers was exposed
to habits of discipline and righteous behaviour. Providing alternatives to the
public house and the demon drink were high on this agenda for discipline and
improvement. Order and respectability were an integral part of the rationale
to introduce gas into the Newmains houses. A report from the 1850s informs
us that supply of gas light into the houses was seen by Henry Houldsworth as

an inducement to workers and families to stay at home in the darker evenings, to read and to conduct home life without the men going to a public house or indulging in other unworthy pursuits out of doors. When James Houldsworth granted eight acres of land for a public park in 1877, he stipulated its use for free exercise and recreation, while emphasising the continuing ban on liquor sales and consumption on that site and elsewhere on company land. From the 1850s, evening classes were available for young workers at Newmains ironworks school where they could listen to and discuss popular lectures given by managers and guest speakers on useful knowledge topics. They could also use the Reading Room Association and the works school library and, from the 1860s, attend a series of winter lectures organised by local clergy who ran the Newmains Mutual Improvement Association. Coltness Ironworks Mechanics Institution served the same purpose of educational improvement, but was always mindful to stay clear of factious dispute on religious and political issues. In the 1870s, alongside the temperance societies, the Young Men's Christian Association took root in Coltness Mission Hall. In later years, the YMCA was to grow into a large, influential organisation zealously supported by the iron and steel employers of Motherwell and Wishaw. The fledgling YMCA served company values in its promotion of religious, moral and physical improvement, respectability and patriotism. Its spirit of fellowship and encouragement of athletic fitness served as 'muscular Christianity' and character building for careers 'as ministers and missionaries, teachers, doctors, lawyers, professions and industrial callings'.[18]

A rosy picture of company benevolence, community gratitude, contentment and deference in this particular iron and coal working company village is expressed in local verse, dating from late nineteenth century:

Robert Russell, iron master, in front of blast furnaces at Coltness Iron Works, c.1900 (North Lanarkshire Council)

Newmains

Oor furnaces are monuments o' engineering skill,
Oor iron tops the market and oor coal's unequalled still;
And the secret o' oor greatness is the energy and brains
Which guide the vast machinery in motion at Newmains.

And we ha'e a famous Mutual wi' influence and power
Where once a week we a' can spend a profitable hour
In brushing up oor intellects or cobwebs frae oor brains,
Nae wonder they are a' sae smart, the folk aboot Newmains.

And then we ha'e oor ministers, kindhearted and sedate,
Wha guide us wi' the greatest care tae Eden's pearly gate,
And in the works o' charity spare neither toil nor pains
Tae alleviate the misery and the sufferings o' Newmains.

And then there's no a public hoose in a' oor little toon
Tae mar its peace and happiness, or cause a single froon;
And yet, alas, there's some we meet can scarcely gang their lanes,
And bring discredit and disgrace on a' aboot Newmains.

But may oor kirks and library, oor Mutuals, schules an' a'
Dispel the clouds o' ignorance or gae them sic a blow
That love and intellectual power shall ever hold the reins
And guide the future destinies o' a' aboot Newmains.

But what would this, oor village be, without the 'Coltness',
A cipher, I am sair afraid, its value would express;
But while the link o' freenship grand between the twa remains,
There will aye be peace and plenty for the folk aboot Newmains.

Lang may the name o' Houldsworth its famous worth still hold
For deeds o' charity and love and enterprises bold;
Lang may it take an interest in a' that appertains
Tae the welfare, peace and happiness o' a' aboot Newmains.[19]

From the 1850s, until their influence was overtaken by other prominent businessmen within the iron and steel sectors in Motherwell, co-partners and managers at Glasgow Iron Company's malleable-iron works pursued a high profile in public life within the company district and in the growing industrial frontier town. They took the lead in local politics, as elected representatives on the burgh council during the 1860s, and the school board in the early 1870s. Works manager, Thomas Morton, was a Liberal councillor for many years, and in 1883–5 served as provost of Motherwell. With undoubted commitment, they and other local captains of industry also promoted civilised values, self help, welfarist and leisure schemes among the workforce, and their intervention within the wider community can be compared with similar types of initiative at Coatbridge and Newmains. However, unlike the Bairds and the Houldsworths, the world view of most Motherwell iron masters and managers was Liberal in politics and religion, although they were no less conscientious in asserting their authority and values in the workplace and beyond. Above them all was John Colville, of Dalzell Iron Works who, from the 1870s, was widely respected among workers as a sensitive and honest employer who practised industrial conciliation. This millionaire iron master also had a distinguished record as street corner Christian evangelist, outreach youth worker, temperance campaigner, and Liberal champion, serving as burgh councillor, civic chief and as MP for North-East Lanark constituency, which then included Motherwell.

Within the Glasgow Iron Company village at north Motherwell, the Primitive Methodist Church was the centre of organised community activity until the 1870s. The Methodist denomination was an influential presence, imported by English managers and skilled iron workers who came into the area in the middle years of the nineteenth century. Likewise, in the late 1860s, John and Robert Williams, of the Excelsior Iron Works, sponsored a Methodist church at Craigneuk to cater specifically for the religious needs of a majority of their workers who came from this English and Welsh noncon-formist background. As church leaders and as employers, they strongly patro-nised and encouraged public worship, Sunday school, temperance drives, adult education meetings, concerts and soirées.

John Colville,
iron master

The Primitive Methodist chapel and hall in Milton Street, Motherwell, was enlarged in 1861 to accom-modate 500 people. Thomas Morton and his main managers were all leading lights in their church, in its social programme and in other local-interest groups. Activities were held in the former works school, converted into a separate community hall and reading room, and in a larger works school built in 1860. The Motherwell Iron Works Band and a Choral Union, with Morton as conductor, were among the cultural activ-ities sponsored by company and church. In the late 1870s, three out of the four Motherwell lodges of Good Templars also met in the Milton Street premises. For

two generations, the experience of common worship, church fellowship, individual earnestness and respectability among this English colony of managers and skilled men was probably instrumental in cementing personal relationships and corporate loyalty. However, this is not to say that such harmony was not strained to the limit, or broken, in the heat of the major industrial disputes that, it will be seen, occurred in the 1860s and 1870s. As for the Scots and Irish iron workers, there was no obvious common identity of culture and interest to bind them to the company. Indeed, contending factionalism of a different kind was already apparent in the expanding malleable-iron district of Motherwell. Two Orange lodges were formed there in the 1860s, and within twenty years, as at Gartsherrie and other parts of Coatbridge, the area had become a stronghold of Orangeism and popular Conservatism. This partisan identity was boosted by fresh influxes of Ulster Protestants and like-minded Scots who found work in the iron industry, at the same time as the Catholic Irish presence was beginning to take root and expand in an area that would remain predominantly Protestant.[20]

The influence and effect of employer interventions to direct and inculcate specific values among iron workers in company towns and villages is difficult to gauge in general terms and must remain largely a matter of conjecture. It would appear that aggressive paternalism and interventionism was more effective in achieving company objectives in smaller villages like Gartsherrie and Newmains, where a single large employer and landlord held sway. In such company villages, also typically dominated by pig-iron smelting, the weight of available evidence suggests that a submissive and obedient workforce was achieved until the closing decades of the century. However, this outcome may have had more to do with the hard realities of authoritarian enforcement of the employer regime in the workplace and occupational divisions among the workers, rather than with the impact of any other influences.

Skilled iron workers who felt a sense of pride and relative security in their craft, income and status were among the aspiring and respectable minority most likely to respond positively to the ethic of self improvement, but without subscribing completely to the values or directive influences of the employer. While employer exhortations to sobriety, thrift and provident living may have had some effect, self-respecting iron workers from all grades recognised and practised those values, and supported employer-sponsored efforts as well as initiating their own schemes. For example, friendly societies were popular and necessary organisations, all concerned with fulfilling welfare functions for members and families, providing an insurance fund against times of accidents, ill health and death. Members often had the option of withdrawing money every year, in which case the friendly society also acted as a savings bank and emergency fund. Most ironworks had such schemes for their workers, although membership eligibility was usually restricted. The Calderbank Iron Works Friendly Society, begun in 1838, was limited to the fit and healthy, of proven upright character, and those 'under no church censure'. Member subscriptions of one shilling a month were directly debited from wages at the pay office, and covered a range of benefits. Its successor, Monkland Malleable Works Friendly Society, had the same rules on membership and welfare payments. It lasted for six years during the 1850s, averaging a hundred and fifty members.[21] However, its existence was typical of both works-sponsored and independent societies that were started and sustained in periods of good trade and regular employment, then collapsed in bad times, to the detriment of members and their families, when wages were being squeezed and workers paid off.

James Baird and other iron masters of that ilk had a reputation as upstanding members of the business community, as public benefactors and as paternalist employers. However, laying aside religious convictions, so much philanthropic effort could be seen as calculated in their self-interest on a

Clydesdale Iron Works band, 1883 (North Lanarkshire Council)

rational cost basis, as it was intended to serve their objectives as employers of labour. In any case, directly and indirectly, the cost of houses, schools, churches and other services and facilities sponsored and provided by iron companies was funded by the workers themselves. The masters made compulsory and arbitrary deductions from wages. For instance, at ironworks schools in Lanarkshire during the 1860s, each worker had to pay a standard two pence per week towards the cost of teacher salaries and maintenance of the building. This was an enforced levy, even if the worker was childless or had no children at school. Moreover, it was an additional cause of discrimination and grievance among Catholic iron workers who were forced to contribute to upkeep of a school which provided religious instruction of a wholly Protestant kind. This issue was not resolved in Wishaw and Newmains until 1874, when the new statutory School Board co-operated with Coltness Iron Company to transfer the levy of Catholic workers towards support of their own elementary schools. Similar arrangements were agreed elsewhere, whenever the Catholic community managed to provide a denominational school. A weekly fee was also routinely charged for the services of a works doctor. Among iron workers there was a running resentment that they had no say in the appointment and choice of doctor, and no agreement to consider a change if dissatisfied with the quality of advice and treatment.

At most large ironworks, illegal and fraudulent practices connected with methods of wage payment, credit and enforced use of company stores were sources of further exploitation. This catalogue of systematic abuse is well documented for ironworking and coalmining communities in nineteenth-century Scotland. Graphic evidence shows that thousands of iron workers, especially in Lanarkshire, were among its victims when the abuse was most rife from the 1840s to the end of the 1860s.[22] The Coatbridge pig-iron masters, in particular, were among the major perpetrators of those malpractices among iron workers and miners.

When James Baird and his brothers owned the firm, company policy concerning consumption of alcohol in the workplace was strictly observed, and workers found under the influence of alcohol were under pain of instant dismissal, accompanied by eviction within 24 hours. Yet, while the company claimed to discourage workers from excessive drinking, there were obvious double standards in its practice of sanctioning and encouraging the sale of hard liquor at stores on the premises. Large quantities of whisky were sold in company stores at all the firm's smelting plants in Ayrshire, and the home base Gartsherrie store outdid them all. Furthermore, by allowing sale of whisky on credit against forthcoming wages, it was a lucrative sideline that took full advantage of the weakness of workers tempted by ready availability of strong drink.[23]

The same conditions applied at most iron company stores. At Calderbank, beer and spirits were available in unlimited supply, and could be consumed in an unlicensed ante room on the store premises. This 'cage', as it was called, was often a notorious scene of disorder, but the business was very profitable. However, in this regard, the Houldsworths at Newmains and Dalmellington were one known honourable exception among pig-iron masters. Their practice was at least consistent with public declarations and company policy. As discussed previously, the Houldsworths pursued a strict policy of prohibition of licensed premises on their Coltness estates. Consequently, their company store at the ironworks there did not stock and sell alcoholic beverage. Yet, although the company mission and message was loud and clear on the issue, its deterrent effect on the workforce must have been limited. Drink culture was strongly entrenched in such industrial communities, and iron workers were not deprived of opportunities to buy and consume alcohol. For example, Newmains workers could always go outside the prohibition boundaries into licensed premises in nearby Wishaw or Cleland.

The typical operation of company stores and associated fraudulent practices until 1870 is revealed in evidence from one ironworks community that was heavily affected by those developments. The Monkland Iron Company store at Calderbank was a large building adjoining the pay office on Main Street. As elsewhere, blast-furnacemen and labourers in the pig-iron smelting department were paid monthly or, even worse, every five weeks. In the malleable department, puddlers, hammermen, rollers and other millmen were by then paid on a fortnightly basis, and prudent, relatively well-paid craftsmen among them were usually in a position to escape direct contact with the worst features of truck store dealing and pay and credit practices. The 'long pay' system and non-cash or part-cash payment of wages led many workers into debt, and was especially hard on those men with low wage packets. Little or no actual cash was paid to those workers who were in the habit of receiving an advance on their wages before the appointed pay day. In such cases, the pay office issued credit lines instead of money, and they were exchanged for goods at the company store or at any other local shop or dairy that had an arrangement to deal in lines. At Calderbank, 75 per cent of the value of lines had to be spent in the company store, and it was easy for the pay clerk and storeman to cross-check the extent to which this ruling was carried out by 'advance men' or their family members. Penalties for bypassing, or 'sloping', the store in those instances ranged from initial warning to stoppage of credit and deferment of wages, and finally to dismissal. Charging interest on an advance payment at the usual rate of 5 per cent on every pound was an additional iniquity. In 1870, more than half the iron workers in Calderbank were caught in this vice of indebtedness to the company. That year, figures submitted to the royal commission which investigated truck and payment systems showed that 440 out of 600 iron workers in the village were advance men. The minority were 'pay men', namely the only workers to receive wages in hard cash on pay day. As long as they retained that status, they were free from the unscrupulous grip of the company store, and could spend their wages in shops of their choice.

As in so many other locations, the Calderbank store had provided a necessary service in the early days when the place was a new industrial settlement without shops. However, by the middle of the nineteenth century the company store no longer had a monopoly of business in stocking and selling general provisions. Yet the company still acted as if it were in the monopoly position, subjecting most of the workforce who were obliged to use the store to blatant profiteering, short measure, inferior quality goods and intimidation. The investigation in 1870 revealed that William Shearer, store manager, who lived in English Row, kept a blacklist of store defaulters. He had also attempted to collect in and burn all credit lines prior to the enquiry, so that damning evidence could not be produced against him in the court hearings at Hamilton.

Although it was found difficult to prosecute companies for such offences, from the 1870s the discredited store system ceased to be an instrument of company discipline or control over the workforce at most ironworks and collieries. In the late 1850s, the Bairds had responded to popular criticism of store practices by removing compulsory spending of advance pay or credit at the store. This mild reform was complemented by setting up a committee of foremen and key workers to run the affairs of each store.[24]

The company stores and attached system of abuses had thrived on the notorious practice of deferring payment of wages to a month or longer, but skilled iron workers had mounted successful challenges for fortnightly and even weekly wages, and were no longer obliged to seek credit and spend all or part of it at the store. Insofar as other shops were available in the locality, they took their custom there, especially in towns and larger settlements where their employer did not hold complete sway. Workers and their families also had a growing and more attractive alternative in the shape of stores belonging to Co-operative Societies. Their large stores in industrial towns and centres were largely a product of worker funds, membership and custom, and they paid out regular dividends on sales.

However, company stores and their lucrative trade in liquor survived in more isolated locations, where the firm used its influence to prevent any rivals from setting up alternative shops in the vicinity. For instance, the store, its liquor shop and drinking 'cage' remained at Merry and Cunningham's iron and steel works in Glengarnock until David Colville and Sons took it over in 1915. The combined circumstances of wartime clampdown on excessive drinking among industrial workers and the temperance policy of the incoming company ensured the downfall of the store's liquor shop and public house, and the store was demolished a few years later.[25]

CHAPTER 4
MASTERS AND IRON WORKERS:
LABOUR RELATIONS, WORKPLACE CONFLICT AND
TRADE UNION RESPONSES c.1860–1920

INTRODUCTION

From the foregoing discussion in Chapters 2 and 3, it will be obvious that iron workers in mid nineteenth-century Scotland formed a highly differentiated sector of industrial labour. In the workplace, each occupational group and section was divided by disparities of skill and grade, status and earnings. Pay systems, including sub-contracting of labour and a variety of fluctuating piece-work and tonnage rates, were sources of further complication and rivalry. Cultural differences around ethnicity and religion were also discriminatory influences, and potentially disruptive of workplace solidarity when support was needed for a wider front against employers.

Trade union organisation, where and when it emerged among iron workers before the 1860s, was limited in numbers and impact, and struggled to survive in an employer-dominated environment. Time-served foundry workers were the first to form a permanent trade union. Originating in Glasgow in the 1820s, the Scottish Iron Moulders Union was craft-based. With 700 members, at most, during the 1840s, it represented only a tiny minority of skilled men within the trade, and its rule-book excluded assistants and labourers. It was typical of the contemporary craft trade unions that represented the sectional interests of the élite among skilled men who were its members. Only the better-paid men among moulders could afford the relatively high regular dues, and this resulted in an exclusive membership.[1] Moreover, leading craftsmen such as pattern-makers in moulding and rollers in malleable plants whose proven skills were in premium demand could negotiate individual earnings agreements with a master or foreman, thereby bypassing collective bargaining and any reliance on trade union backing. As in mining and the building trades, sub-contracting of labour among craftsmen was prevalent and encouraged by masters in most categories of iron production. Such craftsmen exploited the less skilled workers under their authority, and this unequal relationship had the effect of preventing or hindering the growth of trade union organisation and solidarity within an occupational group.

Within the malleable iron sector, head rollers had privileged status as the principal contractors and supervisors of labour teams in the mills. They and other craft rollers could command high earnings at most times. Head rollers, in particular, occupied a powerful position within the workplace. They contracted a price with the masters for specific jobs and orders and took charge of all rolling and finishing operations on the mill floor. Although indispensable as producers of malleable iron, forehand puddlers nevertheless had lower status and earnings than rollers. They hired and paid underhands, but it is entirely mistaken to place puddlers in the same sub-contracting bracket as forehand or head rollers. While a contracting roller dominated a relatively large squad, a forehand puddler looked after one furnace, and collected his wage, usually at fortnightly intervals. His earnings were determined by piecework productivity and tonnage rate, from which he paid one or more underhands a daily or weekly wage. Nevertheless, the employment relationship between forehand and underhand puddler frequently gave rise to tension, especially over wage rates.

Puddlers and millmen were organised in a craft union from the early 1860s, but this was primarily a sub-contractors' union. Their leaders defended and pursued the interests of the respective craft minority and during this period articulated no common cause or unity of action with other sections of iron workers. Such predominant sectionalism and fragmentation had also to contend with implacable employer opposition to any forms of collective bargaining and independent workplace organisation. The combined impact of those adverse influences helps to explain why trade unionism among iron workers was difficult to establish and sustain throughout most of the nineteenth century. In this overall hostile context, blast-furnacemen in Scotland did not achieve a permanent trade union until 1890, but their organisation was exceptional and progressive in that all grades of blast-furnace workers were recruited into membership. However, iron masters in Scotland refused to recognise trade unionism within their own sector. When recognition came, it was ambiguous, limited, and a very late development. Even then, as the century ended, pig-iron masters agreed grudgingly to formal joint conciliation to resolve wage issues only, while masters and men in the malleable-iron sector within Scotland had very recently established formal procedures for resolution of both wages and conditions issues. In the varied and diffuse foundry sector, no such conciliation process existed, and industrial relations were prone to bouts of open conflict into the early twentieth century.

BLAST-FURNACEMEN

As already indicated, faced with authoritarian employers like the Bairds, blast-furnacemen and labourers in smelting plants had particular difficulties in asserting themselves on pay and conditions issues. In the 1860s, Alexander McDonald, leader of the Scottish miners, classified coal and ironstone miners into two categories. He drew a stark distinction between 'honourable men', who were trade union members, organised and able to exert some control over their wages and conditions, and the great majority of 'degraded slaves' who were in the grip of sub-contractors and unscrupulous storemen.[2] If this distinction is applied to ranks of iron workers, then most furnacemen and labourers in the smelting plants came into this second category. At the Baird enterprises, employer control over furnacemen was virtually complete, so that industrial action among their iron workers was almost unknown until the later nineteenth century.[3]

However, despite oppressive conditions and lack of union organisation, furnacemen at plant level pressed for wage increases during upswings of the trade cycle in response to the rising market price of iron, and masters were usually prepared to make some concessions, as in the boom years of 1870–72. Prolonged bouts of depression, declining demand and competitive pressures between 1873 until the late 1880s prompted iron masters to reduce wage costs and enforce wage cuts among most grades of furnacemen. Protest was to no avail, as refusal to comply was met with employer threats and reprisals. In times of depressed market demand, masters stockpiled pig iron and if the men did not accept reduced rates and short time, they could expect several furnaces to be damped down or even blown out. James Dunlop, master of Clyde Iron Works, used this tactic against furnacemen when enforcing wage cuts in 1879.[4] During the 1886 slump, sheer desperation at wage reductions drove furnacemen at the Coltness Iron Works to strike action but, unsurprisingly, this move failed to elicit an understanding response from the company.[5] During the depression years worker morale was low, and any attempts to raise wages from rock bottom levels were easily resisted.

Given such adverse conditions, it has to be explained how, within the next four years, blast furnacemen across central Scotland managed to become unionised, to muster enough collective strength to address grievances and confront the might of pig-iron companies. Growth of trade union consciousness and a more combative approach among furnacemen arose in part from the eventual consequence of owner and management decisions to intensify productive capacity and overhaul supervision of labour within the pig iron industry. In the 1870s and 1880s, greater use of industrial chemistry and technical innovation were introduced to save fuel costs and improve the product, in attempts to make the pig-iron sector in Scotland more efficient and more able to compete with their great rivals in Cleveland and Wales. Furnaces, and the size of charges, were enlarged; temperature of blast was increased, using gas injection; imports of higher quality haematite iron ore were mixed with local ores, and by-products such as gas, ammonia and tar were generated. Those changes were gradually accompanied by a rationalisation of labour deployment in smelting and in other productive operations. Companies removed the sub-contracting role of furnace-keepers, and introduced a layer of management personnel to supervise production and performance of labour.[6] All grades of worker were directly employed, and paid by a wages department. Thus, leading furnacemen and skilled engine, boiler and gas men were placed on the same footing as pig lifters and general labourers, in that they were all subject to foremen and managers, and faced the common predicament of stringent employer controls on tonnage, piece-work and basic wage rates. Within large smelting plants, barriers of craft sectionalism and the gulf between the most highly skilled men and labourers were sufficiently broken down to allow a new-found unity of purpose in an all-grades trade union. The National Association of Blast Furnacemen (NABF) originated in Cleveland in 1882, and extended its membership base further into the north of England by 1886, when it became formally constituted. Blast-furnacemen in Scotland were successfully recruited into membership for the first time in early 1890. They were likely to have been encouraged by the wave of industrial action and formation of unions among other workers throughout 1889–90. Moreover, recovery of market demand and the price of pig iron in 1890, and notification from English branches of the union that they would provide material support in any struggle to redress legitimate grievances in Scotland, rekindled claims for improved wages and conditions in smelting plants.

Furnacemen endured longer working hours, lower wages and worse conditions than most fellow workers in similar work in Cleveland, Durham, Cumberland and Lancashire. In contrast to Scotland, the bulk of iron masters

Overleaf. Blast furnaces, Summerlee Iron Works, Coatbridge (North Lanarkshire Council)

342. SUMMERLEE IRON WORKS, COATBRIDGE.

recognised the trade union as a representative and negotiating body on behalf of its members, and there was an established mechanism of joint employer and union conciliation boards to discuss and settle grievances. Negotiated agreements were in place regarding eight-hour shifts for furnace teams in North Lancashire and Cumberland, and a maximum twelve-hour shift elsewhere; payment of time and a half for day and night shifts on Sundays, and sliding scales for wages and earnings. In lodging their claims, the Scottish branches of NABF sought parity of hours and wages with plants in Cleveland, and did not even attempt to press for the more radical proposal of eight-hour shifts. Instead, particular claims related to overtime payment for Sunday shifts, or the alternative of complete abolition of production work on Sundays. This option was intended to abolish the fortnightly rotation of a double shift of twenty-four to twenty-six hours on Sunday, and replace that

Furnacemen at casting pit, Coltness Iron Works (North Lanarkshire Council)

most punishing schedule with an alternate five- and six-day working week.
Furnacemen also sought a reduction of all 13-hour shifts to a maximum of 12
hours. This move was aimed at eliminating the extra hour that furnace teams
were forced to work beyond each 6 o'clock casting time, when they had to
enlist help from the overlapping shift to finish this vital task. Furnace teams
were short-handed, a consequence of labour-saving and cost-cutting
measures. Managers refused to transfer general labourers from the yard to
assist with casting operations, and did so only in emergencies, when extra
hands would be pulled in to limit the damage and loss caused by any sudden
uncontrolled breakaway of molten iron.[7]

The moderate and reasonable manner in which the workers pursued their
modest claims from the first approaches to employers in August 1890 stood in
marked contrast to the arrogant and intransigent reaction of pig-iron
companies. The Scottish Association of Ironmasters (SAI) was affronted by
the concerted challenge to its power and authority, and determined to resist
and retaliate with all means at its disposal to break the union and drive the
furnacemen back to work on the usual dictated terms. From the start, when
deputations from each ironworks in Lanarkshire made separate approaches to
the employer, masters refused to recognise and meet any union representatives in their official capacity, and continued to uphold this position
throughout the long dispute. The union position, on the other hand, was also
consistent, calling for a joint conciliation board to hear and settle workplace
grievances and disputes. In September, the SAI rejected union demands, and
its member companies terminated contracts of work. This reaction provoked
strike action, and Coltness and Shotts blast-furnacemen were out first, backed
by union support and funds. Smelting companies across Scotland then staged
a general lockout and began to damp down furnaces. By October, only Carron
and the Glasgow Iron Company's smelting plant at Wishaw stayed out of the
dispute. Neither company was a member of the SAI, and they continued in
production. However, elsewhere in Scotland, 72 out of 78 furnaces were
damped down or blown out and 3,500 iron workers were locked out,
indicating that companies were prepared for a prolonged stoppage to bring
the workers to their senses. This intention was further signalled when the first
batches of eviction notices were served at Shotts and Glengarnock.

The union supported 1,200 strikers and lockedout men in Lanarkshire
alone, paying them from funds raised by a weekly levy on other union
members. Each worker received ten shillings a week and an additional one
shilling and sixpence per child. This level of financial support from blast-

furnacemen in England was crucial for several months, until funds were eventually depleted. Some financial support was donated by other trade unions, and had a morale-boosting effect, although such contributions were small and hardly significant in relation to the union's own effort to sustain the welfare of thousands of laid-off iron workers and families. The workers' case and the issue of Sunday labour were highlighted in the press and on public platforms, and drew support from several religious bodies, including the Roman Catholic Church, the Free Church and Congregational Church, but not the Church of Scotland.

By February 1891, with still no settlement in sight, iron masters took further action to intensify the dispute. Foreign blackleg labour was brought in at several plants, including Govan, Gartsherrie, Glengarnock and other Ayrshire locations, to relight and restart some furnaces. Two or three hundred unsuspecting Lithuanian workers, most of them newly or recently arrived immigrants, were drafted into Coatbridge and Glengarnock as strike-breakers. However, this strike-breaking gesture proved unworkable as the combined efforts of raw unskilled labour, managers and foremen were unable to resume smelting operations without the expertise of skilled furnacemen, who refused to co-operate and remained out of contract. The other company measure to exert pressure on workers and families was to intensify eviction threats and enforcement. Again, Baird's workers at Gartsherrie and Ayrshire, and Dixon's, at Govan, took the brunt of this assault, and several hundred families were ejected from company houses.

However, defeat was inevitable as the market price of pig iron continued to decline into March, evictions began to bite, and hunger and debt loomed large as union finances and strike funds became exhausted. In April, with furnacemen straggling back to work and the employers unyielding, the union was forced to concede after a 23-week long struggle.

The iron masters took revenge in the immediate aftermath of the dispute. Tonnage rates were reduced by 20 per cent, and an 8 per cent reduction was imposed on shift wages. The pattern of long working hours remained as before the dispute, including retention of Sunday labour and double shifts on alternate weekends. Prominent activists were blacklisted, and stringent rules prohibited meetings and collection of union subscriptions in the workplace, as employers were determined to smash effective worker organisation and morale. Non-union and immigrant labour was retained.

The recent bitter, resounding defeat of sustained strike action to resolve legitimate grievances in the face of implacable employer hostility had left many blast-furnacemen divided and demoralised. The NABF could no longer claim to represent all grades and occupations within the pig-iron sector. It had lost skilled members to the Amalgamated Society of Steel and Iron Workers (ASSIW), which organised mainly among millmen in malleable-iron works, but also embraced enginemen, boilermen and locomotive drivers in smelting plants. Yet by 1892 NABF in the Scottish area had begun to recover, as resilient organisers managed to recruit 1,000 members from the ranks of 1,500 direct blastfurnace workers.[8]

An eight-hour day for reasonable wages, abolition of Sunday labour, and especially an end to the long weekend double shift, stayed in the forefront of trade union objectives for pig-iron workers throughout the 1890s and into the new century. However, the two trade unions representing the interests of workers in smelting plants had to decide on the strategy and means to achieve their objectives. After defeat and bankruptcy in 1890–91, union leaders were reluctant to sanction the strike weapon as official policy. Instead, they preferred to rely on a moderate stance, and continued to pursue the longstanding aim of a formal process for negotiation, conciliation and arbitration, in a joint body with the employers. In addition, they were interested in the possibility of state legislation that would bind the employers to reduce working hours and enforce other improvements in working conditions. To this end, they decided to campaign and lobby at the political level, to seek and enlist support for key demands such as an eight-hour working day. Meanwhile, they continued to lodge wage claims, while remaining circumspect about industrial action.

Following a conference of employers and trade unions in October 1899, NABF and ASSIW agreed to join a Board of Conciliation for the Pig Iron Trade in Scotland.[9] Each member firm was represented by one delegate from the employer's side, and one elected from the workmen. Although the latter did not have to be a trade union member, this was generally the case, and a union official acted as secretary for the board. The employers recognised the respective trade unions in a representative capacity, although only in relation to negotiation on regulation of wages. As another precondition, the masters insisted on 'freedom of employment', including recruitment of non-union labour. The worker representatives, led by the experienced trade union activist John Cronin, declared their position, firm in their knowledge that fewer than 100 out of around 4,000 employed at blast-furnace plants were not in a trade union. With a virtual closed shop of membership in most smelting plants, non-union labour was not a concern, but they made it clear to the employers that any serious attempt to reverse this position would be resisted thoroughly. By accepting formal conciliation and negotiation on wage-related issues, the employers renounced the provocative lockout weapon against workers, while the trade union leaders renounced the weapon of official strike action. Both sides agreed to accept wage regulation based on tables of sliding scales calculated in accordance with the selling price of pig iron in the Glasgow market. However, trade union proposals for a wider remit to include conciliation and arbitration on a range of working conditions were rejected out of hand. This remained the hard line policy of the employers, despite repeated attempts by the worker representatives to broaden the scope of the Board. Moreover, in 1913, when they argued yet again for the right 'to discuss grievances that might arise at individual works', the employers insisted that masters and works managers at plant level were the proper authority to deal with such matters, with the exception of obvious wage-related issues which came within the Board's remit.[10] It was understood that the worker delegates would intervene and, if necessary, attempt to exert discipline among any members who threatened to take unofficial action to break contract and stop work in local wage disputes with employers.

It is difficult to discern what the trade union side, and blast-furnace workers in general, gained from formal participation and collaboration in this joint representative body, given the Board's limited terms of reference and obvious employer dominance. The employers were at least made publicly accountable for calculation and implementation of sliding scales agreements on wages. However, the wages of unskilled labourers in and around furnaces remained low, and while the case for a basic minimum wage for those workers was made on the eve of war, it was rejected by the employers. For all grades of furnace workers there was a distinct failure to win discernible improve-ments in cost of living, real wages, hours and conditions until the end of the war period in 1917–18. Even then, the improvements in earnings and hours were predominantly the result of Ministry of Munitions recommendations and awards, although trade union lobbying at government level had exerted some positive influence. The ironworking trade unions had signed up to no-strike agreements during wartime, and union leaders honoured them. They held to their reputation as trade union moderates and ruled out official mobil-isation of members in strike action to exert pressure on government or employers around longstanding grievances such as long working hours and weekend shift patterns. For many years, high rates of absenteeism persisted among furnacemen, as exhausted men tried desperately to gain extended bouts of rest and recuperation. A worker explained how it was possible to get some relief from the relentless schedule of seven-day working and twelve-hour shifts. William Davies, a blast-furnace labourer at Dixon's Iron Works since 1908, was on an 84-hour week:

> If you wanted any time off, the only way you could get it without losing pay was to make some arrangement with your mates. What most of us used to do was to work one day of 24 hours straight through, and then take a day off the next week. It was either that, or bring in the by-turn man. He was a fellow who came in at the weekends and did a day for you, but that cost you a day's pay and a lot of us couldn't afford it. We preferred to work it that we did 13 hours on the nightshift, so that the day man got off an hour earlier and had a decent evening to himself. The work was hard, but furnace practice was slower in those days and you could always get a bit of a rest here and there. During the First war we started getting time-and-a-half for Saturday afternoons and Sundays; and later we got the eight-hour day, the best thing that ever happened in my life.[11]

Before 1914, one consequence of the realities of long hours and heavy manual work meant that the actual working week of furnacemen in Scotland remained an average of four shifts, and it was only during the wartime drive for increased productivity in smelting plants that the related problems of unrealistic working hours, fatigue and industrial inefficiency began to be recognised and addressed at government level.

For many years, pig-iron lifters had worked an eight-hour day or less. This established practice was a pragmatic one, determined by the sheer physical demands on workers who endured the most sustained heavy manual tasks in a smelting plant. At the end of 1918, the long-awaited introduction of an eight-hour day for iron and steel workers was signed in a national agreement between employers and trade unions. However, securing its practical implementation was fraught with difficulty, as pig-iron masters in Scotland prevaricated over the supposed complexities and timing of the transition to new, three-shift patterns and redeployment of labour. The related issues of eight-hour shifts, productivity, wage rates and earnings dominated labour relations well into 1919, as workers and their representatives pressed the employers for firm agreements. Employers agreed reluctantly to comply with the eight hours' ruling and, despite worker opposition, insisted on retaining the 'long turn' of a double shift of sixteen working hours at weekends. This position meant that workers gained the benefit of shorter shifts and reduced hours only on alternate weeks, as they were tied to seven shifts and fifty-six hours on the nightshift schedule.[12] Furnacemen also retained the war bonus, including overtime rates for weekend work. Employers were willing to continue those payments, as long as profitable production and industrial prosperity lasted.

However, the new working agreements and wartime gains in wages did not survive. They all came under pressure and were eventually broken by the pig-iron masters after the onset of the protracted post-war slump from late 1920s. By early 1922, the industry was almost at a standstill, leaving only a few furnaces in blast, and working at a loss. The prospect of unemployment loomed for the mass of furnaceworkers, while the skeleton workforces retained in struggling smelting plants were subjected to wage reductions, loss of trade union representation and imposition of harsh managerial controls.

MALLEABLE-IRON WORKERS

A malleable works contained a much larger number of skilled men than a smelting plant. Among the craft puddlers, shinglers, heaters and rollers, puddlers were the largest section, and they were apparently the most combative in asserting concerns over status and grievances. As skilled men at the beginning of the production process, forehand puddlers were often in dispute with employers, usually over tonnage rates and quality of iron produced. Major confrontations between employers and skilled workmen were fought out in the 1860s and 1870s, as each side tested its strength and authority against the other over earnings, working conditions and trade union recognition.

The earliest known evidence of industrial action and trade union organisation among malleable-iron workers in Scotland belongs to the mid 1860s, following the formation of the National Association of Ironworkers in the north of England in 1862. English puddlers had been involved in militant action for improved piecework earnings, and in 1864 newly organised branches of puddlers and forgemen in Glasgow, Coatbridge and Motherwell emulated their example, winning an increase.[13] The employers mounted a concerted counter-attack a year later, staging a lockout after stockpiling bars and plates, and slashing the wage rates.

Trade recovery in 1869 and renewed confidence among forehand puddlers

LANARKSHIRE MALLEABLE IRON WORKS.

Name	Parish	Founded	Closed	Number of puddling furnaces		
				1864	1888	1901
Calderbank	Old Monkland	1839	1887	68	68	—
Dundyvan	Old Monkland	1839	1868	56	—	—
Gartness	New Monkland	1840	1872	18	—	—
Mossend	Bothwell	1840	1900	28	60	—
Motherwell	Dalziel	1845	1903	—	50	33
Merryston	Old Monkland	1851	1885	10	—	—
Coats	Old Monkland	1854		18	31	14
Phoenix	Old Monkland	1857–8	?	—	—	—
North British	Old Monkland	?	1868	6	—	—
Globe	Old Monkland	1868	1884	—	—	—
Scotia	Old Monkland	1884	1897	—	—	—
Rochsolloch	New Monkland	1858		12	14	26
Drumpellier	Old Monkland	1859	1902	19	18	19
Clifton	Old Monkland	1861	1913 (May)	19	20	28
Phoenix	Old Monkland	1861	1921 (Aug.)	26	38	22
Excelsior	Cambusnethan	1863		22	34	20
Coatbridge Tin Plate	Old Monkland	1864		2	14	14
Gartcosh	Cadder	1865		—	7	7
North British	Old Monkland	1868	1927 (May)	—	37	34
Clydesdale	Bothwell	1870		—	—	26
Dalzell	Dalziel	1871.		—	20	—
Milnwood	Bothwell	1872		—	6	9
Crown	Old Monkland	1874	1913 (Feb.)	—	11	12
Milton Tin Plate	Dalziel	1877	1882	—	—	—
Woodside	Old Monkland	1878	1950 (June)	—	10	11
Pather	Cambusnethan	1880	1935	—	12	13
Waverley	Old Monkland	1881		—	16	25
Dundyvan	Old Monkland	1883		—	10	14
Globe	Dalziel	1884	1921 (Sept.)	—	12	21
Brandon	Dalziel	1884	1887	—	—	—
Etna	Dalziel	1887		—	10	19
Coatbridge	Old Monkland	1855	1913 (May)	—	10	10
Stenton	Cambusnethan	1895	1923 (May)	—	—	18
Victoria	Old Monkland	1898		—	—	14
Motherwell	Dalziel	1903	1934	—	—	—
Cairnhill	Old Monkland	1907	1914 (June)	—	—	—
Glencairn	Dalziel	1910	1913 (Feb.)	—	—	—

Lanarkshire Malleable-iron Works (from G. Thomson, *Third Statistical Account of Scotland: Lanarkshire*, p. 51)

again raised the earnings issue. The chosen union tactic was to test out employer response and the viability of strike action at a major works, in this case the Glasgow Iron Company's works at Motherwell. The company refused to consider restoration of the former tonnage rate, whereupon union members declared withdrawal of labour. For six weeks, until February 1870, the majority of striking forehand puddlers were sustained by local branch funds and a levy from other branches and districts. The tactic was successful, as the company had to concede the wage demand after being hard hit by lack of supplies of puddled iron and consequent loss of orders. Puddlers in the country's biggest plants at Mossend and Blochairn agitated for similar increases, which were also conceded.

The union then decided to press the big companies for a fresh tonnage rate increase in line with rising market prices and an arbitration award to puddlers in the north of England. This demand was refused, and a series of rolling strikes was mounted throughout the industry in Glasgow and North

Lanarkshire. Open industrial warfare was declared, as masters closed ranks and imposed a general lockout in all puddling, forge and rolling departments, effectively paralysing production and earnings throughout the trade. Employers in Scotland refused to recognise the principle and practice of arbitration and conciliation as it was applied by masters and trade unionists within the pig-iron sector and the malleable manufacturing side of the trade south of the border. North of England puddlers continued to support and sustain the action of their colleagues, contributing strike levies and refusing to make bar iron intended for transport to malleable plants in Scotland. By June, 400 puddling furnaces were still idle, and the dispute unsettled. However, strike funds had become exhausted in this war of attrition between masters and men. The workers had to admit defeat amid acrimonious division between puddlers and their assistants, who had been laid off without pay; and between puddlers and millmen, who resented being dragged into the dispute and loss of earnings as the result of unsuccessful strike action by puddlers.[14]

Tonnage rates of puddlers and millmen were reduced further at the end of 1870, but continuing rising demand for iron prompted puddlers to call an all-out strike throughout Lanarkshire plants. This was only a partial strike, as in some plants, such as the Excelsior in Wishaw, wages were comparatively high, and the puddlers chose to continue to work. After eight weeks, the strikers were forced back, as a promised levy from the national body of the union was not fully forthcoming. In March, the local press reported the defeat and plight of the puddlers, including chilling news that 'the children of respectable men were begging in the streets'.[15]

Motherwell puddlers had been in the forefront of open confrontation with the employers for no less than 30 weeks within a period of 18 months. They rallied in May 1871, as union members throughout the Lanarkshire area struck work in a call for reinstatement of their victimised leading activist, William Hodge, who had been sacked and blacklisted by the Glasgow Iron Company. However, non-union men ignored the protest and continued to work, and the action was halted after three weeks, with Hodge leaving the district. Thereafter, union membership in the malleable sector in Scotland fell away and was nearly destroyed from the mid 1870s until the late 1880s, when the craft interests of puddlers and rollers were represented within the Amalgamated Society of Steel and Iron Workers.

Despite the lack of union organisation and the grim realities of short-time work, reduced earnings and unemployment during bouts of downturn in trade from 1873, malleable-iron workers still reacted to grievances and resisted attacks on their wages and conditions. However, there were no more large-scale or district-wide confrontations as before, as disputes became largely localised and confined to individual workplaces. The character of disputes also continued to vary, some arising between masters and men, but also others of a sectional kind between and among workmen.

The principal source of workplace troubles from the mid 1870s and into the 1880s was savage wage- and cost-cutting, as employers responded to pressures of competition, irregular order books and declining profits. From mid 1873 to 1876, wages of malleable-iron workers plummeted by nearly 50 per cent from the peak levels reached during the recent boom years of the early 1870s. Such wage cuts provoked reactions in works that, until then, had had a reasonable record of labour relations. For instance, at the Excelsior, in Wishaw, which had been an oasis of calm during the widespread disputes of 1870–71, puddlers resisted cost-cutting in May 1873, and were evicted for breaking contract.[16] Later that year, Excelsior puddlers were instructed to work inferior quality iron without compensation for the additional time and effort involved, loss of heats and of tonnage earnings. Despite an existing agreement on the issue of working substandard iron, the company insisted that puddlers work on regardless, provoking renewed strike action in all departments. Again, the company retaliated with eviction notices, followed by the scrapping of all contractual agreements, dismissal without right of appeal and blacklisting. This harsh dispute lasted for nearly three months until, in January 1874, some workmen were allowed to return on the employer's terms, while others remained victimised and out of work.[17]

In similar fashion, ten years later, at a time of depressed trade and employer provocation, over 100 puddlers and underhands at the Excelsior revolted against cuts in wages and tonnage rates. Shinglers and millmen subsequently joined the strike, but it was a hopeless gesture, as trade union organisation had already been broken, and the masters were able to dictate terms to an isolated workforce.[18]

At another works, Beardmore's Parkhead Forge, the diary of forehand puddler David Willox provides an inside view of labour relations in the 1870s, during boom and recession. He mentions several incidents where fines, suspension and dismissal were imposed on the workforce for lost production and stoppages arising from alleged negligent work and behaviour. Unsympathetic foremen often tried to pin the blame on shinglers for damages to the steam hammer, and millmen were accused of careless operation and faulty maintenance when breakages occurred in the rolls. In a weekend diary entry for September 1873, he records a difficult week for production and labour relations: 'The furnaces have not been working well. Some of the men have been either sacked or suspended. There was a roll broken on Monday night, for which the roller got his leave.'[19]

Application of penalties by masters and foremen was at times arbitrary and unfair, although Willox considered William Beardmore a paternalist employer and reasonable man willing to listen and act justly to resolve the fundamentals of a problem when the full details were presented before him. From experience, Willox complained that puddlers and underhands were sometimes punished when they were not directly at fault during the operation of making iron. Instead, as a forehand puddler and later as a forge foreman, if he could convince or demonstrate to William Beardmore that problems with an unusual or particular charge of iron, or with poor dross for firing, were the real cause of lost heats and quality, more often than not his boss would make a positive response. In the mid 1870s, Parkhead Forge, with its forty puddling furnaces, was one of several malleables experimenting with haematite iron brands from Cleveland and mixing with Scottish pig iron for production of best ship plate.[20] In this context, with 'the furnaces not working well' and the puddling teams frustrated at losing heats and earnings over several days, Willox complained to Beardmore that 'the iron is bad'. Beardmore was at first unwilling to budge but, after demanding and receiving a proper explanation, agreed to act on the problem. The following day, Willox was happy to write that the master now 'resolves upon changing the mixture of iron'.[21]

In accordance with a standard ruling in malleable works throughout the country, forehand puddlers at Parkhead Forge were fined for alleged failure to exercise responsibility for work discipline among their underhands. Willox stated how, one Saturday in June 1873, 'a number of us are fined for under- hands' neglect . . . a source of trouble.'[22] Unfortunately, Willox does not reveal the precise nature of the dispute, but underhands had been on strike for several days, and puddling furnaces were at a standstill. Evidently, on the Thursday, the puddlers had made a settlement with their underhands, but Beardmore decided to penalise the puddlers for lost production. The following Monday, the puddlers made a direct approach to Beardmore, who was willing to reconsider: 'Have conference with our employer today about the fines kept off us on Saturday for underhands neglect. We reason him out of it and get our money.'[23]

Although details are not disclosed, one result of the dispute was the sacking of two foremen for apparent mishandling of the situation. This

decision may help to explain William Beardmore's change of mind about
penalising the puddlers, who were essential production men in a strong
bargaining position. Most probably, the foremen had been slow to take the
initiative to prevent a developing dispute and serious stoppage which proved
costly to the company at a time of full order books. It is not known whether
pressure was, or could have been, exerted on the puddlers to resolve differences with the hands, but it would appear nevertheless that the foremen had
failed as troubleshooters and were made to pay the penalty for lost production.

In disputes about wages, initially a matter between puddlers and underhands, the whole production team lost out. In July 1872, Willox reported that
underhands at Parkhead Forge went on strike because puddlers, including
him, refused to grant them a wage increase. On this occasion, master and
foremen did not intervene, as the men were expected to sort out their differences before too long. However, in such circumstances, production had to
continue and, according to standard practice, forehand puddlers were obliged
to work together without the services of their underhands. This practice
involved two forehands working one furnace, but they received only the
earnings of a single forehand, each man taking an equal share of the returns
for their labour. This working practice and form of payment was called 'level-
hand', and was resented by the better, more productive puddlers, as they were
obliged to divide their usual higher earnings with colleagues, some of whom
did not work as hard or as well as they did. When underhands were in short
supply or, for other reasons, several were absent from work at any one time,
level-hand meant a large wage cut and was often a source of internal friction
and division among forehands. During the dispute in July 1872, when
puddlers were also working in the discomfort of hot weather, Willox revealed
his frustration when 'forehands wrought level-hand and a fine mess they
made of it . . . some getting drunk and others careless'.[24] Given this
predicament, it was clearly in the interests of conscientious puddlers like
Willox to concede to the underhands, and he was relieved that this was done
within three days before considerable earnings were lost.

Although persistent, unaccountable absenteeism from work among
puddlers and hands was liable to result in dismissal, at least while Willox was
a gaffer at Parkhead puddling forge, less severe penalties were imposed for
occasional absence that was not related to family emergencies or illness. For
instance, his diary entry for March 18 1874 makes interesting reading, as it
reveals how he proposed to discipline Irish puddlers who had taken absence
without leave to celebrate a special day in their calendar. Any failure to come

to work already carried the penalty of lost pay, but he intended also to suspend them for deserting work, permitting return only when he was satisfied they were fit to resume responsible work:

> Have had a poor night's work. Three single and one double furnace standing for want of men . . . about a dozen underhands and two forehands off. Yesterday was St Patrick's Day, and most of them, I suppose, were what is called 'wetting their shamrock'. I'll give some of them a week to dry it. It is a shame to see men so degrade themselves with drink.[25]

There is no way of knowing whether the record of labour relations at Parkhead Forge in the later years of the nineteenth century was any better or worse than in other malleable iron plants in Scotland. According to Willox, the state of labour relations depended largely on the character and stance of masters and foremen when dealing with workers. As puddler and forge manager, he claimed to have enjoyed a good working relationship with William Beardmore. However, when his respected master died, and was succeeded by his brother Isaac, relations changed for the worse. He relates how: 'I had a straight turn up with Mr Isaac Beardmore yesterday and nearly got sacked for taking the shingler's part. He is a tyrant of the deepest die. There is as much difference betwixt him and his late brother William as there is betwixt good and evil.'[26]

Apparently, this altercation with an authoritarian and inflexible master was the first of several encounters in which decisions and judgements in his capacity as forge foreman were overruled. Such overbearing treatment was too much for Willox's self-respect, and he eventually resigned his post after being refused a character reference after sixteen years of diligent service as underhand, puddler and foreman.

During the 1870s, William Beardmore at Parkhead was only one of many iron masters who sought to find a mechanical substitute for the troublesome and expensive puddler. However, despite large spending on such experiments, it was found that the resourceful human puddler could not be replaced or de-skilled. For example, at the North British works in Coatbridge, owner Thomas Ellis abandoned experiments with a revolving mechanical rabble as it could not reach fully into the corners of the furnace. It, and other versions, could not compete with the manual dexterity, flexibility and judgement of the conventional puddler and underhand in their application of the ordinary rabble throughout the vital stirring, sifting and forming processes. In any case, in all instances where a mechanical contraption was used, the puddler or an experienced underhand had to be present, keeping watch and intervening, as necessary, to assist and handle the various processes.[27] The puddler was indispensable until the day when his skill was made obsolete by lack of commercial demand for wrought iron, and was superseded by the steel melter, working a much larger furnace in a mass-production setting.

Grievances over wages and conditions continued to flare up in forges and rolling mills before and after the establishment of formal conciliation machinery within the malleable-iron sector. The Scottish Manufacturing Iron Trade Conciliation and Arbitration Board (SMITCAB) was formed in 1897.[28] Malleable-iron plants concentrated in Coatbridge, Motherwell and Wishaw, and the outlying Ayrshire plant at Muirkirk, were the subscribing members, representing initially around 20 firms and over 3,000 workers. Member representation among firms and workmen was on the same basis as in the Conciliation Board for the pig-iron sector. The elected worker representative for each plant was drawn from senior men, contractors, and from the Amalgamated Society of Steel and Iron Workers, although trade unionists did not dominate the representation. However, unlike the other Board, the body for the malleable-iron sector functioned and operated with a wide remit. The formal commitment of its joint representatives to the cause of industrial troubleshooting and peaceful resolution of issues covered the range of conditions as well as wages. Moreover, it had independent arbiters with power to make binding decisions in the event of any failure to agree at the conciliation level, but this source of authority had to be used rarely.

Fixing, monitoring and implementing wages sliding scales for puddlers were essential, regular Board duties, and decisions in this regard appear to have been accepted or condoned by forehand puddlers. However, forehand puddlers did not have uniform rates of payment for underhands, and their actual earnings varied, according to local circumstances and practices. Such variations were often a source of friction and division. For example, in 1897 a Board survey of payments to underhands revealed that, as at Rochsolloch, long-serving, less fit puddlers paid extra money to secure experienced, good quality underhands.[29] In a less reputable vein, forehands were known to offer inducements to entice underhands from other forehands. Other local variations in payment were related to the grade of iron being worked, ranging from common or merchant iron to the very best, and to output in terms of weight.

Wage Rates for Underhand Puddlers					
Works	**Common Iron**		**Best Iron**		
	Wage Rate	Weight per shift	Wage rate	Weight per shift	
		(Tons, Cwts, Qrs, Lbs)		(Tons, Cwts, Qrs, Lbs)	
Clifton	3/4d.	1, 11, 3, 2.			
Clydesdale	3/7d.	1, 10, 1, 11.			
Coatbridge	3/6d.	1, 10, 3, 23.	3/6d.		
Coats	3/6d.	1, 12, 0, 0.	3/6d.	1, 15, 0, 0.	
Crown	3/4d.	1, 10, 1, 13.	3/6d.	1, 10, 1, 13.	
Dalzell	3/5d.				
Drumpellier	3/6d.	1, 9, 1, 0.			
Dundyvan	3/7d.	1, 11, 2, 0.	3/7d.	1, 12, 0, 0.	
Etna	3/7d.	1, 12, 0, 14.			
Globe	3/5d.	1, 12, 1, 0.	3/11d.	2, 2, 0, 0.	
Motherwell	3/4d.	1, 10, 0, 0.	3/8d.	1, 11, 0, 0.	
Muirkirk	3/-d.	1, 4, 1, 6.			
North British	3/10d.	1, 7, 0, 0.	3/10d.	1, 13, 2, 0.	
Pather					
Phoenix	3/10d.	1, 10, 0, 0.			
Rochsolloch	3/11d.	1, 10, 3, 0.	3/11d.	1, 10, 3, 0.	
Stenton	3/7d.	1, 11, 0, 25.	4/2d.	1, 19, 0, 23.	
Tinplate	3/4d.	1, 10, 0, 0.			
Waverley	3/5d.	1, 13, 2, 15.	3/5d.	1, 15, 1, 27.	
Woodside	3/6d.	1, 11, 3, 22.			

Wage rates for underhand puddlers (Scottish Manufacturing Iron Trade Conciliation and Arbitration Board, Minutes, 23 December 1897)

Disputes arose over differential payment and over basic shift payments, as underhands attempted to win parity with other colleagues. At the Waverley Works in 1897, underhand puddlers took strike action and refused to recognise the Board when it failed to support their move for an increase in the wage rate. In attempts to settle this dispute and set a guide for differential payment to underhands, the Board had to intervene to fix average rates per shift.[30]

Wage rates for other teams in forge and mill were not fixed by the Board. Instead, they continued to be determined by local bargaining, firstly between individual employers and subcontractors, and then between contractors and work teams. However, as with puddlers and their underhands, the Board sometimes had to mediate in disputes arising between work teams and their contractor paymasters. For instance, forge rollers experienced fraught relationships with the head rollers who contracted them. Although they carried out heavier tasks than the craft rollers, roughers were the poor relations in terms of skill and pay. They grew to resent the subcontracting system, and periodically voiced demands for its abolition, calling for employers to pay wages directly, coupled with ensuring a more favourable distribution of rewards to the whole team of rollers and millmen. Discriminatory treatment of forge rollers (roughers) was clearly evident in

1916, when contractor rollers claimed they were not obliged to grant this group of workers a share of war bonus payments. The forge rollers lodged a formal case with the Board against the stance of the contractors. After going to arbitration and review by the Board of Trade, the position of the contractors was upheld, as was their continuing authority and status. It is little wonder that such an adverse verdict should have contributed to a growing climate of disaffection among the generality of rank and file workers who were already being denied a living wage in wartime. Owen Coyle, leading union official on the Board, warned in late 1917 of struggling to keep the lid on the tide of 'unrest and discontent that prevails among the lower-paid men in the malleable iron trades just now'.[31]

During wartime, there is evidence of young men deserting the prospect of a career at puddling furnaces, with its gruelling schedules and long shifts. Many volunteered for active service, while more favourable work opportunities appeared in other branches of industry. For instance, in November 1914, a concerned employer complained that 'they could not get a young fellow to take up the puddling trade when they had the steel trade offering better-paid positions without the same hard labour'.[32] In May 1915, a Board member from the Etna Iron Works stated that in the Motherwell-Wishaw area they 'could only get broken down men and aliens to work as underhands'.[33]

Despite problems of recruitment and renewal of labour in puddling plants, continuous production lasted into the shortlived post-war boom. A

Rollers at 9-inch mill,
Etna Iron Works

variation on the newly introduced eight-hour shift pattern was negotiated and implemented by March 1919 and puddlers settled for a productivity agreement based on output. The normal target for an eight-and-a-half-hour shift was five heats, and four heats for a seven-hour shift. On this basis, employers were satisfied with the prospect of an average total of fourteen heats produced by three sets of shift workers within a twenty-four-hour period.[34] However, the new terms and conditions applied for little more than a year. From late 1920, the malleable-iron sector in Scotland began to spiral into recession, closures and decline, bringing within a few years the complete demise of puddling as a viable occupation.

FOUNDRY WORKERS

The unsavoury conditions of casting and moulding work in foundries have been outlined and described in an earlier chapter. How the many thousands of foundry workers scattered throughout Scotland responded to those oppressive conditions is not well recorded, and remains under-researched. The available evidence for active responses, including some resistance to adverse conditions, points to the existence of formal, defensive, collective organisation only among skilled moulders, while it was not until the late 1880s that less skilled and unskilled foundry workers formed permanent trade unions. Before 1850, only a few hundred moulders were at any time members of a friendly society or trade union. This minority was confined to time-served journeymen moulders, craft proud and respectable in outlook who, in their trade societies, were willing to pay high membership dues to qualify for a range of social insurance cum welfare benefits for themselves and their immediate family. Accident, sickness, unemployment and funeral benefits were the friendly society aspect of their commitment to protection against adversity. However, although they excluded from membership, and therefore did not represent, foundry labourers and boys, the Scottish Iron Moulders' Union, from its inception, also had a record of resistance to attacks on wages and conditions, especially when craft positions were under threat.

In the early decades of the nineteenth century, skilled moulders learned the hard way how to organise themselves and to challenge their employers on workplace issues that were to be recurring sources of conflict within the trade into the twentieth century. In a constant struggle to safeguard their own employment, uphold craft conditions, and gain appropriate reward for their labour, they chose to defend their interests by pursuing several restrictive practices, and were known to use strike action when negotiation failed. They concentrated on attempts to control entry and supply of labour and made it a priority to regulate the number of boys who could be allowed into a foundry so that their number never rose above the ratio of one boy to every three time-served journeymen. They sought to limit boy labour to preparatory tasks, including coremaking, before stepping up to casting and moulding operations when an opening occurred. For the same reasons, and to improve their bargaining power as skilled men, they actively opposed subcontracting of labour to foremen. Piece-rate working was also resisted, where possible, as it was seen as a way of getting more work from fewer men, and linked with imposition of increased workloads and speed-up of tasks. Altogether, piece-work payment was regarded as a source of division, unfair competition among the workers, and intensification of accidents, injury and ill- health. Attempts to regulate the time taken to do a particular job, opposition to regular and systematic overtime, and agreement on the length of the working day, were also long-term concerns of this craft union. In evidence given to an 1842 enquiry, the manager of Robert Napier's Vulcan and Lancefield ship engineering foundries in Anderston, Glasgow, reported an informative, though hostile, view of such craft union activities at both works:

> The moulders (ie those who make the moulds and cast the pieces of machinery) are still under a strong combination, and are a bad set of men. If discharged by their employers, they are supported out of the funds of the union. They prevent hands not regularly brought up to the business from being taken in by the master, and are bad workmen often. They are limited by their rules as to the quantity a man may earn per day. If he were starting a new work he would make a clean sweep of them and introduce fresh hands.[35]

The co-owner of Phoenix Foundry, Glasgow, a heavy castings, engine-making works, also testified to an attempted restrictive practice, and the means to counter it:

> There is a strong union among the foundry hands, or, as they are called, 'moulders'. The union chiefly affects this work by encouraging them and apprentices to 'put down', or make much less, for a fair day's work than they can well do: so that the only resort is piece-work.[36]

Moreover, piece-work had long been customary in the numerous light castings foundries in Scotland, where boy labour was most prominent. Trade union organisation and defence of basic working conditions was weak in that part of the foundry sector, and would remain so for many years. Moulders were better organised in heavy castings foundries, where they frequently managed to restrict the number of boy workers and, although unable to eliminate piece-work exploitation, were in a position to counter its more excessive forms. When and where solidarity was sufficiently strong in particular foundries, mainly in large jobbing and heavy casting foundries in and around Glasgow and the west of Scotland, the union sought to secure greater bargaining power by establishing a closed shop of members among the skilled men.

Yet victories in tackling the above list of concerns and grievances were few, limited, and often shortlived, as the odds were usually stacked heavily against successful outcomes. Employers retaliated with one or more weapons at their disposal, including sackings, lockouts, introduction of compliant replacement labour, and resort to the law courts to bring charges against breach of contract and other alleged offences such as intimidation. Several times during the 1830s and 1840s, the small union and its branches had faced bankruptcy and severe loss of members, its meagre funds sacrificed in strike or lockout pay, and in other out-of-work payments.

Of all the challenges to the craft position of the moulder, employer pressure to overcrowd the foundry with untrained labour of any kind, and especially of boys, was the greatest and most persistent threat. It also provoked endless grievance and frequent open conflict. On two major occasions, in the winters of 1846–7 and 1867–8, at times of depressed market conditions, it led to Scotland-wide disputes, after concerted offensive action by the employers forced the issue. In the first dispute, the employers decided to flood foundries with boys and young workers, and prompted a protest strike. The Scottish Iron Moulders' Union was already vulnerable, as support funds were low and many members were unemployed. It was an unequal battle, as funds ran out and the strike had to be abandoned. Members were given the invidious choice of leaving the union and accepting humiliating conditions, or losing their jobs and being blacklisted.

The second dispute caught the moulders' union in a disastrous position, as the employers had the advantage and outmanoeuvred the workmen. Prolonged depression had depleted union funds, many moulders were idle and wages had been slashed. Then, at the start of 1868, the owners dictated a new, harsh set of terms of employment, including complete control over labour supply and work allocation, supervision and discipline and methods and rates of payment. When workers obeyed a union instruction to ignore the notices, they were locked out, and in several foundries were replaced by blackleg labour imported from England. Moulders were forced into unconditional surrender, and union influence was destroyed in most foundries.[37]

Yet, despite such colossal defeats, activists demonstrated the necessary courage and resilience to rebuild membership, funds and credibility so that during the more prosperous years after 1850, craft union membership among journeymen moulders climbed from around 800 at mid century to over 4,000 during the early 1870s. The Scottish Iron Moulders' Association won some concessions in shorter hours, notably a 54-hour week in 1871, but this did not apply in the majority of foundries, where journeymen and assistants were obliged to work frequent overtime. Any gains made in hours, wages and conditions were lost in contests with employers during the trade depressions of the late 1870s and 1880s, and the exclusive craft position of the moulders' trade union was thrown into crisis.[38]

As long as the Scottish Iron Moulders' Union retained its sectional craft mentality and refused to recognise or to organise the growing ranks of semi-skilled and unskilled foundry workers, it increasingly failed to defend its own members, was unable to present a common front with fellow workers against employers, and remained badly positioned to confront the many challenges of changing work processes within the foundry sector. From the 1860s, pipes and many wares, particularly household heating appliances, stoves, grates and other articles in the light castings category, had become mass-produced standardised items that could be prepared and cast by boys and younger men who required little training. Consequently, employers gave out this work to such groups, bypassing the services of skilled journeymen. This reallocation of tasks, usually also on a piece-work basis, provoked countless demarcation disputes, as time-served men protested and resisted employer efforts to displace them.[39]

In the late 1880s, hitherto poorly organised workers in the light castings sector, including semi-skilled and unskilled grades, formed their own union. The impetus to permanent organisation began in 1888 with a strike of hundreds of low-paid, non-union workers in the Falkirk area. Buoyed up by this successful movement to gain a significant wage increase, a rival to the traditional craft union was established in 1889, in the shape of the Central Ironmoulders' Association. With low entry fees and dues, its outlook was

Overleaf. Foundry dressing yard, Coltness Iron Works (North Lanarkshire Council)

characteristic of the more direct, militant approach then developing within a number of emerging, mainly unskilled trade unions towards winning immediate improvements in wages and conditions.[40]

After initial mutual suspicion, the two principal unions representing moulders and other foundry workers in Scotland learned to co-operate with each other from the 1890s onwards, especially to plan and act together to confront the new powerful force of a centrally organised Scottish Employers' Federation of Iron and Steel Founders, formed in 1898.[41] The policy and conduct of the Federation towards the trade unions was similar to that of the iron masters in the pig-iron sector. Whereas the foundry unions would have welcomed a conciliation and arbitration body to discuss and settle disputes, the employers were hostile to such a development. They agreed only to central bargaining on wages issues, while retaining the right to recruit and retain non-union labour, thus opposing union attempts to organise closed shops and restrictive practices.

The more assertive outlook among light castings workers was illustrated in 1905 and 1912, at Carron Iron Works, a former stronghold of non-union family labour. In 1905, Carron moulders were embroiled in a bitter two-month strike over disputed payment for overweight and damaged castings. Company retaliation included eviction from tied houses and blacklisting of workers.[42] In 1912, over 400 moulders struck work in protest against fluctuating wage rates and compulsory overtime. The Falkirk employers retaliated with a general lockout of over 4,000 workers, but the workers' case was won after Board of Trade intervention. Again, in 1913, traditional sectional divisions were laid aside, when over 1,000 Falkirk foundry craftsmen and journeymen struck work in sympathy with their aggrieved labourers.[43]

By 1914, the majority of adult foundry workers in Scotland were organised in trade unions. The largest organisation, AIMS, claimed over 8,000 members, followed by the Central Ironmoulders' Association with 6,000 members, and smaller unions such as the Scottish Iron Dressers, with 1,000 members. In foundries belonging to engineering works, the standard working week was 54 hours, and in organised foundry workshops, wage rates for journeymen were higher than in non-union places, where sub-contracting and low wages still prevailed.[44]

During 1914–18, a vocal unofficial body within the AIMS adopted a militant stance against excessive wartime exploitation of foundry workers and led an influential campaign for a single industrial union to represent all grades of workers in the ironwork sector.[45] Despite opposition from the official leadership within the foundry trade unions, this rank and file movement was strong in the heavy cast foundries of Glasgow, the Clyde and Lanarkshire. Although illegal under wartime regulations, Scottish moulders went on strike for three weeks in September 1917, after growing unrest over the rising cost of living and poor offers of wage and piece rates.[46] The action prompted a significant bonus award from the Ministry of Munitions to moulders and engineering workers.[47] By 1918, the influence of Red Clydeside was clearly discernible within the main craft union, as a militant majority had been elected to the leadership of AIMS, with Tom Bell, a prominent left-wing socialist, president of its executive council.

In the immediate post-war period, renewed demands were made for a forty-hour week and an eight-hour day, and many foundry workers participated in the strike wave of Clydeside industrial workers during early 1919. Although this strike was defeated, concessions were won in the form of a 47-hour working week (down from 54 hours), additional night-shift rates and abolition of compulsory overtime. As we have seen already in the iron smelting and malleable sectors, workers experienced delays to implementation of those agreements. Foundry workers faced a similar predicament, as employers either reneged on, or else objected to, paying the same wages for shorter hours without any guarantees of greater productivity.[48] Meantime, in conditions of full employment, the momentum towards amalgamation of the various foundry unions into one organisation continued apace, culminating in the formation of the National Union of Foundry Workers in 1920. The principal foundry sector unions in Scotland joined forces in this larger Britain-wide entity, but the achievement of greater unity and any prospects of improved conditions were already foreshadowed and threatened by the imminent industrial depression of the inter-war years.

CHAPTER 5
WORKING LIVES IN STEEL:
1870s–1920

If it was nearing five o'clock in the afternoon the wall would be lined with steel furnacemen who would soon start their nightshift. It would be their last few moments of relaxation before commencing their fourteen-hour shift. Most of them were tall strong men who had been born away from Craigneuk, from the Highlands of Scotland, from many parts of Ireland, and a very few from Poland and Lithuania.

Each one would be dressed for action, for there were no lockers or baths or changing rooms then, and all of them would wear heavy nailed boots which, in keeping with the tradition of the district, would be brightly polished. In fact, Mr McFarlane, the steelworkers' manager, would stretch every point to find work for any men who approached him wearing white sweat towels, and heavy polished boots. They were worth looking at and they knew it, they were the labour aristocrats of the heavy industry world. Their wages stood out against other trades like skyscrapers in a town of two-storey buildings. The fact did not make them more prosperous, for the rigours of their work on hand-charging furnaces increased their normal thirsts. Naturally many of them satisfied their thirsts often and long. But they were not degenerates, the harshness of their daily lives rarely seeped into their souls. They were very fine human beings, and I admired them hugely when I was young. I was very proud to see my father, Peter McGeown, standing with them, straight and strong, and as decent as the best of them.[1]

The passage above, from the splendid autobiography of Patrick McGeown, is a moving tribute to the first generations of steelmen, and provides an appropriate introduction to the theme of working lives in the context of the early

development of the industry in Scotland. Like furnace-keepers in iron
smelting, and puddlers in the malleable-iron industry, smelters, or melters,
(the terms are interchangeable for those grades and teams of furnacemen who
made steel), were the key production men in this new heavy industry.
Consequently, steel melters and their support teams of furnace labourers are
given centre stage among occupational profiles in this chapter. Firstly, though,
it is necessary to set the scene for this enquiry, and provide a summary of the
characteristics and development of the steel industry in its formative period.

Steel melter shielding
face from heat and
glare (North
Lanarkshire Council)

THE TRANSITION TO STEEL:
INDUSTRY, LOCATIONS AND RECRUITMENT

Peter McGeown was a forehand steel melter, having started as a melting-shop labourer before progressing through the furnace team grades to No.1 melter, with responsibility for a 35-ton capacity open-hearth furnace. An Irish immigrant from Armagh, he and his son, born in 1897 in Craigneuk, were employed nearby in the Lanarkshire Steel Works, at Flemington, Motherwell until 1914, when they left to continue steel-working careers in the Manchester area. The 'Lanarkshire' – their first and only workplace within the industry in Scotland – was equipped initially with five open-hearth furnaces and three rolling mills. When it began production in 1893, it was one of a dozen steel-works in Scotland, located in the very heartland of this relatively new, and growing, heavy industry. Its larger and more famous neighbour was the Dalzell Works, of David Colville and Sons. Colvilles was already a successful malleable-iron producer when, in 1879, it decided to concentrate on steel production by the tested process of open hearth melting. Siemens melting furnaces had been pioneered from 1873 by the Steel Company of Scotland at Hallside, near Cambuslang. It was the only viable steel making plant until, between 1879 and 1883, several malleable-iron firms whose business depended largely on the Clyde shipbuilding market, made the momentous transition to steel production. The initiative and incentive to invest in steel at this time was provided by the decision of the Admiralty, followed by Clyde shipbuilders, to switch from iron sections to the superior steel for ship plate and marine boilers. Beardmore's Parkhead Forge was the first malleable-iron firm to diversify into steel, followed closely by the Excelsior Works, Wishaw; David Colville and Sons; the Summerlee and Mossend Iron and Steel Company; and the Clydesdale, also at Mossend; while the Steel Company of Scotland built another steel works at Blochairn, in north-east Glasgow, on the derelict site of a once huge malleable-iron plant.

Until then, this crop of new steel plants was furnished with open-hearth furnaces, melting shops and accompanying forge and rolling mills. Plants from the late 1880s into the twentieth century, as at Calderbank and Clydebridge (near Cambuslang), were also of this type. However, there were rare exceptions, which differed in method and technology of steel production. In 1883, at Wishaw, the Glasgow Iron Company built a steel plant on the opposite side of the Caledonian railway from their iron smelting works. At first, they experimented with three Bessemer converter furnaces, feeding them with molten iron from the four blast furnaces directly across the railway. However, the converters were abolished during the 1890s to make way for open-hearth furnaces and production of mild steel to satisfy the demands of Clyde shipbuilders. Merry and Cunningham, at their Glengarnock iron-smelting plant, also installed Bessemer converters in the mid 1880s, but again the preference of Clyde shipbuilders and a place in this lucrative market prompted addition of open-hearth furnaces alongside the converters. Thereafter, the Glengarnock plant remained the sole instance of Bessemer steel production in Scotland. By 1900, the only other pig-iron producers to erect steel plants side by side with existing blast furnaces were at Coltness, near Wishaw, and at Ardeer, on the Ayrshire coast. From the 1890s, the Coltness Iron and Steel Works was an interesting exception, in that it contained modernised blast furnaces and some open-hearth steel production, but no forge and rolling departments. Instead, a large foundry was built for making steel castings for locomotives and ship parts.

Steel was the new, improved iron, with many impurities removed. More flexible and durable, and ultimately less costly to produce than malleable iron, it was rapidly displacing its older rival as favoured supplier, not only for the insatiable shipbuilding programmes of the lower Clyde, but also for railway rolling stock and bridge construction, and other structural and general engineering purposes. By the 1890s, there were ten large steel works in Scotland, and a substantial number of smaller firms producing rolled steel, foundry castings and special tools. Notably, as in the case at Wishaw, several malleable-iron firms traded under the title of iron and steel producers. They did not actually make steel, but processed steel products. While the iron-puddling side of their business had begun to decline, they managed instead to survive and even flourish as the result of service contracts from steelworks whereby their mill plant was used to roll steel billets or re-roll semi-finished steel goods. In 1904, Smith and McLean at Gartcosh Works was an early example of a malleable-iron firm which closed down its puddling plant to concentrate on rolling steel plate, and subsequently became part of the Colville group before 1918. Such links between struggling malleable works and those steelworks that required additional rolling capacity also enabled many iron rollers, heaters and other millmen to retain their jobs. Moreover, transferable skills gained in the iron sector equipped some of those workers for fresh prospects in the new, more modern and larger rolling mills of steelworks.

The advent and rise of steel manufacture between the 1870s and the early

No. 1 plate mill, Dalzell Works, c. 1900 (North Lanarkshire Council)

twentieth century created a second industrial revolution in several established centres of iron production and mining. This intensified development was most significant in the heavy industry communities of Motherwell and Wishaw, and in parts of north-east and east Glasgow which were already industrialised, particularly Springburn, St Rollox and the Parkhead district, where Beardmore's was becoming a giant complex of steel manufacture, including ship plate and naval armaments production. Coatbridge earned the title of 'Ironopolis' of Scotland in the Victorian era, but it was Motherwell (and Wishaw), with its conglomeration of steel-working and allied industry, which became the 'Steelopolis' of Scotland before 1914–18. For the whole period covered in this chapter, the economic and employment profiles of the steel industry in Motherwell and Wishaw make impressive reading. Five of the steelworks in Scotland were concentrated there, and two others were located nearby in this part of North Lanarkshire. The enlarged, reconstructed Wishaw Steel Works was the largest employer of labour in the town by the close of the century. Its workforce had expanded to over 1,000 men and boys, as against only 200 workers prior to the addition of open-hearth furnace capacity. However, by 1913, Dalzell Steel Works was the single largest steel producer in Scotland, with 30 large tonnage open-hearth furnaces and extensive rolling mill capacity. It was then the fastest growing concern in the British steel industry and the largest employer in the Motherwell area, with 2,800 workers. The Lanarkshire Steel Works employed one thousand three hundred workers at the time, and between them the two steelworks employed as many workers as the town's nine collieries. During 1914–18, when Dalzell Works was a major supplier of slab and plate for the navy and merchant shipping, and principal munitions producers in the county of Lanarkshire, the wartime labour force swelled to 5,000. In 1915, at the behest of the wartime British government, Colvilles acquired the steel plants at Glengarnock and Clydebridge, and proceeded to enlarge and modernise their furnace capacity. In 1920, at the height of the post-war boom, the renovated Glengarnock Works employed nearly 3,000 workers, although capacity and workforce were greatly reduced during the subsequent depression.[2]

Directly and indirectly, the growth of the steel industry led to a major increase in work opportunities, and to profound changes in the extent and composition of the working class at plant and community level. When open-hearth steelmaking began in the 1870s and 1880s, the new industry appeared to offer attractive employment prospects. According to John Hodge, steel workers' trade union organiser, men recruited into the labour force in the early years, 'represented all kinds and conditions of craftsmen, such as carpenters, joiners, blacksmiths, iron founders, ex-policemen, miners, and a very few old puddlers; all flocking to the steelworks because of the glamour of the alleged big money which was being earned.'

Hodge then adds a curious comment about the apparent disposition of puddlers towards the emerging rival of steelmaking: 'It is interesting to note that although steel was ousting iron, no puddler would believe it, their minds being inflexibly made up that steel would very soon prove a failure and iron once again reassert itself. Therein lies the reason why so few puddlers entered the steel trade.'[3]

There is no firm evidence to prove or disprove the reality of Hodge's impression about such puddler prejudices or reservations, although Hodge himself was an example of a former puddler who was positive about the prospect of becoming a steel melter. As a young man in the 1870s, he had worked brief periods as an underhand puddler at Blochairn and Parkhead Forge. During the early 1880s, he tried to 'get a job on a melting furnace; fairy

tales were being told of the huge wages which steel melters were earning . . .
I went to Glasgow, saw the foreman of the melting shop in the Blochairn Steel
Works, and was successful in getting a start as a third hand on a melting
furnace.' There is no doubt that, as an assistant puddler, he had certain transferable skills to offer in this regard: 'My old experience as a puddler was a
great asset, knowing as I did something about heat and about slag and the
usual routine.'[4] However, apart from a few 'old puddlers', it is highly unlikely
that experienced forehand puddlers who were still fit and able and holding
down well-paid positions would have been inclined to leave their craft to enter
a steel melting shop unless they were given comparable job grades or wages.

In the early years of the industry, before seniority became the rule for
promotion through the job grades in a melting shop and rolling mill, owners
and managers chose to recruit their workforce in two different ways. For
instance, David Colville and Sons was one of a few firms to handpick its
workers and to manage and pay them directly, while other firms relied upon
contractors to engage and supervise their squads.[5] In both cases, they
promised high wages and quick promotion to ambitious and able young men
who aspired to the arts and skills of steelmaking and finishing. There is no
evidence to suggest that iron workers of various grades and trades who, for
whatever reasons, wished to make a change in livelihood, did not seek and take
advantage of such opportunities to enter the new industry. They had at least
some direct experience of the heat and rigour of an industrial environment,
and many of them had acquired demonstrable skills in their respective trades,
so that they were unlikely to have to start again at the very bottom of the
employment ladder among the unskilled.

On the other hand, raw entrants into the world of steel, who did not have
that background and experience, were also in demand, but in most instances
were engaged initially as unskilled labour. Irish immigrants continued to be a
prominent source of recruits in that category, and were found in all steel-
working communities. Peter McGeown was one such example. Like so many
others before and since, he escaped from rural poverty in Ireland and did
seasonal harvest work in Scotland and England for several years before finally
settling down in his mid-twenties to regular employment at the emerging
Lanarkshire Steel works. In the Craigneuk area, he lived alongside many other
Irish families and single Irish men from similar backgrounds, who also started
at the bottom of the employment ladder in local iron and steel industries.
Smaller numbers of Lithuanian immigrants, many from rural backgrounds,
also found employment as steelworks labourers, notably in the Bellshill,

Motherwell and Wishaw areas. Others were similarly employed and settled in older company houses at Glengarnock, alongside their compatriots at the iron furnaces.

Recruitment of supervisory and skilled labour for early Scottish steel-works during the 1870s and 1880s followed a similar pattern to that of the earlier years of iron smelting and puddling, in that expertise was imported from England and Wales. For example, at Mossend Steel Works, owned by Hugh Neilson, the first cohort of open-hearth melters was contracted and recruited from Wales. When the same owner started Clydebridge in 1886, a core of melters and steam crane men, including some Scottish workers, was transferred from Mossend.[6] At the earliest steelworks village, Hallside, company houses were built on-site for the incoming workforce. There, around thirty houses were stone-built and self-contained and, according to their style, were known as the 'English houses'. Those superior houses were allocated to managers, foremen and top skilled men who were not exclusively Englishmen. The other housing stock consisted of around 150 dwellings arranged in blocks of brick-built, two-storey tenements. Among the skilled contingent, Welshmen were prominent, having come north from Landore Steel Works in 1878 with James Riley, a leading pioneer of Siemens steel production, who was newly installed as Hallside manager. Hence, workers with surnames such as Griffiths, Jones and Thomas became permanent fixtures in the steelworks and the local community, although they were soon outnumbered by Irish and Scottish workers.[7] Hallside village was a separate community but, as the works expanded, it did not accommodate the entire workforce, who acquired housing nearby, in and around Cambuslang, or else commuted on workmen's trains from Glasgow and other towns.

In a rather different setting, Calderbank is an example of a former indus-trial community which was regenerated by the presence of a steelworks. Closure and demolition of the malleable-iron works in the 1880s left a scene of dereliction and empty houses. In the late 1890s, after an uncertain start, steel-working became profitable under a change of owners. In this successful venture, James Dunlop and Company, also proprietors of the Clyde Iron Works, had bought over the old stock of company houses and repopulated them with a fresh intake of steel workers and their families. The familiar pattern of housing provision was again in evidence, the better stock, as at English Row, allocated to managers and top workmen, while the other houses, all increasingly damp, insanitary and overcrowded, were tenanted by predom-inantly Scottish and Irish skilled and unskilled labour.[8]

In some localities, new steel companies did not own and supply houses for their workers, or provided only a small and limited number. David Colville and Sons owned a few company houses in the centre of Motherwell, but the great majority of the workforce had to find rented accommodation from other landlords in a burgh which was already bursting at the seams and struggling to house the rapidly increasing influx of industrial workers. The Lanarkshire Steel Works took no responsibility for housing their workers, as demonstrated by the experience of the McGeown family who lived across the boundary in the burgh of Wishaw, one of the worst-housed urban areas in Scotland. In the

A labour-intensive operation, taking heavy rolled steel plate to shears, Dalzell Works, c. 1900 (North Lanarkshire Council)

fourth ward, which took in Craigneuk, housing stock was primarily single-room and two-roomed dwellings built by coal companies in the 1840s and 1850s, and sold to local property speculators, shopkeepers and tradesmen when mining declined towards the end of the century. The McGeown parents and three children lived in this type of small, older house. They rented a single room in Cowie's Square, a block of fifty houses consisting of ten two-apartment dwellings and forty single ends. Their ground-floor room had a fireplace, an inside sink with cold-water tap, and gas lighting. Cramped living conditions allowed little space for furniture. There were two curtained-off recess beds in one wall; a wooden chest for storing blankets which served as an extra seat; two chairs and a table and some shelves along another wall. Before 1914, Cowie's Square was one of many properties that were officially condemned as insanitary and overcrowded, but such regulations remained a dead letter owing to the critical housing shortage. As sole breadwinner with a young family, it is unlikely that Peter McGeown could have afforded a move to more roomy accommodation but, even if he had wished to do so and could manage to pay a higher rent, tenants such as the McGeown family had no other option, as there was no alternative rented accommodation for industrial workers in the burgh, and properties were fully occupied. As Patrick McGeown remarked ruefully about such living conditions, after a long, hard shift, and in soiled clothes, 'it was a poor place for a man to come home to: one room, with no bath, no instant hot water, and a lavatory at the end of the close which eight families shared'.[9]

TASKS AND WORKING CONDITIONS

At all steelworks throughout the first half-century of the industry in Scotland, the bulk of tasks in the preparation and making of molten steel in open-hearth furnaces depended on hard manual labour, dexterity and considerable powers of physical and mental endurance. Machinery and appliances for lifting and positioning, such as stationary and mobile overhead cranes, were introduced from early on. However, machines and devices to assist melting shop and furnace labourers were not a prominent feature until the very end of the period covered by this survey. Instead, investment in such efficiency and labour-saving measures was made mainly elsewhere, during the stages after melters had done their work at the furnaces, and for tasks which could not be carried out by manual labour.

As an example of those priorities, crane operators worked alongside casting pit teams to ladle molten steel from the furnace. Steel ingots, of various weights and sizes, were then allowed to form in the cast-iron moulds. However, they were many times heavier than pig-iron billets, and even when cold were impossible to hoist manually. Consequently, several workmen at one time, using muscular strength and hand tools for levering and manipulation, were needed to support any mechanical lifting and processing of large ingots. As ingots had to be moved several times while hot, such tasks required crane operators to lift the still roasting metal from the casting area and place them in soaking pits to retain their heat. Cranes were also used to hoist and transport hot ingots to the first set of rolls in the cogging mill. The rectangular slabs which emerged from this process were then mechanically lifted and positioned for further rolling into plate or other shapes and sections. Before cogging mills were introduced in the 1890s to flatten ingots into slabs, a shingling team at the steam hammer dealt with this forging operation in much the same way as their counterparts carried out the task in the malleable iron works. However, one vital difference for respective shingling teams to contend with concerned the sheer bulk and heavy weight of a steel ingot as compared with the much smaller units of puddled iron, which were less difficult to manipulate and forge. The steam hammer was soon abandoned for heavy ingot work in most steel plants, as it was found to lack the necessary strength and precision. However, the conventional steam hammer and teams of hammermen were still deployed in tasks like forging steel axles and wheels.

In large rolling mills which were periodically improved for greater efficiency, as at the plate mills of David Colville and Sons, the extent of manual labour was eventually reduced to a minimum. Where, formerly, bulky plate had to be manoeuvred with great difficulty by a squad of workmen and brought in bogies to the cutting shears, a power-driven table on rollers was devised to load and convey the plate for this purpose. However, where conventional steel-plate mills continued to operate, a considerable number of men were needed to push forward, guide, and turn the slabs through the rolls. In the most up to date mechanised rolling mills, tilting gear, mounted on a carriage, run on rails and operated by levers from a gallery, dispensed with the majority of movements and adjustments formerly carried out by assistant workers using bodily exertion and hand tools. Yet, even after 1918, in some rolling mills within Scottish steelworks, and especially in malleable-iron works where steel was re-rolled, older, labour-intensive plants had not been replaced by more powerfully mechanised efficient versions. In those plants, manual assistance was still required for cleaning, descaling and setting the rolls and, to a greater or lesser extent, for push- and pull-over operations.[10] John Morrison, a long-serving roller at Blochairn Steel Works since 1914, recalled that 'the old mills were hard work. The sheet metal was very heavy, all tong work, and it had you running up and down like a whippet. It was easy enough when you got the knack of it, but you were gey tired at the end of a 12-hour shift.'[11]

The extensive yards of every steelworks were laid out with an abundance of railway track, and small steam-powered locomotives transported materials

Cogging mill, rolling a steel ingot, Dalzell Works, c. 1900

and products in, around and out of the premises. Nevertheless, labouring squads had still to shift all sorts of heavy materials to and from wagons into ordered heaps and containers in the yards and stores. Using heavy iron hand barrows and shovels, they unloaded and stacked constant supplies of coal, sand, pig iron, iron ore, iron and steel scrap, firebrick, clay, lime and other minerals to feed and maintain the furnaces.

Moreover, in melting shops, open-hearth furnaces were charged by hand. This was a labour-intensive operation involving the team of melters and support workers. It was not until the 1890s that machine charging of furnaces was introduced in a Scottish steelworks, namely at the Dalzell Works, Motherwell.[12] However, this innovation, so much welcomed by furnace teams, and which was already standard practice in modern steelworks outside Scotland, was by no means widely adopted until the likes of Clydebridge, Glengarnock and the Lanarkshire were transformed by furnace and melting shop reconstruction between 1915 and 1920. Where machine charging was introduced, the manual labour of chargewheelers was still required to arrange the necessary supplies of pig iron, scrap and other materials and sort them into boxes. Then it was the turn of the charge driver, in his electric-powered machine, to take over, roll up with his load of full boxes to the required position, and finally tilt and tip them in orderly fashion directly into the furnace. Peter McGeown, for instance, in his 20-year career in melting shops at the Lanarkshire Works until 1914, had to endure the repetitive and brutal drudgery of cold metal, hand charging. Even after becoming a first hand melter he had still to take his share of shovel wielding to load the large furnace.

For support teams of melting shop labourers in and around the furnaces, exhausting manual work was a constant feature. Drawing from direct experience and careful observation, Patrick McGeown has provided a graphic account of the working conditions of this section of the labour force. He starts by relating the circumstances of his own experience of becoming a labourer in the melting shop, reminding us that this harsh working environment was no place for physically undeveloped boys straight from school at 14. After an extended period at school without gaining any qualifications, and a brief stint as a barman at the steel workers' local pub (the 'Beehive'), it was as a strapping 5ft 10ins tall 16-year-old, that the young McGeown began labouring at the Lanarkshire steelworks in early 1914.

He describes his first task, as a member of a five-man team, emptying a wagon of firebricks on to the melting shop floor. Sacking was provided to wind round his hands for some protection against the abrasive brick.

Although this class of work was unskilled labour, he indicated the systematic way in which this unloading task was accomplished, and 'soon got used to it'. The first man 'lifted two bricks clamped evenly together and swung them easily into the second man's hands. He swung them diagonally to the third man, who repeated the action to the fourth man. The fifth man stacked them neatly on the floor'.

After going home for lunch at midday, he returned with great reluctance and helped the team to unload a second wagon of bricks before the shift ended. 'I had more than enough, and my fingers were so crooked with the continual action that it was painful to straighten them.'

A day later, the foreman ordered the whole melting shop gang of labourers to strip out 'the roof and linings of the B furnace that was due for a general rebuild. Some, the wreckers, worked with hammers and steel wedges and bars. Others threw out the bricks they displaced, from the furnace bath. The rest of us filled them into barrows and wheeled them away.' The typical job of refurbishing a big open-hearth furnace was an arduous and lengthy undertaking, and in this case took two weeks.

His next task was to help cut residual slag from the chamber underneath the bottom of the same furnace. As he explained:

> The function of this chamber was to trap the semi-liquid dust and debris that came with the waste gases as they left the furnace on the way to the chimney stack. It had become clogged up with the wear and tear of weeks of steelmaking. We smashed the steel wedges underneath the dark solid substance, and levered it apart with the steel bars. It was warm work, and very enclosed, and we sweated freely. Lack of space compelled us to work in relays of three men each, the one group taking over while the other group rested. Rather strange to say, I liked the job where many more dreaded it. I fancied myself with a 14-pound hammer, and took pleasure in crashing it with all my force on the steel wedge. It was very heartsome to see the slag break up with every clout I gave it. Later I found it could be heartbreaking when the wedges didn't budge despite my most determined efforts. I enjoyed the rest, too, as we sat with jackets thrown over damp shirts and drank strong sweet tea.

Three weeks later, while on the nightshift, he found that removing slag from another furnace proved a much more daunting and frustrating task:

There were six of us and as usual we worked in groups of three, and this time we had to fight for every shovelful. There was no smoothness at all in it, and the wedges became blunted with our efforts. Each night we started at six o'clock and worked steadily to first supper at nine. There was an hour break which I spent at home, and would gladly have stayed there. At ten we resumed and worked steadily through till second supper at one in the morning. This was a long affair till two thirty and really was the boundary of our intense effort. From then on, we took it easy, the deadly tiredness of night shift was upon us, and we had bought our ease by our earlier efforts.

McGeown could also have added that gutting and clearing out furnace chambers in a confined space to a depth of 20 feet below ground was dusty and noxious work, as the squads were exposed for sustained periods to the harmful effects of breathing in waste dust and gas. However, there were no health and safety regulations for such a task and no 'permit to work' restrictions which would have been required for the same type of operation in more recent times. For the bricklaying squad coming in after them to complete the skilled job of replenishing the linings and walls of the underground chambers, the debris and most of the dust had been removed, but their working conditions were still a danger to health on account of dust from silica sand.

The labouring squad was also called in to help deal with any unexpected situations or emergencies. During a cold snap in February 1914, McGeown and another man were detailed for several days to build and sustain coal fires near all the important water pipes around the whole works. This job did not cause him any problems or difficulties, unlike the hectic scene facing the squad whenever they had to contend with a breakaway of molten metal from a furnace, as an unfortunate result of heat control failure. This problem bedevilled even the most conscientious melter in his handling of volatile furnace conditions. He recalled his first experience of this hazardous occasion of firefighting:

It happened just beneath the sillplate on the middle door . . . when the metal ceased flowing we hosed it straight away until it was black. Then we hammered steel wedges under the ragged mass, which might have weighed fifteen tons. Once the wedges had lifted it a trifle we inserted steel crowbars to raise some more. Then we slung steel ropes round it

and a steam crane tugged it away in large ragged pieces. All the time
the stifling atmosphere was filled with the steam of dirty water, bad
tasting stuff it was too. We had to stand often on the metal to tug the
steel ropes tight, and that burned our feet as well as our boots. It was a
three hours job before we put sweeping brushes on it.

Although they performed necessary work in and around the furnaces,
labouring squads occupied the bottom of the job ladder in melting shops. Yet,
while accepting that their work was not skilled in the formal sense of the term,
McGeown emphasised the importance of learning the knack and know-how
of proper and efficient handling and lifting of heavy tools and materials, if
only for self protection and the safety of workmates. He put an eloquent and
strong case for the art of manual labouring from his own experience of good
practice and that of other workmen in steel plants, whether as labourers,
chargewheelers or melters: 'It is essential to know the right way to shovel,
hammer, hold a wedge or a crowbar, carry loads, and to fill wheelbarrows.
There is rhythm in these actions which protects the heart and lungs, and
brings serenity to the mind. Without that rhythm the muscles shriek. The
chest is strained, and the mind infested with frustration and anxiety.'

He was grateful to his first squad gaffer for showing him how precisely to
use a long-shafted shovel: 'He showed me how to stand and how to dig the
blade into the material, how much to lift, and how to swing it into, or from, a
wagon. The tiresome way is to hold the shaft and haft rigidly, the lightsome
way is to let the shaft pass through the loosely clenched lower hand in the act
of swinging.'

The same principle applied in swinging a heavy wrecking hammer: 'Grip
one hand firmly at the shaft end and the other lower down, and as the hammer
rises let the lower hand slide up the shaft until it grips firmly just under the
other hand to take its part in the crash down'.

He found that the correct way to load a big furnace barrow with the likes
of heavy lump manganese was to 'spread the material evenly on the forepart
and over the wheel, and not beyond one's strength'. Overloading threatened
to snap the shafts and provoke a well-earned curse of reproach from the
gaffer, but in such situations it was more important to avoid getting a strained
back which, in his experience, was 'a vicious thing' and where there were 'no
prizes for weightlifting and vanity'.

He reckoned that 'the most dangerous job and the simplest one was pig
lifting. It just had to be done the right way. Each long stick of iron weighed

from one to two hundredweights; we labourers handled only the few that fell from the chargewheeler's flat barrows. I watched the chargewheelers, the experts, before I attempted to lift one.'

His description of lifting pig iron the correct way would have been familiar to right-doing labourers in the iron industry: 'each man upended the pig with two hands, the hands being protected by leathers, then steadied it on the floor vertically, and gently lowered the top end on the right thigh until the other end swung in balance. From that position, they carried the pig away, rather in the fashion of one approaching with a battering ram.'[13]

The position of chargewheeler was regarded as one step up the ladder from that of a member of the labouring squad. The range and type of experience and practical knowledge gained in this job as a furnace support worker was also essential preparation for entry to the lower melter grades. As a labourer, McGeown worked alongside chargewheelers, and observed how they assisted with hand charging operations at the Lanarkshire steelworks. A few months later, his first post in a steelworks in the Manchester area was as a chargewheeler, but in a larger and more modern works where the open-hearth furnaces were charged by machine, and his workload did not include barrowing heavy materials to furnace platforms. Whether hand-charged or machine-charged, furnaces had to be supplied with various additional materials throughout a shift, such as manganese for the final, tapping stage of the melting process, and crushed limestone (dolomite) for repairing the furnace bottom after each charge. Chargewheelers carried out those supply tasks, and at times actively assisted with filling operations at the furnace. They were answerable to the melting shop manager, but worked closely under the direction of the leading melter.

In the steelmaking process itself, the leading furnaceman within the team of production workers was the first hand melter. He was assisted by at least second and third hand melters and, in the case of large-capacity furnaces, fourth and fifth hands. The first hand was in charge of all furnace operations and, although responsibility for specific tasks was delegated to second and third hands, he supervised the whole processes of charging, melting, tapping and repairs. His craft and competence were the product of years of accumulated practical experience of observing and wrestling with hot metals and their chemical reactions. In McGeown's words, 'on basic open-hearth furnaces, the melter's craft is not in his hands but in his eyes. Through years of gazing in the white heat of furnaces he acquires a sort of secondary sight, as if his eyes have special compartments for judging furnace temperatures.

Previous to the increased instrumentation on melting shops, the melter's eyes were almost his whole guide to controlling heat.'[14]

Moreover, if the No.1 melter was a skilled craftsman who probably had no theoretical knowledge of what steel actually was, he had gained long practical expertise and wisdom in heat control, and had learned to understand the behaviour of furnaces and their contents. With that necessary knowledge base, he was usually able to make confident, timely and correct decisions, anticipate and rectify problems and, with the efforts of his colleagues, produce a satisfactory standard of molten steel. It was the responsibility of the melting shop manager to order up the composition of furnace charge and to inform the first hand melter what category of steel he and his team were expected to produce as, for example, a low-carbon mild steel. The first hand knew what to do as he had most likely carried out this familiar remit many times in his long experience.

McGeown's recollections and comments help to provide a composite and graphic picture of the melting shop scene throughout the steelmaking process in the years before modern furnace improvements and instrumental testing came into being, with its precise monitoring and measurement of temperatures and properties of molten metal. Until the coming of such breakthrough in measurement technique and laboratory analysis to test the accuracy of the steelmaking processes, the success and quality of the end product depended largely on the applied practical skills, technical competence, instincts and intuition of experienced first hand melters.

Before the furnace was heated for production, the bottom, roof and linings were inspected briefly as being fit for purpose. The gas-flamed injection which provided the fuel was fired up in readiness for the waiting charge, which was at the same time being loaded systematically on to the furnace platforms. In their working gear, the melting team wore heavy boots and were equipped for torrid conditions: 'Their flannel shirts absorbed the sweat, while retaining their heat, and the sweat towels were a god-send. Their heavy sailcloth aprons protected their legs from the heat, and that was their job, anyway, experts in heat . . . inside a melting shop they were the nearest thing to firebricks.'[15] The first hand melter was also equipped with protective blue-glass spectacles for gazing into and judging the roasting surge of furnace contents.

The first hand melter directed the hand charging operation which, at the Lanarkshire, could take up to three hours for a furnace with production capacity of thirty five and forty tons. This size of furnace needed over forty

Overleaf. Melting shop scene: preparing to hand charge the furnaces. Note pig iron and scrap piled ready. (North Lanarkshire Council)

tons of charge, and was a huge physical task for a melting team of four men to accomplish in such a time. This explains why the chargewheeler's assistance was welcome, but the whole busy undertaking required the additional services of a flying squad of mobile labourers. 'Slasher-in' was the name of this category of labourer, and their 'strength-sapping job was moving from furnace to furnace, where charging up was taking place.' Their contribution was to help shovel in limestone and scrap and, using a long paddle, throw in solid pig iron.[16] In this fashion, assistant labourers and melters knew how to line the furnace bath with pig iron: 'each man slid a stick of iron from a neat stack and walked leisurely forward. In turn they placed each stick on a long flat-ended iron rod known as a peel. Immediately the man holding the peel moved it swiftly inside the furnace, and neatly turned the iron on top of the previous one.'[17]

The next charging job was to shovel lime and iron ore into the bath.

> The operation was lengthy and exhausting, and resting between whiles was necessary. This caused no delay, for the flame would be still doing its work in melting down the materials. The last part would see the heaviest steel scrap being manoeuvred in by the peel. It would take four to five hours before the charge melted into liquid and was ready for the refining stage.

The melter kept a watchful eye on the furnace contents, especially during the melting and final stages. He saw and knew that when the mixed charge was boiling freely from end to end, the phosphorus, carbon and other impurities were being transferred from the metal to the slag. Getting the boil right, and avoiding the dangers of overheating, was 'the important thing on steel furnaces'.[18] At intervals, he also tested the appearance of the molten metal by taking samples. This was done by dipping 'a long spoon through the furnace door, and passing it swiftly through the bubbling slag to the metal beneath'. The sample was then cooled by being thrust into water, hammered down and fractured. By looking at the grain and colour of the broken metal samples, and by applying the knowledge acquired over the years, he was able to make a very accurate assessment of the emerging results. He then considered whether any further adjustments were needed to the molten metal as, for example, to add lime or ore, before deciding when it was ready for tapping. Having made this decision, he consulted his immediate foreman, the sample passer who, as quality controller, inspected the latest samples, and delivered his verdict. Only

Tapping molten steel
into ladle, Dalzell
Works, c. 1900 (North
Lanarkshire Council)

when satisfied with the quality of the metal did he exercise his authority to make the final decision and order the tapping operation.

Almost invariably, by the end of the nineteenth century, the sample passer was a former first hand melter of long experience and proven capability. In later years, the samples and his assessment would have gone to a trained metallurgist in the works laboratory for testing and confirmation. However, until then, assessment remained the responsibility of the first hand melter and his sample passer supervisor. Examples of leading melters with such vast experience, responsibility and authority included Duncan McNeill, John Wilson and Robert Dunlop. McNeill, a Highlander, settled in Motherwell in the 1870s. He worked at the Globe Malleable Iron Works and transferred to the melting shop at Dalzell Works when steelmaking began there in 1880. In over 40 years of service at the Dalzell, he progressed through all the grades as melter, and in his time was one of the most experienced melters in the country, with practical knowledge of steelmaking ranging from the original ten-ton furnaces to the latest 100-ton furnaces in the modernised No.3 melting shop.[19] John Wilson had a versatile experience of working life in both iron and steel. He had started out as a boy at the rolls in Mossend Malleable Iron Works before becoming a puddler in 1890. He transferred to Clydebridge steelworks, firstly as a stoker at the gas furnaces, and then as a junior melter. He progressed to first hand and in 1900 was promoted to sample passer in the No.1 melting shop, a position he still retained in 1920.[20] However, the most prestigious of our three profiles is that of Robert Dunlop, who started working life in Motherwell Malleable Iron Works, before finding employment and preferment in the new steel industry at Dalzell in 1885. There, he learned melting shop practice under Jim Dawkins, leading melter. He reached the grade of first hand melter and in 1898 was promoted to sample passer and foreman in the new No.3 melting shop with responsibility for 60-ton furnaces. In 1922, with 37 years' service at Dalzell and in charge of the largest furnaces in the country, he was at the top of his craft as a much respected senior sample passer.[21]

As first hand melters, all those men, and Peter McGeown among them, had long, direct experience of the art that was steelmaking in the first half-century of the industry in Scotland. Despite the exhausting hardship of furnace work, for the leading melters as craftsmen, there was, in Patrick McGeown's words, an attractive side to steelmaking in those days:

> To the first hand melter, there was great satisfaction as he watched the metal stream from his furnace into the waiting ladle. He had an awareness of creation; hours previously this surging white-hot liquid had been tons of solid limestone, steel scrap, and hot iron. He had controlled the huge flame which played over the metal, saw that it did its work, and that it didn't damage the furnace's brick roof or linings. Hour after hour he had tended it, watched for every change in the liquid, increased the slag contents with more lime, or thinned it out with iron ore. His junior melters were every bit as interested as he was. It was their money too that was filling the ladle, and their sweat too that put it there.[22]

Of course, there were times when the process did not work out smoothly, and remedial action was required to salvage their wages and reputation. For instance, at the tapping stage, sometimes 'the liquid didn't gallop out of the furnace generously, but trickled out in a miserable taplike stream. That wouldn't suit anyone, and least of all the foreman who was responsible for tapping the charge successfully. The melters would rush hurriedly to the front of the furnace, and clear the obstruction away with long iron rods. The liquid, if it was in good condition, would spurt away again, the melters would wipe their streaming brows, and the foreman would assume his former attitude of omnipotence.'[23]

Even greater mishaps could occur to frustrate the whole melting team and the foreman. The potentially disastrous instance of a breakaway of molten metal tearing in a fiery stream through the furnace bath and around their feet, has already been described. However, the collapse of a furnace bottom during any of the stages of the melting process could be just as threatening, and also required the urgent attention of melters and labourers. It was an essential task of melting teams to carry out any repairs to the furnace bottom after each tapping operation, to make it ready for the next heat and the oncoming shift. As McGeown explained, furnace baths were composed of crushed dolomite which, 'when shovelled into the holes and crevices left by the charge, became part of the bath proper. But it was only successful when applied in a very high furnace temperature . . . a very warm and uncomfortable affair' for the melters. 'It was a split-second action; one went to the open furnace door with loaded shovelful, took lightning aim, swung, and retreated. Even a second's delay could cause active burning to the body.'[24] Normally, this heavy, unpleasant and routine task of fettling the furnace was carried out within a short while but, depending on the condition of the furnace, it sometimes took hours to accomplish and prolonged the shift. Despite care and commitment, the bottoming repair operation could turn out for the worse. Again, McGeown supplies the essential detail of such an incident, while relating the story of his father's unfortunate experience:

My father was suspended for one week, and he was very unhappy about it. The bath of his furnace, wherein the liquid metal lay, had given way and the metal had poured out on the floor. It had been a scene of chaos as the sparkling metal tore its devouring way, and the sweating melters had shovelled banks of dolomite to divert it. It was cleared away afterwards when it solidified and cooled, and would go back into the furnace to be re-melted. Since my father had been responsible for the repair of the furnace bath, he alone was suspended. It was considered that he had failed in his duty to make the bath solid enough to bear the metal charged into it. So far as he was aware he had performed his duty with the same efficiency as any other time. When the furnace had discharged its metal he and the other melters had shovelled in the dolomite used for such occasions. They had filled in every worn part and had taken time to do the job properly. He could swear to that, but the element of chance, good or bad, was always in steelmaking at that time. He had been unlucky and there was nothing he could do about it. He didn't feel guilty of slipshod work, and the management didn't say that was so.

Fettling at the Lanarkshire Steel Works (North Lanarkshire Council)

However, apart from the loss of a week's pay, there was another important consequence of a suspension of this nature, as it ruined the confidence of the first hand melter; 'and without that his judgement of heat and the condition

of his charge was impaired. Suspension turned a melter into a bundle of nerves and hesitations; it made his working hours a misery and would remain that way for a long time afterwards'.[25]

At the conclusion of the tapping stage melters remained on duty in the burning heat. At the last minute, they shovelled manganese into the molten metal, while others wielded heavy hammers to smash a long iron rod into the taphole to release its flowing contents into a chute and down into a large heated ladle. They also ensured that the slag was poured out separately into containers.

Thereafter, responsibility passed to the forehand teemer who, with his crew of pitmen, took charge of the ladle and its contents for pouring and casting operations. The teemer also supervised the action of the crane operator, who manoeuvred the ladle into ready position over the waiting ingot moulds in the casting pit. The special responsibility of the leading hand, the teemer, deserves attention. The intricate process of transferring the molten charge from ladle to moulds had to be conducted with the utmost skill, care and accuracy, in order to ensure proper and timely flow, and avoid dangerous and wasteful spillage. It was essential to keep the pit side and the cast-iron ingot moulds dry and free of extraneous dirt before casting, and to avoid damage to ingots while they were mechanically removed to the soaking pits or the mill. Unfortunately, whereas we know something of the working lives of melters and furnace labourers, little is on record for the individual experiences of teemers and pitmen for this period of enquiry. However, McGeown reminds us of the dangers encountered by pit-side workers, particularly from casting cranes loaded with molten metal. They were potential 'death traps' and 'a sight to terrify the bravest teemer or pitman' as he 'watched a ladleful of wild metal bearing down on him, with its gases lashing over the side'.[26]

THE HUMAN PRICE OF STEEL

Stresses, strains, injuries, occasional fatal accidents and constant danger, were obvious features of steelmaking in this period. However, only impressions of the record of industrial accident and injury and of inadequate health and safety provision in Scotland's steelworks are available to us. In evidence to the Royal Commission on Labour (1892), John Hodge, leader of the steel melters' union in Scotland, stated that, while fatal accidents were few and unusual, there were many 'small accidents' – men losing a toe or a finger, or getting burnt. He confirmed that steelworks were dangerous places, and was especially concerned about the lack of handrails and guards to protect workmen from falling into pits and containers, and being hit by moving vehicles such as cranes and wagons. He condemned factory inspectors for their gross inefficiency, claiming that, 'in some of the works, if they do visit them, they have always got their eyes shut'. Moreover, he voiced concern about the scandalous absence in Scotland of official investigations into the causes of fatal accidents. He cited the example of a man who fell from a platform into a ladle of molten metal, yet there was no coroner's inquest, as would have been the case in England.[27] John Cronin, leader of the steel millmen, gave evidence of frequent casualties, 'maiming, such as losing legs, fingers or toes', and the occasional fatality.[28]

The incidence and pattern of accident and injury, as evidenced by the union leaders in 1892, is confirmed from random sampling of local press reports of accidents at Dalzell and Lanarkshire Steel Works for several years between the 1880s and 1913. However, the newspaper record for 1899, in the case of the Lanarkshire, and for Dalzell in 1913, appears to report an unusually higher incidence of accidents and fatalities than in other years.[29] While no definite comparative analysis is possible, there is nevertheless an indication of a likely reason for this increase, in that major extensions to furnaces and plant were taking place in those particular years. To elaborate on this point, of the five reported fatalities in 1899 at the Lanarkshire, four involved contracted workmen who either fell or were struck by falling parts while engaged in extension work between September and December. In 1913, a similar pattern appeared to prevail, prompting editorial comment that 'the ambulance wagon is a common sight in the streets of late'.[30] The report went on to blame the unusual series of accidents on pressure to complete extensions, and on temporary and outside workers who were allegedly unprepared for the unfamiliar internal structures and surroundings of large steelworks. Allowing for human error, nothing was said about the possibility of other causes, such as the lack of guards; of inadequate or non-existent scaffolding; the failure of ropes and chains in lifting and suspension gear and liability on the part of employers and contractors for poor provision of safety cover.

The works doctor attended an injured worker at the scene, applied treatment where possible, then arranged to send the worker home or, if required, ordered the ambulance wagon to take the patient to hospital. For seriously injured workers at Glengarnock who needed urgent treatment and surgery, the journey to hospital in Glasgow must have been a long, tortuous

business. There is no doubt that many cases there and elsewhere that deserved
hospital attention did not get the opportunity. For one Glengarnock melter,
who was burned about the body while working at the Bessemer steel furnaces
before they were dismantled in 1920, the treatment and aftercare were
primitive. Joe Smith explained:

> Ma faither wis brought home. He was burnt – claes were burnt aff
> him. See, when you're drawing in those bogeys from the vessel, slag
> keeps bubbling and this yin must have been right full up . . . the wye it
> bubbles oot and it caught alight. Ah think they took him hame in a
> horse-drawn cab, aye. An he come in – oh, he wis an awfae state. And

Tapping molten steel,
Dalzell Works, c. 1900.
Note works
locomotive waiting to
take full ladle to
casting pit (North
Lanarkshire Council)

would you believe the treatment he got efter that, leeches pit on his back, leeches! This wis a doctor's idea, for bad burns. He was quite a bit aff before he was right again for workin'.[31]

In the case of hospitalised casualties from steelworks within Lanarkshire and Glasgow, destinations were the Royal Infirmary, the Victoria and the Western,

Steam crane hoisting ladle into position at casting pit, Clydesdale Steel Works (North Lanarkshire Council)

while the Eye Infirmary catered for injuries of that nature. Before 1914, horse-drawn ambulance wagons from Motherwell were replaced by motor-driven vehicles. Each steel workforce made annual charitable donations and contributed special levies to support the various Glasgow hospitals. In common with major ironworks, steel workers also paid a separate weekly fee (3d in 1914) for the services of a works doctor.

Patrick McGeown does not recall any serious injuries suffered by his father in twenty years as a furnaceman at the Lanarkshire Works although, for the older man and others like him, long hours and harsh working conditions always threatened to debilitate health and wellbeing. In 1914, the 45-year-old melter was 'fit and well, but he found the going still hard. His shirts were just as wet with sweat as ever they were. All her married life my mother had noted anxiously the state in which he arrived home. She knew the danger signals too well, the eyes far back in his head, the voice hoarse, almost inaudible, from his strength-sapped lungs. My mother looked after him well and got him the best fillet steak from the good Scots butchers. They called it "melter's steak" in Craigneuk, for only the better paid steel furnacemen could afford it.'[32]

This chapter ends where it began, with McGeown and other melters waiting in late afternoon to start a 14-hour shift. In Scotland there was a long-standing discretionary custom among melters to rearrange their exhausting six-day schedule of 12-hour shifts on alternate weeks, preferring to work a longer shift in the cooler conditions of evening and night time, and reverting to a ten-hour stretch in daytime. However, on the eve of the First World War, McGeown was determined to pursue a better prospect than continue to endure the hours and conditions of the Lanarkshire Steel Works or of any other steel plant in Scotland. A new start beckoned for him and his two sons, as they left for Lancashire to earn a living at a modern steelworks where machines charged the furnaces and melters worked eight-hour shifts.

CHAPTER 6
TRIALS OF STRENGTH:
CONFLICT AND CONCILIATION IN THE
STEEL INDUSTRY IN SCOTLAND 1880s–1920s

We believe in the peaceful settlement of differences, we believed in it fifty years ago when in the climate of trade union opinion at that time it was almost heresy to do so. We never believed there was anything attractive about a strike, it being at best an ugly and painful necessity. As the records show, however, when the behaviour of an employer left no alternative but the strike, it was never shirked, but we never sought a fight under those conditions.

Lincoln Evans, former general secretary,
Iron and Steel Trades' Confederation,
in preface to *Men of Steel*, 1951

A CLIMATE OF CONFLICT

Contractors and leading hands in melting shops and rolling mills started out as big money men in the early days of the new industry. However, in the cut-throat market conditions of the depressed 1880s, they encountered a series of attacks on earnings and conditions, as steel masters competed with each other to reduce labour costs, and individual contractors and workmen quarrelled about tonnage rates and other due payments. As John Hodge stated, 'During these early days there was no Union. Consequently, there was no sustained unity of purpose amongst the workmen in combating these continual reductions. I cannot recall a single strike which took place in those early days where the men fought successfully against a reduction in rates of pay, and if they fought, defeat was invariably their portion.'[1] By the end of the decade, having learned from bitter experience that bouts of spontaneous strike action were no effective answer to employer aggression and contractor greed, significant

numbers of melters and millmen turned to trade union organisation to defend
and support their livelihoods as key workers.

Disputes in the 1880s centred on wage rates and manning levels. At the
Steel Company of Scotland's two works in 1881, furnacemen and millmen
were on strike against wage reductions, for six weeks at Hallside and for three
weeks at Blochairn. Acute depression in Clyde shipbuilding during 1884 hit
demand for steel plate, provoking cutbacks in wages and a five-week dispute
throughout the supply industry. At Motherwell, David Colville, junior, sacked
the striking head rollers and hammermen and promoted second hands to their
positions, while the melters conceded only after he had promised a
compromise deal on wage rates.[2] In autumn 1885, further wages cuts up to 20
per cent were imposed at Blochairn and Hallside and third hand melters were
removed from each furnace. A protest strike resulted, and when Dalzell
Works followed this lead on wage cuts and de-manning, melters and
hammermen at Motherwell also came out after serving necessary notice. They
were incensed at the deceitful, high-handed conduct of David Colville, as he
had twice broken verbal agreements to withdraw wage reductions and phase
in reinstatement of third hands. On the second occasion he had added insult
to injury, punishing the melters with an arbitrary pay cut to defray the extra
cost of coal consumed in relighting the furnaces.[3]

While there was, as yet, no trade union challenge to their authority, when
it suited them, steel masters like David Colville and James Riley approached
workers on an informal basis to gauge opinion about practices and conditions.
At this time, in the 1880s, steelworks were still relatively small. Dalzell had
eight open-hearth furnaces and employed fewer than fifty melters. Masters
knew most, if not all, of those furnacemen and often as not had employed
them for their proven qualities as steady, reliable, skilled men. Indeed, David
Colville knew John Hodge and his family very well. He had persuaded Hodge
to leave his third hand melter post at Blochairn to come to work at Dalzell.
William Hodge, John's younger brother, already worked there as a third hand
melter. Their father, William Hodge, an iron worker and trade union activist,
had worked at Dalzell in the 1870s, and was latterly a foreman there.

In his memoir, John Hodge recalled workplace relations with David
Colville, starting with the disputes in 1885–6, and the sense of grievance
which led to the formation of the steel melters' union. He recounted that the
firm of David Colville and Sons then had a great public reputation as good
employers, but recent unjust treatment of the men did not square with that
reputation. 'Mr David Colville, senior, founder of the firm, was a gentleman

David Colville (senior), founder of Dalzell Iron and Steel Works

of very high character, but at this time he did not appear to take any very active part in the business. John Colville was the leading partner and the eldest brother of three; he was a very excellent gentleman.' This father and son, as explained in earlier chapters, were paternalist iron and steel masters, and John was a conciliator. However, David Colville, junior, 'a big, bluff, blunt, outspoken individual' was an entirely different character.[4] This ambitious, ruthless, aggressive steel master was actual boss in the workplace. He was also rare among Scottish steel masters in that he had solid personal knowledge of melting shop practice, which was to his advantage when recruiting and dealing with furnacemen and overseeing steelmaking operations. With foresight, prior to the iron firm's entry into the steel industry, his father had sent him to Hallside to learn the steelmaking trade. After schooling at Hamilton and Glasgow Academy, the 17-year-old son trained under James Riley as a third hand melter. An able learner and worker, he was fast-tracked to first hand within two years, finally working in the laboratory to pick up practical knowledge of metallurgy before returning to Motherwell in 1879 to begin his career as steel master.[5]

John Hodge led deputations of Dalzell workers in various deliberations with David Colville in late 1885 and early 1886. Hodge was an articulate and well-informed spokesman, putting the case for retention of third hands at the furnaces, and quoting the Glasgow financial press on movements of the market price of steel to argue for improved wage rates. He demanded and got agreements in writing, threatening to expose the devious master publicly in the newspapers if he continued to renege on his word. Hodge's version of this series of encounters during the dispute in late November 1885 gives an impression of the fraught state of industrial relations which led the workmen along the road to trade union representation:

After rather a stormy interview, Mr David Colville calmed down and made some alterations with respect to displacement of the third hands. We said we would go back and report. We afterwards met him again and entered into an arrangement for re-starting the furnaces to begin the following week on a reduction of 10 per cent, but a modification of his other claims [i.e., on furnace manning]. At the beginning of the next week the men found they were to re-start on terms different from those which had been arranged, so did not start, and the furnaces were again let out. Some days afterwards, we met Mr Colville again, and entered into another agreement, which slightly varied that previously arranged. I said: 'Now, Mr Colville, we want this in writing'. He said: 'Why?'. 'We entered into an agreement previously and you broke it. We want this agreement in writing.' He retorted: 'Will that make me keep it?'. 'No,' was my retort; 'the man who breaks his word will not keep his bond.' He roared with laughter, declared that he admired my cheek, and finished up in saying, 'You dictate.' A shorthand writer was brought in, and the agreement dictated, which was signed by Mr Colville and myself; and then he said, 'What value is that agreement to you?' I said, 'Well, it is like this, Mr David. If you break this agreement, we can hand it to the newspapers to print and let the public know what kind of man you are, but we cannot print a verbal agreement.'[6]

John Hodge, trade union leader, steel workers

However, Colville had a vindictive streak when crossed to this extent. The third hand melter, Hodge, being too 'damned clever' and in the front line of the workers' action, was sacked and blacklisted from any further work with the firm. Hodge also recorded David Colville's petty, mean-spirited sacking of his brother two weeks after resumption of work; the master telling William to warn 'his big brother to write or speak no more damned lies about him'.[7] In early 1886, John Hodge managed to find another melter post at Parkhead, but meantime he had become unpaid elected secretary of a new trade union, soon to be known as the British Steel Smelters' Association, which had been born out of the recent dispute at Motherwell, Hallside and Glasgow.

At this time, around 500 furnacemen worked in steel plants in Scotland. In January, 1886, after informal contact and a newspaper advert, the first call to form a union attracted 66 melters to a Glasgow meeting. On 6 February, the new union was formally constituted and membership contributions submitted. Hodge recalled how, by mid 1886, 'we had succeeded beyond our expectations' in the recruitment drive within Scotland. Substantial numbers of melters in each of the Glasgow and north Lanarkshire open-hearth furnace plants were enrolled, with the important exception of Mossend, where workplace relations were particularly oppressive. During the Glasgow Fair

Holiday week in July, Hodge and Donald Galbraith, union president, made their first foray into England to recruit and organise members, and met with a ready response, forming workplace branches at Elswick, Consett, Spennymoor, Stockton and South Bank.[8]

THE MOTHERWELL DISPUTE: 1886

The new union and its members faced a difficult baptism in a two-month-long struggle to resist wage reductions at Dalzell in autumn 1886. During the course of this industrial conflict Motherwell became the scene of major disturbances, as strike action by melters and hammermen was countered by an employer lockout and imported blackleg labour, provoking violent riots and emergency police control of the town. As this whole episode and its consequences are of vital importance for the theme of this chapter, they justify a detailed account.

One day in August, David Colville imposed a 10 per cent wage cut, effective from midnight. Adopting a hard-line stance, the employer was provoking and deliberately testing out the resolve of the melters and the strength of the new union. He had already torn up existing contracts and placed his production workers on a day's notice. The men stood firm, and informed a furious Colville that unless he withdrew this latest wage cut, at midnight they would turn off the gas and leave the charges in the furnaces. He refused to reconsider, steel production was stopped and for the first time a strike began with official trade union support.

David Colville's strike-breaking strategy was twofold. Firstly, he was determined to secure the commitment of the top millmen – rollers and shearers – to continue working during the dispute by giving them loyalty contracts and freedom to employ their own labour. Secondly, to restart steel production he decided to lock out the striking melters and replace them with blackleg labour. The first objective was easily accomplished, but attempts to recruit outside labour to resume furnace production proved a frustrating business, taking over a month to achieve. Meantime, melters who occupied the firm's few company houses were notified to leave the properties, as they had broken their contracts of work. They handed in their keys, and left peacefully, avoiding forcible eviction at the hands of sheriff-officers.[9]

The strike-breaking strategy of this major employer inflamed tensions in the town. It encountered determined but orderly union resistance among steel

No. 1 plate shears,
Dalzell Works, c. 1900
(North Lanarkshire
Council)

workers and widespread hostility from other workers, notably local miners, who were also in dispute over wages and conditions. Throughout September, Dalzell Works and local railway stations were picketed day and night to detect any strike breakers. In the second week of the dispute, it was known that David Colville had gone to South Wales to recruit furnacemen. According to Hodge, at Motherwell station Colville had gibed at pickets and disclosed his intentions to import fresh labour, declaring that 'he would go to H——, but he would get men to fill their places'. One of the pickets, an Irishman and melter, John Overend, gave the witty reply: 'For God's sake, sir, don't take a return ticket.' [10] It seems Colville was not readily successful in his mission, as the first and only contingent of around twenty strike breakers did not arrive until the start of October. The company had organised makeshift living accommodation for strike breakers inside the works and, although the union had objected to the local authority about this arrangement on the grounds of insanitary conditions, their protest was overruled.

On the evening of Monday, 4 October, the strike breakers arrived by train from Glasgow. Their movements were already detected, and a crowd had gathered outside Motherwell railway station before discovering the intention to smuggle the carriage directly into the steelworks. At the rail junction leading into the works, according to various reports, a crowd of hundreds of men, women and boys charged and stoned the moving carriage, breaking all the windows and injuring some of the occupants. The carriage had to be reversed onto the main line and the strike breakers taken back to Glasgow while police reinforcements were summoned to restore order. Later on that evening, another carriage was attacked in the mistaken belief that it also contained blackleg labour. On this occasion, the mob had stoned the police, who retaliated with a baton charge.

In the confusion of events, there are conflicting reports of what happened in the violent fracas of that evening. In 1892, giving evidence on conditions of labour to a parliamentary enquiry, John Hodge maintained that one of the Colville partners had stood 'on the footboard of the carriage and brandished a revolver, and was going to shoot all hands'.[11] Writing in his autobiography over forty years later, Hodge does not repeat this most serious accusation, but instead refers to Archibald Colville as being 'very foolishly in the crowd watching operations. How he came into conflict I never quite rightly made out, but he got a blow from someone which split his lip and knocked two or three teeth out'.[12]

Next day, the town was swarming with mounted police guarding the railway station and entrances to the steelworks. Crowds were not permitted to form, and police escorted a special train from Glasgow carrying strike breakers into the works. Steel production was resumed, but not at anything like full capacity and, although a strong police presence was maintained in the town throughout the duration of the strike and lockout, union members carried out peaceful picketing in accordance with the law . Hodge and other union activists managed to talk to the Welsh melters within days of their arrival, and explained the circumstances of the dispute, exposing the apparent dishonesty of the steel master who had told them they were coming north to start production at a new works. Half of the strike breakers were persuaded to leave Motherwell, their return fares and other expenses paid by the new union.[13]

Seven weeks into the dispute, it was already clear that the company was facing defeat in this contest with organised workmen. A small squad of blackleg labour was inefficient and unreliable, and a poor substitute for experienced, skilled melters Moreover, it was successful picketing that depleted this makeshift workforce and effectively brought steel production to a halt, prompting David Colville into a complete lockout at the Dalzell Works. This was a desperate measure which did not have its intended effect of bringing the workforce to its knees in surrender and, within days, he had to concede defeat. On 20 October, Colville offered to settle on the same wages and conditions as at Hallside and Blochairn, where tonnage rates were higher and contracts were on 14 days' notice. Certainly, steel prices had begun to recover by then, but an immediate outcome of the dispute was a breakthrough for the new union. Melters and hammermen had refused to be intimidated by a leading employer, and had survived the struggle, not least with the aid of weekly strike and lockout benefits of 15 shillings for married men and 10 shillings for single men. However, Hodge had to admit later that 'it had been a fight to the finish at Motherwell' and the men could not have held out much longer than two months as union funds were almost exhausted.[14]

As well as using up meagre union funds to sustain members and families during the dispute, the union provided bail and other legal costs to fight a court case. No arrests were made on or immediately following the disturbances of 4 October, but on 19 October six men, including three melters, two other steel workers and a miner, were arrested in connection with those events. They were charged with mobbing and rioting, and stood trial at Hamilton in January. Hodge recalled the scene of the trial:

> There could be little doubt of the fact that the police apprehended the wrong men. In two of the cases, a very strong alibi was put forward. Strikers' wives were among the witnesses. Well do I remember how neatly every woman was dressed, and the Judge who heard the case was greatly impressed by the clearness of their testimony, which the cross-examining counsel was unable to shake.[15]

In cases which, in Hodge's opinion, should never have come to court, the jury found no obvious evidence for mobbing and rioting convictions, and declared five of the accused not guilty of the single reduced charge of common assault. The union member who allegedly assaulted Archie Colville was given the option of a one month prison sentence or a £5 fine, which was paid immediately.[16]

The repercussions of the Motherwell dispute had lasting consequences for the conduct and shape of industrial relations in the steel industry in Scotland. In one important respect, the conflict was a humiliating climbdown for the principal steel master David Colville. He had failed to destroy the infant melters' union and the experience led him to reconsider his approach to labour relations, eventually adopting a less abrasive stance. The struggle was a positive experience for the melters' union, as it had passed its first real test and demonstrated to steel workers and masters its commitment and credibility. Millmen had rejected early overtures from the newly-formed melters' union to join them in membership. They were not yet convinced about organising themselves and began to do so only after the inspiring example of the Motherwell melters and subsequent consolidation of trade union influence in winning wage increases at Dalzell, Hallside and Blochairn, had provided the impetus. During 1887, James Riley, that most astute manager of men and resources at Hallside and Blochairn, was the first steel master to recognise the melters' trade union as a representative negotiating body, and David Colville came to accept this view in 1888. Riley, in particular, quickly assessed the practical value of the moderate, responsible behaviour and character of the new trade union and its leadership, and the potential for a relationship in which both sides desired a combination of industrial stability and peace, productive efficiency, and its due rewards in enhanced profits and earnings. When the Scottish Millmen's Union was formed in early 1888, Colville and Riley also recognised its status, though only after some initial mutual distrust and hostility. Nevertheless, as will be seen, at the close of the 1880s, a few steel masters remained fiercely opposed to any challenge to their absolute authority.

At this stage, the steel melters and millmen were reluctant militants who preferred direct negotiation with individual employers to win redress of grievances, while reserving the threat of strike action to enforce concessions. For instance, at those works where the melters' union branches were sufficiently strong, reinstatement of third hand melters to furnaces, and abolition of the abuse known as the 'gaffer's furnace', were achieved by reasoned argument backed up by union pressure. The issue of third hand melters was tackled during 1888, Riley being the first to concede that manual loading, smooth operation of melting processes and repair work at any of the ten- or twelve-ton furnaces required regular servicing by more than two furnacemen. The 'gaffer's furnace' had originated with the contracting system, but it remained a major grievance in those steelworks where furnace contracting was no longer practised. It allowed the foreman samplepasser in the melting shop to appropriate the first hand's share of tonnage rates from the highest producing furnace. This meant that the foreman was paid by the

melters instead of by the firm, and the earnings of the men on this furnace
were relegated one grade down to accommodate payment to the foreman. On
such occasions, all hands incurred a serious reduction in wages, although they
were still doing the same work and hours as colleagues on neighbouring
furnaces. Eventually, in May 1889, the melters had to force the issue at
Motherwell and at Beardmore's, Parkhead. At both works, they effectively
threatened strike action to remove this notorious practice. The union's case
was also conceded at Hallside and Blochairn, resulting in improved earnings
and morale among furnace teams.[17] However, this abuse persisted for several
years at other works, where foreman contractors continued to run and control
melting shops and furnacemen were not yet sufficiently organised to counter
such adverse conditions.

Efforts to abolish the 'gaffer's furnace' were a prelude to a more concerted
assault on the whole system of contracting within steelworks. It was an
iniquitous system of wage payment, whereby furnace, forge and rolling mill

Melting shop, Dalzell
Works, preparing to
charge (North
Lanarkshire Council)

underhands were paid time rates while all the benefits of increased output and tonnage rates were appropriated by individual contractors. Some rolling mill contractors did little work for huge earnings and were occasionally away from the workplace for several days. The respective trade unions of melters and millmen were determined to end contractor power and exploitation, and to hold the firm responsible for direct employment and payment of all skilled workers and underhands. Wherever a workplace branch of the melters' union secured recognition, an end to contracting at open-hearth furnaces was soon negotiated. Accordingly, the contractor rate of earnings was redistributed in agreed proportions throughout the furnacemen grades, who were all put on piecework instead of a low day wage, while the former contractor was obliged to revert to first hand melter on an equal basis with other leading hands. Similar agreements were pursued and achieved in several steel mills. In the course of early struggles on this issue, when assisting organisation among hammermen and rollers, Hodge discovered that discerning owners and managers like Riley could be persuaded of the good business sense of ending the contract system in this department. Companies gained in various ways from making this change: in rising output, as process workers now had the incentive to earn a bonus linked to productivity on top of a basic minimum wage; in better management and direct supervision of work; in efficiency savings and, not least, in reducing a source of constant trouble and resentment in the workplace.[18]

However, at two steelworks, employer resistance to union recognition and to any meaningful concessions on wages and conditions provoked lengthy disputes during 1888 and 1889. In the first dispute, the newly formed Scottish Millmen's Union took action against wage cuts at Clydesdale Works. An official strike lasting for nearly four months was supported by member funds and voluntary donations, but it ended in defeat. Although the melters joined the strike, managers outmanoeuvred the men with the promise of concessions on rates, and then withdrew them after they realised that the strike was far from solid.[19] While managerial opposition to change was its principal barrier, according to Hodge, on this occasion, the efforts of both unions were also frustrated by the distracting, reactionary influence of Orange and Catholic divisions among workers.[20]

During autumn 1889, both labour organisations faced a similar stern test and an even greater setback at Clydebridge Steel Works, where the principal partners, Hugh and Walter Neilson, were staunch opponents of trade unions. After making little headway since the works had started production in 1888,

John Cronin and other activists from the millmen's union finally succeeded in establishing a small branch of around thirty members. Many were soon victimised and sacked for their trade union activities. The record is not entirely clear, but the union decided to take a stand, risking support for a strike among its small core of members, while hoping to encourage other workmen to come out in solidarity. However, the resulting response was limited and uneven, as fewer than 100 men joined in the dispute. The melters' union executive also backed the strike, but it failed to influence Clydebridge furnacemen, who were not union members, and they continued to work. The company replaced sacked and striking millmen with blackleg labour, and loyal contractors instructed the recruits. The dispute dragged on for nineteen weeks, by which time many men had gone back to work. Although the union had managed to find employment for some of the others in English mills, it had to concede defeat. It was an ugly dispute, with frequent tussles among strikers and blacklegs, and several arrests for alleged illegal picketing. All who were found guilty were allowed the option of fine instead of imprisonment, with the sole exception of the millmen's general secretary, John Cronin, who was sentenced to 60 days. Despite extensive public protest and a Court of Session appeal funded by Glasgow Trades Council, the conviction was upheld. Cronin served the prison sentence, thereafter resuming his trade union duties in April 1890.[21]

Such disturbing events and episodes prompted influential men on both sides of the steel industry to press for ways to avoid and settle costly disputes. One important outcome of their initiatives in 1890 was the formation of the Board of Conciliation and Arbitration for the Manufactured Steel Trade of the West of Scotland, the first formal joint board of this kind within the iron and steel industries in Scotland. Its constitution, including equal representation among member owners and workers, was modelled on the North of England joint conciliation board which, as was discussed in Chapter 4, had influenced industrial relations within the malleable-iron sector in Scotland.

Among employers, James Riley and David Colville, and leading trade unionists John Hodge and John Cronin, were the prime movers behind the new body. After a difficult start, this joint body helped to defuse open industrial conflict within the steel sector, although many of its decisions can be reckoned of questionable value to the workers who came within its rulings. For various reasons, during the early 1890s its influence and impact within the industry were more limited than the founding members had originally hoped and intended. Only three companies were members of the board at the outset

– the Steel Company of Scotland, with representation from Hallside and Blochairn; David Colville and Sons, Dalzell and William Beardmore, Parkhead. This situation prevailed until 1899, when two other firms joined: Clydesdale (according to Hodge, influenced by a change in management) and Wishaw (after Riley had become works manager of that plant). In the 1890s and 1900s, despite this commitment to the board, there remained several notable omissions among steel companies whose owners and managers refused to participate in formal mechanisms of negotiation and conciliation or otherwise showed any signs of a progressive and collective approach towards industrial relations. New arrivals to the industry in the 1890s, including the Lanarkshire Steel Works at Motherwell, and James Dunlop at Calderbank, also came into this opposition category, as did established firms at Coltness, Glengarnock, Clydebridge and Mossend.

The board was also severely limited in the composition of its worker member participation. It represented millmen, but not melters. Reasons for this exclusion can be traced to disagreement among the interested parties concerning the basis of representation and terms of reference for the

No. 2 plate mill, Dalzell Works (North Lanarkshire Council)

proposed board. The Steel Smelters insisted on direct union representation, a position that was rejected by the millmen and the masters. Eventually, the core of steel masters and leading millmen agreed on terms to form a board, but did so after failing to win co-operation from the melters' union and the wider ranks of furnacemen. Without inclusion of representation from melting shop workers, the remit of this forum throughout its existence until 1922 was confined to regulation of wages and conditions of workers in the steel mill sector instead of the whole industry.

Board deliberations for the early years are of particular interest. They reveal the dominance of the masters and the inability of the millmen to make much impression. Important decisions went against the millmen despite vocal representation by John Cronin and colleagues. In the downturns and difficulties between 1891–95, masters continued to behave in the usual way, by slashing labour costs. There was an informal agreement within the board that millmen's rates were determined by the fluctuating price of ship plate in the Glasgow market, but no mechanism such as sliding scale tables existed to make precise calculations. Consequently, on two occasions, proposed wage cuts went to arbitration, and were both upheld.[22] On another occasion, in 1892, William Beardmore ignored the board, imposing wage cuts of 20 per cent, and provoking a strike among indignant Parkhead rollers.[23] Rollers and shearers also felt aggrieved by a board ruling to withdraw extra payments for disposal of accumulations of scrap from cut bars and sheets. Together, this series of attacks on millmen's wages and earnings wiped out the value of increases that had been won during the temporary upswing of the late 1880s.

Such adverse decisions and rulings aroused considerable resentment among millmen, although lower paid men had been exempted from the cuts. However, the millmen were not grateful for this concession. In 1893–4, further discontent was expressed during abortive efforts to draw up detailed occupational sliding scales, as the masters refused to include clauses intended to guarantee the principle of a basic minimum wage for low-paid labourers.[24]

The core group of masters were also united against proposals to fix standard working hours and stoppage times at weekends. When the issue was first raised in 1895, millmen's representatives hoped to win agreement on an early Saturday afternoon finish to their working week. Leading for the masters, David Colville considered the proposal to stop mill work at 1 p.m. or at any other fixed hour as 'absolute nonsense'. He insisted on continuing flexibility for Saturday working to accommodate busy production and finishing schedules arising from the last casting of the week on Friday night or

Saturday morning. He argued that, in competitive conditions, companies could not afford the additional costs of keeping ingots and slabs in soaking pits or reheating furnaces until they were rolled on Monday.[25]

While David Colville held fast against any changes to Saturday working in the mill department, in another respect he was the exception among steel masters in Scotland in that he continued to uphold the practice of refusing to make steel on Sundays. At the Dalzell Works, open-hearth furnacemen started their working week at midnight or early on Monday morning, whereas at other steelworks this shift started much earlier in the evening. The disputed position on the absence of standard hours for weekend work in mill departments was compounded by simultaneous demands from the melters' union. In unionised melting shops, as long as furnacemen were expected to work fourteen-hour evening shifts and ten-hour dayshifts, they wanted at least the benefit of free time and rest at weekends. Their immediate objectives included a free Saturday and complete abolition of Sunday working, so that the final furnace charge for the week would be worked on the Friday night-shift, and the first shift of the following week would commence no earlier than midnight on Sunday. Again, the majority of steel companies turned down such proposals, unwilling to make any changes that they thought were likely to restrict production and give an advantage to competing firms.

At trade union conferences in the early 1890s, millmen and furnacemen had debated the issue of shorter working hours, including the principle of eight-hour shift patterns over a twenty-four-hour day. However, while there was agreement on continuing to campaign for, and negotiate, shorter hours, opinion among melters was divided on an eight-hours' system. Opponents of

Pit side at new melting shop, Dalzell Works (North Lanarkshire Council)

this proposal felt vulnerable, as they were influenced by the experience of reduced earnings during recent years of wage cuts and trade downturn. They were convinced that changing to such a radically different pattern of working hours in such bad conditions then and in the future would not improve their earnings position, and would perhaps make it even worse. Although eight-hour shift schedules had been introduced in some steelworks in the north of England from 1897, conservative forces among masters and men prevailed on this issue in Scotland. In consequence, the two-shift pattern of longer hours, worked by a divided army of compliant and unwilling labour martyrs, persisted there for another twenty years.

'STORMING THE LAST BASTIONS OF REACTION IN THE STEEL TRADE'. CONFRONTATION AT MOSSEND

Meantime, the steel smelters' trade union continued to build and consolidate its base as representative organisation for melters, ladlemen, teemers and pitmen, and gas producers. Committed to winning standard agreements on a district-wide basis, it had to confront the remaining core of non-union firms, where the worst rates and conditions generally prevailed among underhands and, in some cases, masters and contracting foremen ruled by fear and intimidation. In this context, the principal 'rogue employers' within the steel industry in Scotland at the end of the century were the Neilson family, who controlled Clydebridge and Mossend. James Neilson, at Mossend, had earned a notorious reputation as a fervent opponent of trade unionism. His actions there in 1899 provoked a confrontation which lasted for over 15 months, and resulted in the longest running single dispute in the history of the steel industry in Britain.

The dispute began in October 1899, when Neilson discovered that his fortress had been penetrated by the melters' union. He sacked the branch secretary and fifteen others, expecting a collapse of morale instead of the concerted resistance that followed. Hodge had met Neilson in an attempt to resolve differences, but after the employer had made false promises regarding the victimised men and improvements in wage rates, the trade union decided to give the aggrieved men official backing. By this time, the British Steel Smelters was well established, with 11,000 members in Scotland, England and South Wales. It had full-time regional organisers and possessed financial resources to fight for recognition among recalcitrant employers like Neilson and bring an end to working conditions which were far behind the 'country rates' agreed with other steel masters. The strike won solid support, not only from furnacemen, who toiled without the help of a third hand melter, but also among the majority of millmen, who were persuaded to throw off the shackles of contractors and join the melters' union. Nearly 500 skilled and unskilled men were out, leaving behind a skeleton workforce.[26]

This display of solidarity prompted Neilson to lock out the strikers, order up eviction notices, and organise a hunt for sufficient blackleg labour to resume steel production, as the dispute occurred during a period of good trade. Over 80 families were evicted from company houses during November and December. Aided by trade union funds, alternative housing was found after women and children had been provided with communal feeding and temporary overnight accommodation in a large marquee.[27] Meanwhile, supplies of blackleg labour were recruited from Belfast, but early efforts to secure further supplies from elsewhere were relatively unsuccessful. Arrivals from Hawick, told they were replacing steel workers who had been called up to serve in the Boer War, agreed to turn back when union pickets informed them of the company's lying conduct. However, Neilson did manage to source a considerable number of recruits from the ranks of the National Free Labour Association, a union-smashing organisation which had assembled thousands of potential strike breakers for ready intervention at trouble spots like Mossend. The organisation's recruiting agent, Graeme Hunter, worked closely with Neilson, who paid for his strike-breaking services for a whole year. Hunter's reserve army of scab labour was billeted inside the works and at other company premises nearby. At changeover of shifts, the employer and the recruiting sergeant often led their men in a military-style parade to and from the works. According to reported allegations which were not challenged or rebutted, many of Hunter's 'free labour' mercenaries were disreputable characters. While off duty they went about in groups and were prone to boisterous, drunken exploits and insulting, offensive behaviour towards women and girls. The police did not caution or apprehend them for such misdemeanours, or for taunting pickets and other workmen. On one notable occasion, they stoned police who were there for their protection, but no action was taken against them.

The hardship of evictions, police protection of strike breakers at work and outside working hours and alleged heavy-handed policing of pickets, leading to numerous arrests and convictions, were controversial aspects of a nasty, protracted dispute. According to J.T. McPherson, assistant national secretary of the melters' union, and leading organiser of the Mossend workers, the divisive language of sectarian abuse was also evident during this dispute. For example, strike breakers of Protestant persuasion from Belfast had been told that there were 'too many Catholics in the works, and [they] were there to replace them'. In the same vein, a foreman had claimed that the dispute was a 'Fenian strike'.[28]

Such public displays of force and intimidation caused offence amongst strikers, their families and other members of the predominantly mining and iron-working local communities of Mossend and Bellshill, but they acquitted themselves with remarkable restraint. There were only a few incidents of retaliatory violence, involving assault on blacklegs. Convictions led to prison sentences of up to forty and sixty days, including the excessively severe punishment of three young women who were imprisoned for thirty days for hurling stones and filth.[29] Nevertheless, in the face of massive provocation from professional strike breakers, pickets conducted themselves responsibly and obeyed McPherson's instructions to stay out of trouble. Trade union accusations of police bias against pickets were taken seriously and the law officers were ordered to tone down their approach after the Lanarkshire Liberal MP, steel master John Colville, who was sympathetic towards the striking and locked-out workmen, had interviewed the chief constable on this matter.[30]

The commitment to stay out for elementary justice and decent conditions remained solid throughout this extraordinary long dispute. The basic needs of men and families were sustained by regular weekly allowances from union funds and occasional donations from other worker organisations. Morale was also boosted by rallies, demonstrations and concerts, and celebration parties giving a hero's welcome home for everyone who had been imprisoned for the cause.

However, the manner in which the dispute finally ended was by no means conclusive or decisive in terms of victory or defeat for either side. In early November 1900, Neilson appeared to break the deadlock without conceding trade union recognition. He agreed to re-employ the bulk of the workforce, but gave no guarantees about further employment conditions. Sensing a compromise deal, 'the union decided to call the strike off.' It had spent £30,000 (a huge financial commitment for that time) to support the

James Neilson,
iron and steel master,
Mossend

strike and the fight for recognition. 'While the union regarded the result as a draw, since it did not establish recognition, it had taught a lesson to the Neilsons and others likeminded.' This is a valid verdict, as the commercial reputation and viability of Mossend Steel Works had already been severely weakened by the prolonged dispute. To run a steelworks for so long with blackleg and unskilled labour was a costly, inefficient and ultimately ruinous undertaking, and undoubtedly forced Neilson to reconsider his position. Signs of deteriorating quality of product were also visible to the union and the locked-out workmen: 'The reports which came to the branch, and which no efforts of management could prevent, was a series of wasted metal, damaged furnaces and machinery, and plates returned below quality.'[31] Neilson was the loser here, but was too obstinate to admit that his steelmaking business was facing ruin, although the company's coal mining enterprises and iron smelting plant at Coatbridge remained viable. When steel production was eventually resumed at Mossend, blacklegs were dismissed, most workers were reinstated and a trade union presence was established. However, the works failed to make a full recovery, and by 1902 it stood closed and derelict.

The saga of poor industrial relations at Mossend was to continue under a different owner. Beardmore's of Parkhead bought the redundant plant in 1905, and re-equipped furnaces and mills for production of armour plate. However, George Neilson was installed as general manager, and 'the old traditions of the family found expression in his management. Every man who was engaged had to sign a book that he would not become a member of a trade union, the wages were less than the standard, and the conditions worse. Notwithstanding this, we persevered in organising.' James Walker, Scottish organiser of the British Steel Smelters, 'haunted the works gate like a shadow', distributing handbills and engaging the men as they entered and left the works. 'The firm tried all sorts of dodges to have him shifted, but the police were neutral, and told Walker exactly what he could do and not do.'

Meanwhile, Hodge pursued the issue of union recognition and employment conditions with a direct approach to William Beardmore, who met union leaders in London. The company had state contracts for navy work, which were subject to fair wage agreements. Such contracts were being worked at Mossend at less than recognised rates, while the Parkhead men, who were organised and working at the proper rates, were aggrieved at being denied a share of the contract work which had gone to Mossend instead. The union warned Beardmore that unless he took action to stop such practices, it would alert government officials and publicly expose the company's breach of

agreements. Acknowledging this possible threat to his contract status, Beardmore undertook to remove the embargo on union recognition at Mossend, and to remedy the wage disparity. However, again, during the following months, it was only organised pressure, involving the trade unions of melters, millmen and cranemen which finally forced both issues to a satisfactory conclusion at Mossend, as George Neilson had been slow to pay the standard rates and continued to intimidate workmen against joining a trade union.[32]

In the lead-up to the First World War, the right to collective bargaining was also established after persistent efforts to organise workmen against hostile management regimes at Clydebridge and Lanarkshire Steel Works. Hodge had exerted his considerable authority at Clydebridge, after having journeyed

Melters taking
samples from furnace
(North Lanarkshire
Council)

from the union headquarters at Manchester to meet owners and managers. He claimed to have convinced them of the business futility of industrial slavery at the plant, with its low wages and excessive hours, its exhausted and discontented men and its detrimental consequences for output and productivity.[33] While some subsequent improvements were made to hours and conditions, union recognition and negotiated standard rates at plant level came about only after a long struggle by activists and interventions by Walker, the full-time organiser.

The able, confident, intelligent and articulate James Walker had worked as a melter at Parkhead. As a promising activist, he was awarded a trade union scholarship to study at Ruskin College. A full-time regional organiser with socialist convictions, Walker honed his speaking and negotiating skills in the busy round of meetings with workmen and bosses, and earned his formidable reputation as a committed and tough-minded trade union official.[34] Such qualities were required for successful troubleshooting at the Lanarkshire Steel Works before 1914. The young Patrick McGeown tells how he 'often saw Jimmy Walker in the Craigneuk main street, always accompanied by steel melters, and always off to meet the melting shop manager and try settle some grievance or other. The branch meetings were held in private houses and very often some sneak told what had transpired to the manager. This man would victimise the householder by suspending him on some trivial grounds. It was Walker's job to get the suspension removed. My father, a quiet, tongue-tied man when at a meeting, had a great admiration for the determined and loquacious Walker.' However, McGeown is certainly mistaken in his comment that: 'As far as I know my father never worked in a non-union melting shop.'[35] Whatever inroads had been made earlier to organise furnacemen at the Lanarkshire Steel Works, a fresh struggle had to be conducted in 1910 to re-establish a trade union presence in the two melting shops.

During early March 1910, Walker convened at least one recruitment meeting with melting shop workers from the Lanarkshire. According to a press report, he put the case for trade union organisation in the workplace and enrolled 100 members to form a branch of the Steel Smelters. A mass meeting on 26 March decided on steps to win union recognition and resolve various grievances. Management retaliated swiftly, sacking three union activists on alleged disciplinary grounds, and testing the resolve of the new branch. Around 160 men voted for strike action to gain reinstatement, union recognition and redress of grievances. The dispute revealed the usual set of inferior working conditions and practices associated with an oppressive regime in a

steel melting department. Grievances included the 'gaffer's furnace', an abuse
which had been removed from the scene in other works; wages of furnace
labourers at well below the standard rate; excessive working hours on weekend
shifts; unsafe arrangements for internal transport of heavy ingots and absence
of safeguards in the casting pit of the new melting shop. In response,
management agreed to reinstate the victimised men, and conceded the wages
issue, but requested a month to sort and settle the remaining concerns.[36] In
October, after a growing feeling of unrest at management failure to act on
outstanding grievances, furnacemen and pitmen gave strike notice. This
threatened exercise of trade union power at the workplace, involving local
branches of smelters, cranemen and boilermen, and promises of support
from the millmen, was sufficient to bring management into line with other
steel firms. Albeit grudgingly at first, they began to accept union recognition,
collective bargaining processes and negotiated agreements on a wide range of
workplace issues.[37]

The maturing strength of the leading trade union in the industry, the
British Steel Smelters' Association, was reflected at workplace branch level by
1914, with firm representation in all open-hearth plants in the country. From
a position of strength, union leaders and executive members were also better
placed to pursue their preference for centralised direct negotiations with
organisations of steel masters. The union negotiated an important standard
ruling for promotion of steel-furnacemen based on experience and length of
service. Promotion by seniority was intended to give them some security of
prospects, to rise through grades with associated earnings. In later years (see
Chapter 7), this seniority ruling was strictly applied among production teams
in melting shops and mills.[38]

For years, melters and employers had each been divided about the merits
of formal detailed sliding scales for regulating wages, but the steel smelters
and a core of principal employers in Scotland and England finally reached
agreement on the issue. The North of England Melters' Sliding Scale
Agreement of 1905, with the newly formed Steel Ingot Makers' Association,
was the first national agreement in the steel industry. The original signatories
among firms and their worker representatives in Scotland were from William
Beardmore and Co., David Colville and Sons and the Steel Company of
Scotland, and it is no coincidence that they were the same group of firms
which had led the earlier initiative of this kind in 1890, to form the Board of
Conciliation and Arbitration for the Manufactured Steel Trade of the West of
Scotland.

The terms of the 1905 agreement formed the basis for regulating wages of melting shop workers and other steel occupations over the years. It remained in operation until 1940, when the system of calculation was changed to incorporate a cost of living index. For many years, the market price of steel was the primary indicator of wage regulation, and favoured the higher-paid skilled men who got most benefit from piece-work and tonnage rates, especially during the buoyant wartime and post-war years 1915–20. However, before 1914, many unskilled men in labouring work within steelworks were still grossly underpaid and on time rates, and were not covered by sliding scale agreements. Unorganised or poorly represented, they were neglected by the craft-dominated major trade unions. It was left to the Gasworkers and General Workers Union to organise among such groups of low-paid men as, for instance, at Dalzell Steel Works, where hundreds were in the local branch from 1912 until 1920.

To meet the demands of uninterrupted wartime production, the joint board system of employer and trade union representation for regulation of wages and conditions became fully established at all levels in the iron and steel industry and was extended to all manual grades. The employers conceded 100 per cent trade union recognition, and trade union officers enforced discipline among their members, ensuring that wildcat strikes and any other forms of rank and file unofficial action on wage issues during wartime were avoided. By 1917–18, sliding scale calculations were made more acceptable to disgruntled lower-paid steel workers when the base level was augmented with special wartime bonuses and cost of living awards.

In 1917, following initiatives led by the steel smelters, several trade unions in the iron and steel sectors agreed to dissolve and merge into an amalgamated organisation called the British Iron, Steel and Kindred Trades Association (BISAKTA). The formation of this big industrial union, and the accompanying emergence of its related national governing body, the Iron and Steel Trades Confederation (ISTC), created a power base of members, funds and resources with greater potential for negotiating, winning and enforcing agreements. As if to encapsulate the moderate, responsible image of mainstream trade unionism in steel, John Hodge, that canny, pragmatic Scot, principal architect of the British Steel Smelters Union, Member of Parliament since 1906, Minister of Labour and Minister of Pensions in the wartime government of Lloyd George, was elected president of the ISTC. However, for at least three years, Hodge and the ISTC faced problems in Scotland with trade unions that did not come under the auspices of the new organisation and had to be cajoled into accepting its central authority.

The first inter-union dispute was with the Operative Society of Bricklayers, whose members included steelwork squads occupied in the vital tasks of furnace building and repair. In October 1919, after employer refusal to negotiate demands, 350 men took strike action for a minimum weekly wage and an increased hourly rate, halting steel production from Glengarnock to Wishaw and causing thousands of workers to be laid off. After the third week of stoppages the bricklayers accepted the ISTC offer of mediation, but rejected the recommendations of the arbitration decision.[39] Frustrated by the continuing action of the bricklayers, the collapse of arbitration and the damaging effects of the dispute on his members, James Walker, now Scottish Division officer for the ISTC, made this critical, revealing observation:

> The action of the bricklayers is a splendid illustration of the effect of sectional trade unionism, as it means that a small group, without consultation with, or consideration for, a vast body of men with whom they are employed, can dislocate the whole industry and throw thousands of men idle . . . One would have thought that, with the continued failure of these demands on the part of small groups of workmen, it would have taught them a lesson and would have shown them that real success can only be achieved by all the men in one industry acting as one united body on behalf either of the whole or any section within the industry.[40]

Walker's standpoint, and that of the ISTC, on the supposed advantages of direct centralised negotiation conducted by a large representative organisation rather than by a small trade union, appeared to be vindicated by important recent successes in winning improved terms for many occupations and grades of steel workers. The National Eight Hours' Agreement of February 1919, negotiated by major steel employers and the ISTC, aided by the Amalgamated Society of Steel and Iron Workers, was one such achievement. This historic agreement reduced working hours, fixed starting and finishing times and set out the new three-shift pattern for production workers and millmen. Employers supported this measure as it guaranteed 24-hour production and promised greater co-operation and output from workers whose shifts were now shorter and less exhausting than before. Also in 1919, the other substantial achievement involving the ISTC as principal negotiator for the workmen was improved hours and wages for steelwork labourers. In

Scotland, Walker had led the negotiations on behalf of those unskilled workers, who gained a 47-hour week instead of the usual 58 hours, and a raised minimum wage, thus compensating for the neglect they had suffered before and during the war years.[41] The employers accepted the Eight Hours Agreement and the labourers' settlement only after winning concessions on downwards adjustments to rates for higher-paid melters and rollers, whose tonnage and productivity earnings had soared in relation to those of less well-paid colleagues. From the ISTC standpoint, this breakthrough in major negotiated agreements appeared to stand in marked contrast to the galling difficulties with the bricklayers, whose actions were considered counter-productive not only for their own interests but also for the better interests of the wider steel-working community. Faced with a stalemate position which was not of their own making, Walker and ISTC branches lost patience. At this late stage, they strongly advised the bricklayers to go back to work, pending further negotiations on their claim, and offered to intercede on their behalf at the negotiating table if they adopted this course of action. Foreman brick-layers were already returning to work after six weeks, and the bulk of their workmates, isolated and overruled, voted to return on the terms recom-mended by the ISTC.[42]

Early in 1920, Hodge was in Motherwell, asserting the authority of BISAKTA and ISTC and propounding the advantages of a single, powerful representative body to replace separate, sectional trade unions that still insisted on independent status. He had been encouraged by the recent decision of the Amalgamated Society of Steel and Iron Workers, most of whose 10,000 members were millmen in Scotland, to vote in favour of changing to the new order. He now targeted 900 labourers at Dalzell, who wished to remain members of the General Workers Union. The ISTC already represented nearly 80 per cent of 5,000 workers at the huge iron- and steelworks. Only the labourers and a few non-union men had not yet complied. The ISTC was intent on persuading or compelling the labourers to transfer membership and to commit the non-union men to join their ranks, aiming for a 100 per cent closed shop of ISTC members. To force the issue with the firm and impose their will on the dissident labourers, ISTC branches at Colvilles threatened strike action, intimating their refusal to work alongside this minority. Management colluded with the coercive stance of the ISTC and posted notices giving the non-compliant workmen a week to make the required decision, or face the consequences.[43]

In the early 1920s, ISTC branches also proved capable of mobilising their

26-inch bar mill,
Dalzell works, c. 1900,
for rolling iron and
steel bars

forces at workplace level to prevent employers from reverting to unacceptable practices. For example, in 1924, moves to bring back contracting in the plate mill and to extend working hours at Blochairn were repulsed after Walker had ordered the local branches to stop work. Production was effectively closed down for a fortnight until the issue was resolved in favour of the union. Around the same time, ISTC vigilance and the threat of strike action also led to withdrawal of contract notices at Parkhead.[44] Such examples of collective action among steel workers were entirely defensive in character, and intended to remove obvious grievances at particular workplaces. The actions were also entirely consistent with the tradition of a pragmatic, moderate trade unionism and upheld the long-standing official position of steel union leaders on limited use of the strike weapon. Industrial peace was preferable, but not at any price, and strike action was seen as a last, necessary resort. However, even defensive actions of this kind were rare in steel plants in Scotland during the years of prolonged depression within the industry between 1921 and 1934, as the ability of BISAKTA/ISTC to protect their members and resist attacks on hard-won agreements and conditions was increasingly sapped by the ravages of slump and closures, mass unemployment, short-time working, loss of earnings and the drastic decline in trade union membership and resources.

CHAPTER 7
WORKING LIVES IN IRON AND STEEL
1920s–1980s

This chapter continues thematic coverage of working conditions and practices in iron and steel plants in Scotland. After an introductory section on the traumas of the interwar years, conditions of blast furnace and foundry workers are reviewed briefly before concentrating on production workers in the principal sector, the steel industry. In this survey, the survival and elimination of traditional tasks and methods, the impact of technical developments on the workforce in iron and steel and of other changes in the working environment, are investigated and observed against a background of fluctuating fortunes and crises within both sectors of heavy industry. Fortunately, apart from the evidence of conventional sources and official records to assist our enquiry in the modern era, we can benefit more than ever before from the personal testimony and living memory of former workers. Such informal sources help provide inside knowledge and representative impressions of labour experience and of workplace relations in the iron and steel industries, and their contribution is most welcome.[1]

IN SLUMP AND RECOVERY: 1920s–1930s

As in mining communities, memories of hardship during the lean years of the 1920s and the worldwide slump of the early 1930s were embedded in the minds of more than one generation of iron and steel workers. Looking back over 44 years of working life, William Kelly, a long-serving mill hand and furnace heater at Etna Iron Works, recalled:

> It's not the hard work I remember so much as the times when there was no work at all. There was the 1921 and 1926 strikes, and then the

depression, with the slack time. We were getting maybe three or four shifts a week, and then it was two, and sometimes only one. The company did their best to give the men something: you usually got one shift out of it. After that, it was the dole and the Means Test. We didn't starve, but it was not much of a life. The district was in a terrible state. Nearly everything had closed down.[2]

Likewise, for Thomas Campbell, a blast-furnaceman at Clyde Iron Works:

There's nothing to compare with the hard times we had then, because in those days there aye seemed to be something wrong with the iron and steel trade. During the slump it was extra grim, very little coming in, a lot of mouths to feed. They used to say in those days the butcher called at the Clyde Rows six times a week, once with the meat and five times looking for his money. I went back to the pits when the times were bad. You see, in those days, Clyde Iron Works had its own pits – the Easterhill and the Dolly, we called them – and that was where I had started. Quite a few of us would change our jobs back and forward when we had to in the bad times.[3]

John Dempsey, a mill man at Glengarnock, recalled how the iniquity of the means test in the early 1930s compounded the misery of long-term unemployment and forced family units to break the law to survive:

This is where ma father and ma mother got the hard en' o' it. Because whenever we got a job in the Guide Mill, ma father didn't get anything. He was unemployed and we were supposed t' keep my father. If ah worked for three month, then he got nothing – which forced us t' say, 'We've left the house.' Ma eldest brother was married, so we'd all say, 'We're living with ma brother.' That was to get something from the Labour Exchange when we weren't working; and something for ma father to get because he couldn't say that we were in the house keepin' him.[4]

Thomas McKune, a charge wheeler at the Lanarkshire Steel Works in 1913, promoted to the melting team after returning from war service during the First World War, recalled the full employment, high tonnage and good wages earned at new machine-charged open-hearth furnaces in the boom of 1919–

early 1920. Thereafter, his working world went downhill for several years. However, it would appear that he was rarely out of work, as the Lanarkshire managed to keep open. In this respect, he paid tribute to 'the sheer hard work and determination' of the works manager, Mr Gray, who 'was a fighter and had to be. Things were so bad that the millmen were coming in in the morning to find out if they would be working or idle at 2 p.m. But Mr Gray used to put his hat on and go out himself to find orders. Today [1957] the minimum run in the mill is about 200 tons. In those days, we were changing rolls for five tons. It was a terrible struggle.' This situation continued until Colvilles Ltd took over the Lanarkshire in 1936. McKune had feared the

Machine-charging at open-hearth furnaces, Clydebridge Steel Works (North Lanarkshire Council)

worst, expecting that his workplace would be rationalised out of existence. The opposite occurred, as the furnaces were enlarged and modernised. 'The time we thought we were finished, we were in fact making a fresh start.' With the onset of economic recovery, once again, instead of years of 'working short time, there was work for all of us'.[5]

McKune's experience of 'working short time' through all, or most, of the interwar recession and slump, rather than having been laid off completely for long periods, was probably not unusual among steel workers not in regular employment during those fifteen years. Moreover, his experience may well have been more common and typical than that endured by many iron and steel workers hit by long bouts of unemployment, including those who were made redundant, never to return to their workplace or trade. Only estimate figures are available for the scale and extent of unemployment and short-time working among steel workers with regard to year and plant/location, although there is a record of temporary and permanent closure of iron and steel plants. In the boom year of 1920, around 25,000 workers were employed in steel manufacturing and rolling plants in Scotland. The numbers of iron workers in smelting plants, and in puddling and rolling, is not known, but was considerably less than in steel. It is reckoned that around 25 per cent of iron and steel workers were out of work for months on end and for even longer when vital coal supplies were cut off during the mining strike and lockout of April–June 1921, and as a consequence of the huge shipbuilding yards of the Clyde going into recession in 1921–2. In the steel heartland of Motherwell and Wishaw, the Dalzell and Lanarkshire works shut down their furnaces and melting shops for several months, before resuming production at reduced capacity. There were permanent casualties among malleable iron plants. Puddling ceased forever at Dalzell in 1921, and Muirkirk also joined the scrapheap.

However, the main casualties of this first post-war recession in iron and steel were workers in iron smelting plants, as furnaces at all Scottish locations were closed down for long periods. In the Coatbridge area, Calder, Carnbroe and Langloan closed forever, and all surviving smelting plants relit their furnaces only at the end of 1922. Renewed conflict in the mining industry, and its long-term effects on coal supplies and on jobs created a similar crisis at iron and steel plants in 1926–7, giving rise to popular memories of the drastic stoppages and hardships of ''21' and ''26'. For other years during the 1920s, the unemployment rate among iron and steel workers in Scotland is reckoned at no less than 15 per cent, although this bold figure disguises a higher rate in particular years; and much worse was to follow in the catastrophic slump of the early 1930s, when closures devastated whole communities.[6]

Despite the few years of exceptional unemployment (1921–2, and 1926–7), it would appear that the majority of retained steel workers (but not iron workers) were in regular employment for most of the troubled 1920s, although this experience was less certain during the early 1930s. However, among those steel workers not in regular employment, it is possible to account for incidence of short-time work as against outright and sustained unemployment. For instance, when work was in short supply in steel plants that remained open during this chronic recession, the practice of 'working round' was an informal agreement among workmen and managers. There is no way of knowing the extent to which this arrangement was applied in steel plants, but it consisted of sharing out available shifts as far as was practically possible. It was done in order to avoid the hardship of prolonged redundancy, but also to continue wage earning and thereby maintain the right to claim unemployment benefit. Perhaps this arrangement applied more in the case of skilled men. For example, McKune was a melter and a vital production worker and, along with others in the same category, such as rollers, was likely to retain at least some shifts as long as furnaces and mills were kept in operation, even at much reduced capacity. It was also the practice to retain a skeleton staff among ancillary workers, for essential maintenance.

Moreover, it is known that shutting down open-hearth furnaces and mills was a rare and short-term occurrence in the majority of steelworks that weathered the long recession of 1921–35. How those steel firms survived during this period, managed to keep their gates open for business and most of the workforce at least partially employed, requires some explanation. Hallside is an interesting case here. According to its historian, the steelworks was by then a relatively small concern, although its workmen could turn their hands to a variety of products, which proved to advantage during the lean years. 'Hallside could take on short runs the bigger works could not tackle economically; and with its ability to roll billets, rails and all shipbuilding sections it could range wide in its search for orders.' In similar fashion to the Lanarkshire Works, as reported above, 'Hallside operated its mills and melting shops from day to day, taking on orders of as little as 20 or 30 tons and then sending the men home until another order came along.'[7]

However, there is another explanation for so many steelworks managing to keep open for business, and this was intimately connected with their ownership structure and the continuing viability (albeit much reduced) of their main traditional customer-base in shipbuilding. During the boom in 1920, all steelmaking firms in Scotland were bought by leading shipbuilders, aiming to secure direct supplies of plate and sections in the expectation of a continuing rising market demand for all types of ships from the Clyde, Belfast and Tyne yards. However, although demand for new ships was greatly reduced from the end of the post-war boom, the order book for ship construction, particularly for cargo and passenger liners from the Clydeside yards, remained remarkably resilient through most of the 1920s and until the collapse of 1931–4. A decade of relative decline in shipbuilding on the Clyde, followed by sharp collapse, had disproportionate effects on employment in the dependent steel industry. While some consequent job loss and short-time working was typical of the 1920s, the crisis of the early 1930s in a dwindling shipbuilding sector had a much more devastating impact on the ranks of steel workers as outright unemployment reached record figures and opportunities for any gainful employment were greatly diminished. In short, jobs and work prospects among steel workers continued to be heavily dependent on the fluctuating fortunes of the shipbuilding industry.

The steel industry in Scotland shed around 5,000 workers in the late 1920s and early 1930s, and the dominant Colville combine's rationalisation programme had further impact on a depressed employment scene. Closure of Calderbank steelworks in 1931 turned the village into an industrial wasteland. The Bellshill community suffered closure of Beardmore's Mossend steel plant, while transfer of Stewart and Lloyds tube works to Corby in 1932, and partial closure of Clydesdale steelworks, inflicted further employment casualties on this beleaguered locality. All smelting plants in Ayrshire were swept away in the depression years, although Glengarnock was given a future as a remaining outlying centre of steel production.

A gradual climb to economic recovery was under way by 1934–5, as order books for the Clyde shipbuilding yards were renewed, and government contracts were awarded for naval rearmament. It was this upturn, more than anything else, which restored employment for many iron and steel workers in the west of Scotland, and gave a reprieve to ailing staple-heavy industries in urgent need of investment and modernisation. In their principal plan for steel the Colville combine had, by the mid 1930s, decided to concentrate on developing integrated blast furnace and open-hearth capacity at a rebuilt Clyde Iron Works and Clydebridge complex, while investing further in enlarged open-hearth furnaces and additional mill capacity at Glengarnock and at its Motherwell base of Dalzell and the Lanarkshire Works.

Clyde Iron Works. Blast furnaces, demolished in late 1930s to make way for modern furnaces

BLAST-FURNACE WORKERS

At Shotts Iron Works, young Archie Henderson was a furnace-filler working eight-hour shifts and the occasional gruelling double shift at weekends:

> Although my physical endurance was extended many times later [as a coal miner], I never had a more searching test than what I got early in 1920, when I started as an auxiliary filler. I was called out one Saturday night to fill the iron-ore barrow of No. 2 Furnace. The furnace had to get the full tally, or darg, of 44 charges. This I did and serviced a 'cast'. Then I had to continue on to the Sunday dayshift and do the same again. Eighty-eight barrows of ore, each barrow weighing 16cwts, and two casts – that I did.
>
> The work was hard and very heavy. I was in turn for promotion and got a filler's job on No. 3 Furnace. Only strong men could do that work. Forty barrows had to be filled with a load of coal weighing 15 cwts; and fillers attended the cast of molten iron. That was the average day's work. Each alternate fortnight a filler changed from the coal barrow to the iron ore barrow. The work had to be done in all conditions and weather. For me, the main fault of that job was the rotation of shifts – daytime, afternoon and night. Being bound to such a scheme of work made social activities almost impossible.[8]

At Clyde Iron Works, Thomas Campbell recalled how the plant –

was pretty small in those days before Colvilles took over, and nearly all
the work was done by hand. There were only five old hand-filled
furnaces, usually with four of them working, and you were lucky if you
got 350 tons a week out of the best of them. The furnace-fillers started
out from the Rows for their shift on Monday morning, all in their clean
white moleskins and blue flannel shirts. Modern trousers wouldn't
have lasted a month then with all the shovelling at the barrows.
Moleskins – white for the men on the ore barrow and black for the coal
barrow – they lasted a year.[9]

Although, by 1920, machine charging had replaced hand charging of open-
hearth furnaces in steelworks, in Scotland's antiquated iron smelting plants
this labour-intensive practice persisted until modern blast furnaces were built
at Clyde Iron in the late 1930s, and latterly at Ravenscraig in the late 1950s. In
the 1920s, Joe McAulay was employed at Glengarnock's 40-year-old blast
furnaces before the plant was closed and demolished in 1930. His valuable
testimony confirms that furnace operations, tasks and division of labour were
essentially unchanged since the late nineteenth century. The keeper had
overall responsibility for furnace operations and his team of second and third
man, two charge fillers at the top of the hoist and the barrow men below. At
the age of 14 he had started as labourer, shovelling lime and ore into barrows
for the furnace charge; when 16, he progressed from filler on to the furnace
team, as third man. His responsibilities at this grade included clearing up after
casting, and cleaning the runners leading to the pig beds, as well as collecting
hand tools and materials, such as clay, for furnace repairs. He did not get an
adult wage until he was 21, and was paid a paltry 5s. 9d. per shift. The leading
members of the furnace team, keeper and second man – the slagger – were on
tonnage rates, while lower grades of furnacemen and labourers were only on
a shift rate. He did not mention whether this was the result of local agreement
or the policy of the blast-furnacemen's trade union.

As a young man, McAulay was promoted to slagger, like his Lithuanian
father before him. As such, he worked closely with the keeper, monitoring the
boiling metal and the slag. He did most of the heavy, hot, manual work at
tapping time, hammering a long bar into the taphole to release the molten
charge, servicing at the cast, removing bogeys of slag and organising and
carrying out furnace repairs. He helped the keeper to supervise casting, and

the flow into pig-bed moulds. He remembers seeing the last of the pig lifters in their coarse leather aprons and gloves dislodging and lifting the solidified bars into waiting bogeys.

McAulay noticed the introduction of some mechanisation in and around blast furnaces during the 1920s, including crane-operated ladles to remove slag and the erection of elevated 'breakers' to receive full beds of pig bars by overhead crane uplift. However, though welcome, this limited removal of manual processes did not alter the inherent dangers of furnace operations, as he confirmed that the old furnaces were not in good shape, needed constant fettling and fundamental repairs and were accident prone. Sudden collapse of the hot charge was not infrequent, blowing open furnace doors, weakening brickwork and causing the team peril and much bother.[10]

The change from manual labour to machine-assisted and power-driven operations at blast furnaces was more complete in the modern plant at Clyde Iron from the late 1930s. Its three furnaces were mechanically charged, movement of the charge was externally regulated, pig casting and moulding machines had overtaken the need for ground-level pig beds, overhead magnet cranes lifted tons of pig iron bar and liquid iron was transferred to fleets of containers. By the 1950s, each furnace had a control room with instrument panel, including indicators of blast volume, gas pressure and temperature recorder, and a visual record of the molten metal. The controls were operated by the keeper, and sited for a clear view of tapholes and ladle positioning. He manipulated a piston-type gun to lengthen and straighten the taphole, and an oxygen lance to make final openings. The keeper had become a skilled technician, as well as team leader and troubleshooter, while he and other operators also had to possess an 'intimate knowledge of the smelting characteristics of a variety of ores.'[11] At the time, Thomas Campbell, local secretary of the National Union of Blast-furnacemen, claimed that, at the transformed Clyde Iron Works, 'all this mechanisation has come in, and from the very start it has never cost a man his job. The works have kept on growing, so if a machine displaced a man there was always another job for him.'[12]

Ravenscraig's blast furnaces were the final addition to iron production capacity in Scotland, but even their technological modernity could not prevent or avert the danger of occasional violent blowouts and other severe incidents. In early January 1982, No. 3 furnace exploded when being recommissioned after the holiday break. Fortunately no one was injured, but it could have been otherwise, as excessive gas pressure inflicted heavy damage, causing a large fallout of molten metal and ash.[13] A year earlier a furnaceman was

Casting at No. 3 blast
furnace, Clyde Iron
Works, 1970s (North
Lanarkshire Council)

killed and five others injured, with burns, during a maintenance operation. According to a newspaper report headed 'Survivor tells of steelworks death horror', the men were on platforms trying to undo a blockage, when the fixture and materials broke away, and they had to jump for their lives while being showered with burning dust and ash.[14] The next fatal accident at Ravenscraig occurred over three years later, when a controller at No. 1 blast furnace was caught in a blowout and hit by a flying chunk of red-hot metal.[15] In such circumstances, a former manager admitted that 'the blast furnace department was a place where you felt that time wasn't always on your side.'[16]

Every furnace worker has stories of scares, near misses and human error. Ian Murray recalled how he and a mate were bringing a furnace back into blast again, when they experienced carbon monoxide poisoning. They were sitting on the floor keeping an eye on it and having a chat, but when he got up he felt his legs were like rubber. He realised they 'had slipped up' as 'the furnace generates carbon monoxide, and so the leaks should be lit with a newspaper as they come out'. They had failed to do this and were affected by the gas. However, it was a lucky escape from unconsciousness and possible death, as both men managed to get to the ambulance room, their breath sampled, and were treated with an infusion of soda water 'poured down your gullet'.[17]

FOUNDRY WORKERS AND MOULDING SHOP CONDITIONS

In Chapter 2, the notoriously unsafe and unhealthy conditions of foundry work, especially for moulders, were emphasised. It is questionable how far conditions had improved into the modern period, as indicated in the following accounts. In the early 1930s, the 80-yard long moulding shop of Shanks and Co. sanitary wares foundry at Barrhead was described as a 'cauldron of blazing heat and grit-laden air'. The piece-work wages, at £5 a week, almost double the local average wage if you had work, were earned in the hardest, most desperate conditions. To one observer –

> it was unbelievable. Slave labour! I knew those that worked in the foundry. They used to make cast iron cisterns, in a box, with sand. They ran the sand into one box, then into the other, in two halves, to make one pattern, and then smoothed off the shell they'd made, and lifted the holder of molten metal. They had two holes in the top, and they'd pour the molten metal into that. This was all done by hand. The same with cast iron baths. It was really brutal work . . . it was dirty work, inasmuch as there were no masks, and there was all this sand. Pneumoconiosis was rife. They just thought it was chest disease. The foreman had the power of life and death over them.[18]

Andy Wilson, who entered Shanks' moulding shop at 14, described his working life: 'Apart from fatigue and soreness, the swallowing of dust particles was distressing, nostrils choked constantly. The normal daily experience was to cough and spit for several hours after finishing – almost solid black clots.' The dangers of hauling two-wheeled cup-shaped bogeys of molten metal over uneven passageways from furnace to moulds were ever present. Each team had to contend with –

'the heat of the white-hot metal, the odd mistake at the tapping point, the odd metal spill from bogeys filled to the brim and pulled slowly by two men walking backwards (one looked backwards; one steadied it, looking forward). Apart from being too narrow, the aisles were badly pitted and holed sometimes. I never saw any maintenance work done on them. Were there Safety Regulations in those days? If so, they were completely ignored. The moulding shop could never have passed the most basic, rudimentary, safety requirement.[19]

Also in the 1930s, Jack Summers left school at 14 to be an apprentice iron moulder at R.Y. Pickering's wheel and axle works, Wishaw. He left after a year and nine months, saying this decision 'was the best thing I ever did in my life, because it was the worst, most hellish job you ever were in. There were huge stoves fired for days, using coal. After moulding was done, the surrounding sand was hosed down and you couldn't see for clouds of dust and smoke. The blackened sand turned to dust. The moulding shop was worse than the mines for dirt and your lungs were filled with it, you spat blood sometimes.'[20]

A contemporary survey revealed that less than 10 per cent of young men who came into foundries stayed on, as the great majority were repelled by the squalid conditions of smoke, fumes and silica dust pollution, cheap labour and no prospects in 'a blind alley job'.[21] Such atrocious conditions also repelled Jim Gardner, a leading activist in the National Union of Foundry Workers who, from the 1940s, was determined to eradicate them from moulding and dressing premises. Of all problems facing the foundry worker, where mortality rates from occupational disease were higher than for coal mining in 1936, 'there are none more urgent than health.' In two influential campaigning pamphlets based on his working experience and research in Central Scotland, he identified the worst offenders as being among older, light castings iron foundries, with their 'ramshackle dilapidated buildings, primitive sanitation and ventilation, badly constructed runways, poor lighting, the danger of open pits and sand heaps, box parts in chaotic confusion, dust inches thick on the floor and coated on everything under the foundry roof; and producing all kinds of disabilities and diseases such as rheumatism, sciatica, dermatitis, bronchial and lung diseases including the dreaded silicosis, pneumoconiosis and tuberculosis.'[22]

By all accounts of this time, including Gardner's reckoning, working conditions and the workplace environment were more orderly and acceptable in new, and more modern foundries, in most large and heavy castings iron foundries attached to major engineering works and shipyards and in the few steel foundries in Scotland. Those types of foundry usually had stronger trade union representation, and workers were protected from the dirt-cheap wages and sweatshop conditions that prevailed in so many others. Gardner noted that the modern foundry was 'comparatively free from smoke nuisance from badly fitting stove doors, and from coal and coke fires for drying jobs in the moulding pit all year round', although increasing use of machine moulding continued to create additional dust problems and the need for adequate ventilation.

In Fullwood Foundry at Mossend, part of the Colville combine since 1915, long-serving craneman John Adamson observed the changes in his workplace where the principal activity was casting ingot moulds for the steel industry. For forty years, he had a 'bird's eye view' of everything going on in the moulding shop:

In the old days, there was hardly any mechanisation. I used to see them spreading out the sand for the moulds, watering it, and bringing it together, and packing it into the moulding boxes by hand. I'd see them hand charging the heating furnaces, and a heavy job it was unloading all the pig iron by hand. In the old days, with all that handwork, and no

Moulding shop,
Hallside Steel Foundry

ventilation, the dust used to rise in clouds. The men were white with
it, white faces, hair, clothes; and as it rose up there were times when I
could hardly see what I was doing. It was like driving a crane in a pea-
soup fog, and fumes coming up too. Now, between the machines and
the ventilation, the air's clear all the time. There's hardly a man
wearing a mask, and with the new baths coming along there's a
tremendous difference. I've seen huge changes. But the biggest change
of the lot is the way dust has gone, that used to blow up to my cab.[23]

However, the workplace improvements at Fullwood had come only in the
period after 1945. New knock-out equipment and dust-extraction plants were
installed. Introduction of controlled water blast speeded up the dismantling
of mould cores and abolished one of the least pleasant jobs, but the men had
to wait until 1956 for amenity blocks, lockers and baths which allowed them
to go home without dirty working clothes and grime.[24]

From the 1930s onwards, the foremost concern among industrial health
campaigners was the reduction and elimination of the permanent menace of
dust particles at all foundries, particularly of silica dust – the principal cause
of debilitating and fatal lung disease. Their campaign efforts exerted pressure
on governments, factory inspectors, occupational health professionals,
employers and on foundry workers themselves, to tackle this menace by all
available means. Although preventive measures, X-ray and regular medical
testing, safer and cleaner working equipment and practices were carried
through from the 1950s, and the working environment in the dwindling
number of foundries in Scotland had been transformed by the late 1970s and
1980s, there is nevertheless at least one unfortunate conclusion. If dust
control was the objective, then that was achieved: but the dust menace was not
eliminated. Finding, funding and implementing safe substitutes for silica sand
and other known toxic agents in the foundry workplace was never a
government or employer priority and, as a consequence, foundry workers
continued to suffer and face premature death.[25]

STEELMEN: THE MELTING SHOP

Teams of melters making steel in open-hearth furnaces was the principal
method of production in Scotland until final closure of this type of plant in
the 1970s. The latest in technology of bulk steel production, the basic oxygen

furnace, was in operation only at Ravenscraig from the early 1960s. From the 1920s, open-hearth production was continued at Dalzell, the Lanarkshire, Clydesdale, Clydebridge, Hallside, Blochairn, Parkhead, Glengarnock, and was in operation at Ravenscraig from the late 1950s. Apart from Clydebridge (from the late 1930s) and Ravenscraig, where blast furnaces fed liquid iron to steelmaking plants, it was a measure of the backwardness of the industry in Scotland that steelmen in other open-hearth plants had to work in traditional mode with furnace charges of cold metal instead of hot metal. However, since conversion from hand charging to machine charging after 1918, furnaces had been enlarged. The new melting shop at Clydebridge, with 300-ton tilting furnaces, and Ravenscraig, with 240-ton capacity, had the largest furnaces. Capacity elsewhere ranged from 90 to 150 tons, but Blochairn and Hallside had smaller 60-ton furnaces.

Tasks and responsibilities of members of open-hearth furnace teams remained essentially the same as before, although it will be seen that some changes in furnace efficiency and in the melting shop environment had an impact on working conditions and practices. A profile of duties, progression routes and division of labour in a typical melting shop between the 1920s and the 1970s can be revealed with the help of information provided by former steel workers from Glengarnock and Motherwell.

John Ramsay did a skilled job as crane driver at Glengarnock during the 1920s. From stockyard wagons, he lifted and transported materials into steel boxes to feed the melting shop's six furnaces. Ramsay used a magnet crane to lift and deposit scrap for the box-trimmer, whose job consisted of sorting and placing the tangled metal in orderly, even fashion within the container, to make ready for uplift by the driver of the furnace-charging machine. Ramsay was promoted to charging machine driver in 1927, and remained in that responsible job until his retirement. The magnet crane operator had displaced the charge-wheeler with his heavy hand-barrow loads of cold metal and lime, but manual labour was still the order of the day for the junior ranks. For example, the box-trimmer job was dirty, heavy and hazardous, and the lime boy was at the bottom of the melting shop pecking order. Sorting barrows of burnt lime, which inflamed naked skin and eyes, was usually a hated job, and boys hoped to progress quickly to the next step up, as box-trimmer.[26]

Harry Mclean stepped up from box-trimmer to furnace helper, the fourth and lowest melter grade. In his case, working on a 100-ton furnace, two fourth hands were required for general labouring jobs in and around the furnace. A helper was also dogsbody, tea-maker and message boy. He also drilled and bored samples, and took them to and from samplepasser and laboratory. As third hand, Mclean was responsible for giving out and maintaining furnace tools, and for making up any last minute additions for furnace or ladle as ordered up by the sample passer at tapping times.[27]

Second hand melters confirmed that they bore a large burden of heavy work, and shared major responsibility with the first hand. The No. 2 melter was in charge at the back of the furnace, preparing and organising tapping operations. At tapping time he braved the tremendous heat, and physically opened the taphole by pulling out the clayfired plug, before hammering in a

Melter using oxygen lance to pierce tap hole: last tap at Glengarnock, 22 December, 1978 (North Lanarkshire Council)

long bar to pierce the taphole and release the surging metal. He needed 'lungs of brass and stamina of a bullock to open tapholes'.[28] He had to ensure that the metal flowed freely from the tapholes, and that slag passed into the chute separately from the molten iron. After the furnace had drained off, he then had to seal the taphole, his team using rabbles from the front side to insert a packing mixture of coal and magnesite. Finally he organised immediate repair of the taphole, in order to keep this vital part of the furnace in good working condition. As a second hand explained: 'the taphole was about four or five feet long. We patched it up as far as it was able to take the charge. Whenever the pipe lost its length, you had to replace it.'[29] Latterly, the strenuous task of opening tapholes by manual hammering was relieved only when oxygen lances were used to burn out the blockage and release the flow of molten metal.

The second hand melter also organised fettling of the furnace hearth. This task remained a bugbear for melters, as it was an arduous manual labour job requiring a lot of time, effort and care. As a fourth and third hand melter at Dalzell in the 1950s, Alex Fraser recalled that 'the shovel was never out of your hand'. Fettling was 'done with the door about half open. You had your glasses on, and you threw dolomite into the holes and built up the banks of the furnace again. It was very hot and hard work.'[30] An official source informs us that fettling machines were in use at Clydebridge and the Lanarkshire in 1957, but part of the job had to be done with hand shovels and rabbles.[31] When Fraser became a third hand melter at the brand new Ravenscraig open-hearth furnaces: 'we had a machine for fettling, but in saying that, we had to shovel sometimes, so it was still hard work.'

Melters occasionally assisted colleagues on other furnaces as, for instance, with difficult fettling operations and at busy tapping times. If a taphole was blocked or clogged up, second hands helped each other to repair or burn it out. If available, second, third and, sometimes, fourth hands would assist at a furnace that was ready to tap although, apparently, the first hand always stayed at his own furnace.[32] The second hand was understudy to the first hand, and relieved him at meal and other times.

As ever, the first hand was in overall charge of the furnace, its operations and his team. During later stages of the melt and in the final decision to tap, he liaised closely with the samplepasser foreman. From the 1940s, leading melters had to cope with technical changes and improved processes at open-hearth furnaces. In 1954, David Graham had been a first hand melter at Dalzell for 15 years. Recently, his job had changed somewhat, but not his responsibility and craft, as expressed in this journalist's account:

In the vast No. 4 melting shop, his place is at a huge instrument panel on which every dial has a message for him on the state of affairs in the incandescent furnace under his charge. In the climate of astronomical temperatures, draughts, and pressures under his control he cannot afford to make mistakes. All is well while the furnace is roaring away at 1,600 degrees centigrade. But let it get any hotter and the melter may soon be in trouble. Fifty degrees more and the thousands of bricks lining the inside of the furnace begin to melt and the whole process is in jeopardy. Where margins are so fine as that, unwavering efficiency is indispensable. Melters had few scientific aids and managed their furnaces largely by instinct born of long practice. Things are different now. But if modern steel workers have machines and instruments to help them, these have in no way diminished their responsibility. Today the aim is greater accuracy in production of better steel, and the emphasis is still on skill.[33]

In 1962, a newly retired first hand melter at Dalzell confirmed this experience of change:

Melting is a far simpler process than it was when I began. Then you depended on the eye of the sample passer and not much else. He sent examples to the laboratory like we do now; but there were sometimes serious delays, as the laboratory was quite a distance from the melting shop and samples had to be carried there by hand. The sample passer often had to back his own judgement. Now you push buttons. You watch the instruments, and they tell you if something is wrong. Then you go to the furnace and have a look at it, and you spot the trouble straight away. You have a big responsibility – you could easily cost the firm thousands of pounds if you spoiled the melt and if you damaged the furnace – but the instruments have made melting much simpler and more of a science than it was before. The method of sampling too has improved. Samples are sent to the laboratory by Lamson tube and returned in a matter of minutes by tape machines – a boon to the sample passer.[34]

Some first hand and second hand melters did not have the necessary confidence to adjust to technical changes such as instrument panels. For instance, at Glengarnock in the middle 1960s, they encountered difficulties when furnace firing was converted from gas to oil. Oil firing of open-hearth furnaces was introduced there and at most other steelworks for reasons of cost, speed and efficiency. For melters, the process was a lot cleaner, although noisier, as oil was steam injected into the furnace, but they were relieved of the wisps and clouds of black gas that hung throughout the melting shop. Traditional gas firing and maintenance of gasports and chambers was troublesome, although melters were used to handling levers and valves to regulate air flows, flame and heat, trusting their practical experience and relying on eye-judgement without the aid of any recording instruments. However, although most leading melters did learn to adapt to working faster oil-fired furnaces, others failed to do so. A melting shop manager explained how melters were given in-house training on an oil-fired furnace. 'A few men decided it was too fast for them', knowing that making errors in heat control 'could do a lot more damage to brickwork if you weren't careful'. Moreover, they either resented, or could not cope with 'this imposing panel', which was new and formidable, and registered all their movements. Many men were suspicious that temperature clocks and control panels would take away their jobs, instead of just helping supervision of the melting process and improving the quality of their end product. The new technology deterred 'some second hands, knowing they had to step up and take the responsibility of a first hand, and didn't feel they could do it'.[35] A first hand melter at Glengarnock who coped with this challenge reported that they lost a lot of experienced men who

Open-hearth furnaces: melting shop, Glengarnock Steel Works, 1950s

could not, or would not, adapt, and it is likely that similar experiences occurred at other steelworks.[36]

On the same size of furnaces at Glengarnock and the Lanarkshire in the 1960s, oil firing reduced tap to tap time from around thirteen and fourteen hours to an average ten and eleven hours. The difference was even greater at Ravenscraig's four new, and much larger, oil-fired, open-hearth furnaces, where Alex Fraser was a third hand melter, then second hand, between 1959 and 1963. The Craig's furnaces 'took a lot of looking after. The furnace team had the same duties more or less as they had at Dalzell, but because it was a more technical, modern melting shop, everything seemed to go quicker and you were tapping about every seven or eight hours. When they built the fourth furnace, that was tapping 300 tons every six hours, so the wages were pretty good.' But he had to pay for them, as he was caught in a blowout and suffered some burns.[37]

For decades, steelmen worked an eight-hour day, on a three-shift pattern of 6 a.m.–2 p.m.; 2 p.m.–10 p.m. and 10 p.m.–6 p.m. A 48-hour week and shift arrangements were a legacy of the national agreement of 1919. That agreement also included abolition of productive shift work on Sundays. However, this condition was conceded by the ISTC in the mid 1920s in a deal that reintroduced Sunday shifts from 2 p.m. onwards in return for raising the base rate of wages for lower-paid shop floor workers. Around 1950, the industry changed to continuous production over the whole calendar week and

Open-hearth furnaces; melting shop, Lanarkshire Steel Works, 1950s

shift working on Sundays became the norm. Apparently, melting shops at Glengarnock and the Lanarkshire Works deviated from this pattern of an inclusive 21-shift week and instead operated a 19-shift week which started at 6 a.m. on Sunday and finished at 1 p.m. on Saturday. As a works manager at Glengarnock explained, production started at 6 a.m. on Sundays, when what was known as the lying-in charge was tapped at all operating furnaces. Placed in the furnace on Saturday morning, this was a heavy, condensed charge consisting of good quality scrap and pig iron. It required only the attention of a second hand and helper, who came on the Saturday nightshift at 10 p.m., fired the charge and looked after it until ready for tapping first thing in the morning. Then a hectic scene followed. Furnaces rarely tapped at the same time, but they did so on the Sunday morning shift. For the sample passer and the casting pit foreman – the teeming observer –

> 6 a.m. Sunday was a critical time. With all six furnaces sitting boiling and maybe three ready, it was pure hell. I've seen us tapping six furnaces in less than two hours and that takes a lot of going, I can tell ye. You never got your head up, because if you made one slip, it held everybody up, and you had to decide right, between yourself and the sample passer. There was maybe a few arguments deciding which order to tap and where to teem them, so there wouldn't be delay to any furnace.[38]

In all casting operations, teeming roasting liquid steel from the nozzles of a 100-ton loaded ladle into trains of ingot moulds was concentrated, stressful and very hot work for pit-side men. A casting pit team was a mobile unit, servicing several furnaces. It usually consisted of a couple of senior men, who were first and second teemers; at least three assistant teemers at the moulds; first, second and third hand ladlemen; a slagger and a mould washer. During and after teeming operations, they interacted closely with cranemen and locomotive drivers who brought in and removed mould trains. Principal teemers had responsibility for taking initial test samples from the ladle, and sending them for analysis. As leading melter and sample passer had done earlier, they also made any final additions to the hot metal, to reach required standards before commencing the main business of teeming.

Teeming into ingot moulds at Lanarkshire Steel Works, 1977 (North Lanarkshire Council)

Ian Murray, a teeming observer at the Lanarkshire Works between 1952 and 1977, recalled how the whole operation created a lot of mess and waste. For instance, slag flowed from a furnace in a cascade system into four large

pots, leaving inevitable spillage. The solid residue of metal spillage while teeming into the moulds also left an accumulation of spent scrap that had to be removed for safety reasons. Ladles had to be dried off, fettled for reuse, and heavy stoppers removed, cleaned and reset with precision into bar fixtures inside the ladle.

Pit-side workers had to get accustomed to the heat, grime and time pressure of teeming and casting and, as Murray also recalls, the ever-present dangers under your feet and above your head. Pit muck was often a combustible and explosive mixture, sending flames high up in the air. Some potentially disastrous incidents occurred, and he relates two, in particular, involving crane failure. On the first occasion, crane brakes failed to hold the weight of a full ladle when lowering the load towards the mould train. Realising what was happening, the driver managed to shout a warning as the ladle hit and toppled a slag pot, spilling its contents. The only human casualty was the crane man, who caught a scorched face from the rising heat. The second incident was even more serious, and 'it was fortuitous that no one was hurt or killed'. A crane was hoisting a full ladle over the casting pit when, without warning 'there was an almighty bang' and he and others fled in fear for their lives. A casting on the hoist drum had broken, and the fault caused the ladle to drop. The ladle stoppers melted, discharging the hot metal load onto the pit floor. The pit men had escaped, but they and the maintenance crew had the unenviable task of extricating a damaged ladle, tangled ropes and fixtures, and a mess of 90 tons of rapidly solidifying steel.[39]

STEELMAKING AT RAVENSCRAIG: BASIC OXYGEN FURNACES

The revolutionary process of making steel in an oxygen blown furnace converter came on stream at Ravenscraig in January 1964. There, the only Basic Oxygen Steelmaking (BOS) plant in Scotland was installed by the end of 1963, with melting shop and two 100-ton converter furnaces. Oxygen-injected heat had long been used for cutting and welding metal, and was in more recent use to open furnace tapholes. However, the open-hearth process was not technically equipped for production of the specific high-grade, low-carbon strip steel needed for the growing market in motor-car bodies, washing machines and other consumer white goods. The new converter process, patented in Austria, quickly and ruthlessly burned impurities out of the iron to enable production of precise formulae of quality steel which could be rolled out into coiled sheet in the new strip mill. The BOS plant was not planned as a replacement for Ravenscraig's four modern open-hearth furnaces, which continued to operate: instead, the objective was to create additional capacity and greater versatility in steel production at the giant complex.

In simple terms, the furnace was an egg-shaped vessel similar to the conventional Bessemer converter, but much larger and with a solid base. It was charged with molten iron and scrap. A three-metre long, water-cooled lance was lowered into the charge. At high velocity, the lance blew oxygen and powdered lime on the surface of the charge, producing intense heat, a violent reaction on the molten metal and a fast boil. Up to 100 tons of iron was thoroughly refined in less than 30 minutes, the vessel was tipped, and steel poured into a teeming ladle standing on a transfer car below the converter.[40]

Alex Fraser, then a second hand melter at Ravenscraig's open-hearth furnaces, made a successful application to transfer to the BOS plant in December 1963. He was among the first batch of recruits to be trained up in the new production processes. He remembers being present at the momentous occasion of the first tap, 'at half past five on Friday night, January 31st, 1964. I stayed all night. The Austrians were there', to supervise the process and train around a hundred men for working three shifts. 'They sent over a squad of operators, engineers and foremen to teach us how to work a basic oxygen furnace. They did that from January until about June. On 16 April, I got my first vesselman's job, and had my own team under me.'

Outlining his experience as first hand melter between 1964 and 1983, he remarked that the oxygen furnace was, 'very, very fast. You could turn out 125 tons of steel in half an hour; or sometimes it took three quarters of an hour.' The furnace charge was –

> about 25-ton of scrap and then 90-ton of liquid iron coming from the blast furnace. You put the vessel vertical, and you lower the lance. It's lowered by push button down into the furnace and, as it enters, the oxygen is switched on and it ignites. It goes down so far and stays there. And then you start adding burnt lime and other materials. You got all the impurities out because there's so much turbulence inside the furnace.

Asked whether the oxygen process was safer to work than an open-hearth furnace, he found it –

hard to say. I mean we've had blowouts in the oxygen furnace where the slag has come right over the vessel, landed on the floor, covered the whole floor. We've had tae run for our life, you know. We know now why these things happened, because as the years wore on, we got more technical and got more feedback from the chemists and research people. So we got better and better.

He claims that some former open-hearth colleagues at Dalzell and Ravenscraig were sceptical, curious and a bit jealous of the new methods, quality of product and the earnings. Their attitudes were reminiscent of those expressed by iron puddlers towards the new-fangled open-hearth steel production over 80 years earlier:

Some of the open-hearth lads used to come down to watch it, and see what was happening. But they still couldn't believe we were making steel as quick as that. They kept saying, 'It canny be good steel'; but we knew we were making good steel. It was still hard work and dangerous work. At first a lot more technology attached to it. I learned more in the oxygen shop than I ever did at Dalzell and Ravenscraig open-hearth shops, working with technicians and chemists. I could talk the same lingo to them because of that, whereas years ago I wouldn't have known what they were talking about.

In the early 1970s, the two original oxygen furnaces were removed and three new vessels installed. This meant 'more technology and controls, but these were completely changed again in the late '70s. It was far more modern, more computerised, and was really first class. I must say the training we got in the Craig was always first class. Any new equipment, any new procedures or any new schemes, they put us on courses for a day or two.' Later, leading furnaceman Fraser became a unit trainer of Ravenscraig production apprentices and experienced men alike. He also gained a well-earned City and Guilds certificate in steelmaking, as if he had anything to prove.[41]

WORKPLACE AND INDUSTRIAL RELATIONS: 1920s–1970s

In his final annual report as chairman of Colvilles (1916–55), Sir John Craig paid tribute to the workforce for a long history of industrial peace:

Basic oxygen steel
making at
Ravenscraig. The ladle
of molten iron is
poured into the
converter (North
Lanarkshire Council)

It is remarkable that during my long connection with the Company, there has never been a stoppage in the works arising from a strike of our iron and steel workers. There have been incidental stoppages arising from outside sources but it is noteworthy that the last general strike in our works was in 1886.

He then praised the positive role of the ISTC,

which has represented our labour in such a statesmanlike manner that without strikes it has steadily gained higher wages and improved conditions for its members. The relationship during all these years has been of a cordial nature in spite of many differences of opinion. Yet, notwithstanding these difficulties, we have never failed in the spirit of conciliation to solve the problems of working conditions and rewards.[42]

The statement above is remarkable, all the more so in that it is a true summary record, at least for Craig's period as chairman. In all that time, production men avoided taking industrial action, and the few strikes that occurred were among craft trades, maintenance workers and labourers. There is also no doubt that the relationship between Craig and the workforce, and especially the production men organised by the ISTC, was one of genuine mutual respect. They appeared to share an expressed corporate loyalty to the Colville enterprise, although it is unlikely that the bulk of workers subscribed fully to Craig's notion of 'the Colville family'. The son of a Dalzell puddler, Craig had been with the firm since his start as an office boy 60 years earlier. As a successful captain of industry, Craig also had a singular, selfless devotion to Colvilles, and he mixed an acute business sense with a paternalist approach to the workforce.

Craig felt a moral obligation to keep Glengarnock open in 1930, as closure would have devastated a whole community whose livelihoods depended on steel work. He was even more insistent in this regard during deliberations through the 1930s and '40s on expansion and restructure of the steel industry in Scotland. He gave a powerful reason to oppose recommendations to locate a giant new integrated deepwater steel plant on the Clyde at Erskine: to avert the drastic prospect of closure, unemployment and other social costs to workers and families in the existing Lanarkshire steel heartland. His paternalist and welfarist leanings were also shown in 1946 when, in a private contribution, he bought a mansion at Skelmorlie and converted it into a convalescent home and rehabilitation centre for injured steel workers.[43]

However, during Craig's regime, notably at his Dalzell base, recruitment and preferment policy was decidedly in favour of good-living young men from Protestant backgrounds. A particular Colville recruitment ground was in church-related activities and clubs such as the YMCA, of which Craig was a life-long champion. It can be said that Catholics knew not to bother to apply for managerial and white collar jobs, although this type of discrimination was less evident in other areas of employment, as at shop floor level. Moreover, while the Colville regime accommodated and encouraged responsible trade unionism among the manual workforce, it refused to recognise trade unions and collective bargaining among managerial and white collar staff, whose posts carried a works pension as well as expectation of compliant loyalty.

Since the end of the 1930s, return of relative full employment and rising earnings had created favourable conditions for the reassertion of trade union membership and influence in the workplace. Managers exercised their traditional responsibility and power to recruit and appoint staff, and to promote to foreman grade from shop floor ranks, for example, first hand melter to sample passer. However, their powers of preferment and promotion were circumscribed in one important respect, as they knew not to interfere with, or override, the promotion by seniority agreement operated by the ISTC among production men and other members in melting shops and rolling mills.

Sir John Craig, 1956

Every member had a seniority number which was his for life in the industry, and determined his place in the promotion line. As a former Scottish Divisional Officer of the ISTC explained:

> We were very, very strict about it. We guarded it very jealously. We knew exactly where we stood in promotion. We knew that so and so was retiring, or somebody had died, and so on. We knew the next man to move up. If he didn't move up we, as the branch officials, wanted to know why. We had men refuse promotion because they didn't want responsibility – what was known as stickers. They just wanted to remain where they were. Fair comment.[44]

The seniority system and the right to a place on the promotion line was a safeguard against managerial favouritism and abuse in selection of men for promotion, but the system also had a downside. Unless a worker was leaving for a position at a new works, a move elsewhere usually meant dropping down the promotion line, so this condition discouraged plant to plant mobility. It meant that ISTC members either stayed in one place or with a single firm for all, or nearly all of their working lives in steel, and that their careers and prospects were often determined by the fortunes of one company. The system also discouraged a militant outlook. Members already benefited from industry-wide agreements, high productivity earnings or prospects of promotion with higher wages, and they were reluctant to take any action which would have an adverse effect on that security and stability. The élite were the well-paid senior hands who also dominated the affairs of the union branch, and served as representatives and negotiators at local and wider levels.[45] Men further down the promotion line were accustomed to wait their turn for next steps up and the higher earnings that accompanied those moves.

Consensus on the seniority scheme and a common stake in regular production and its material rewards made a huge contribution to industrial peace between ISTC members and employers from the busy post-war period to the early 1970s. However, ISTC and other trade unions in steel plants still had to intervene to gain some respite from the heat and grime of melting shop and mill, as workplace facilities for manual workers were often rudimentary. Basic amenities such as clean drinking water, running hot water and showers, decent toilet facilities, lockers and changing rooms, canteens or separate accommodation for eating and resting, were not installed in some older plants – for instance, Glengarnock – until the 1950s and 1960s.[46]

Apart from those concerns, the climate of industrial relations within steel in Scotland changed for the worse in the late 1950s and into the 1960s, as grievances over working conditions and practices erupted into disputes and strikes. It was not the older plants but the new Ravenscraig-Gartcosh complex which was the scene of most disputes and issues. Safety issues predominated when steel erectors stopped work on three occasions in 1956–7, including a walk-out of two thousand men after five colleagues in a fifteen-month period had been killed in accidents at Ravenscraig. In June 1957, a general strike of craft trades followed a disputed wage claim and staff blacklegging on their jobs. After the hot strip mill and cold reduction plant were operational, an alleged 32 strikes occurred between May and September 1964, involving mill production workers, engineers and other craftsmen. Most stoppages were short and unofficial, and were settled the same day. Issues included demarcation disputes, automation and manning of rolls and machinery, and productivity bonuses. This spate of disruption provoked Colvilles' chairman Andrew McCance into a furious denunciation of irresponsible trade union power.[47] Unrest continued, as blast-furnacemen and ore plant workers struck over wages and abnormal conditions. In January 1965, 700 men brought the strip mill to a standstill over alleged victimisation of a trade union activist. Further strikes at Ravenscraig in 1965 included cranemen, labourers and electricians, mainly over wage claims but, in the electricians' case, the dispute was exacerbated by staff cover of strikers' jobs. In July 1967, blast-furnacemen were on unofficial strike for a fortnight, their action coinciding with the dissolution of

Tapping molten iron:
Ravenscraig blast
furnace (North
Lanarkshire Council)

the Colville Company and its transfer to the nationalised British Steel
Corporation. In February 1968, the hot strip mill was closed when production
men took unofficial action over management demands for new shift patterns
and overtime, and in September, bricklayers at Ravenscraig, Gartcosh and two
other plants were on strike over yet another demarcation issue.[48]

Brief scrutiny of disputes at Ravenscraig, Gartcosh and other plants
during this period reveals that production men in mills were rarely involved.
However, a conspicuous feature is the no-strike record of melters. This would
appear to confirm their propensity, and especially that of the ISTC, to settle
issues around the table. As for other workers implicated in industrial action,
it is too easy to pin blame on trade union cussedness or on mindless militancy,
thereby to divert attention from real grievances and management short-
comings before and after the second nationalisation in 1967. Whatever the
verdict on the 1960s, in the fateful years to come, the world of steel and of its
workers in Scotland was to be plagued by even more uncertainty and trouble.

CHAPTER 8
CLOSURES, PROTEST
AND REDUNDANCY
THE FINAL YEARS OF STEELMAKING IN SCOTLAND

CLOSURES AND REACTIONS: THE 1970s

In autumn 1974, a respected journalist proclaimed that, 'no domestic issue in Scotland has generated as much controversy in recent years as BSC plans for steelmaking.'[1] A year earlier, the British Steel Corporation had published its *Ten Year Development Strategy* for a profitable and competitive industry. Its startling proposals for reshaping the steel industry in Scotland comprised a mixed programme of rationalisation and closures; modernisation and expansion. In a projected sweep of ageing, obsolescent and uneconomic processes and plants, all open-hearth furnaces and melting shops at Clydebridge, Dalzell, the Lanarkshire, Glengarnock and Ravenscraig, several rolling mills and the blast furnaces at Clyde Iron Works, were to close by 1978–9 or earlier. On the other hand, major investment was earmarked for an additional plant at Ravenscraig, and for a deepwater terminal and direct reduction iron ore plant at Hunterston, as the first stage in a long-term plan to develop a large, modern, integrated steel complex. Continued support was also promised for specialist steel production at Hallside and Clydesdale Tube Works, and for plate mills at Clydebridge and Dalzell.

However, it was not the prospect of record investment at Ravenscraig, Hunterston and elsewhere which grabbed the headlines: instead, it was the prospective loss of 7,000 jobs by the end of the decade which created a public furore, and fuelled anxiety among steel workers in plants destined for closure. This bad news came during a continuing economic recession which had recently seen an appalling spate of factory closures and redundancies in textiles, mining, marine engineering and shipbuilding, symbolised by the crash of Upper Clyde Shipbuilders. The decline and closure of Clydeside shipyards – a vital customer base for so much of Scottish steel plate and sections, and of jobs – was already an obvious source of worry for the workforce in the older, and more vulnerable, rolling and finishing plants.[2]

Rollers at Clydesdale
Steel Works, c. 1980
(North Lanarkshire
Council)

The essentials of BSC plans for rationalisation and investment in Scotland
were endorsed by the incoming Labour government when, in August 1975,
Lord Beswick delivered his review report.[3] Amidst growing concern over a
revised projected total of around 6,000 net job losses, there was some encouragement for steel workers, as indicated by Beswick and Tony Benn, in the
government's approach towards the industry and its workforce. There were
distinct signs of a less stringent and more sensitive consideration of issues,
such as delay to scheduled closures for up to an extra year or so; cases for
retention of particular plants on grounds of viability (thereby saving jobs
which were to go in the original plan) and levels of compensation payment for
workers who were to be redeployed within the industry or were to be made
redundant. The government also signalled a renewed commitment to regional
development policy in areas hit by heavy closures and high unemployment,
above all, to the North Lanarkshire steel belt which was about to bear the
brunt of impending job losses within the industry, and to the Garnock Valley,
where 50 per cent of male employment depended on the Glengarnock plant.

Agreement and understanding on those problem issues had been reached
with government ministers and BSC after lobbying by, and consultation with,
trade union bodies, MPs and local councils in Labour-dominated steel heart-
lands. Campaign activity at various levels had also begun in 1974, intensifying
through 1975, to combat and defer closures, to save jobs and to create alternative sources of employment. The Motherwell District Council area, the
historic centre of steelmaking, faced the bulk of proposed closures, and

around 2,400 lost jobs in the short term. The cuts were due at Dalzell's open-hearth furnaces and two mills (1,030 jobs); Lanarkshire's furnaces (400 jobs); Ravenscraig's four, relatively modern, open-hearth furnaces (400 jobs) and Clydesdale's furnaces (600 jobs). With local unemployment already running high, there was increasing concern that most job losses in steel could not be absorbed or replaced, leading to unacceptable levels of unemployment and strain on workers, families and services.

In May, over 1,000 local steel workers participated with fellow workers in a major rally and demonstration, carrying their case to the seats of power in London. In a day event, which received national coverage on the BBC and ITV, they marched and lobbied MPs at Westminster, and demonstrated outside BSC headquarters and the Trade Union Congress.[4] The timing of this protest had been provoked by an announcement from BSC chairman, Monty Finniston, of up to 20,000 imminent redundancies across British steel plants, and thus bringing forward intended closure plans. After successive years of profitable operations, this threat was a drastic response to the inflationary crisis of 1975, falling demand and escalating costs of steel and forecasts of a colossal deficit within the Corporation for the coming year. The chairman's threat was averted after intervention by the government and the Trades Union Congress; but there is also little doubt that the strength of feeling demonstrated by the steelmen in their London protest had contributed to reconsideration of BSC's emergency measures.

The BSC and TUC Steel Committee (including Scottish representation) negotiated a six-point plan to manage the continuing crisis, including co-operation to share declining orders among plants, and handle plant closures and workforce reduction with the minimum of hardship.[5] However, this truce did not dispel unease among steel workers in vulnerable plants such as Dalzell and Clydebridge, where production was down to a single furnace in October.[6] Steel workers expressed their concerns again at national level with a second demonstration in London on 21 October. The principal focus of their lobby of parliament was to win firm commitment from BSC and the Labour government for funded programmes to redeploy and retrain workers facing redundancy in areas of high unemployment such as Motherwell and Cambuslang.[7]

The downward spiral of demand and production continued into 1976 after the government had secured loans from the International Monetary Fund to stave off the balance of payments crisis. Loan conditions led to a government squeeze on public spending, forcing BSC to abandon its development strategy. The impact on the steel industry in Scotland was dismal, as development and expansion were stopped at its principal centres. Construction of electric arc furnaces at Ravenscraig was curtailed; and at Hunterston where, since 1973, millions of pounds had been poured into the deepwater terminal and iron ore reduction plant, plans for oxygen and electric arc steelmaking plant were also abandoned. Moreover, in a further internal reorganisation of BSC in 1976, a separate Scottish division was formed; but by 1977–8 its vulnerable position was exposed, as losses per ton of steel production were greater than Teesside and South Wales. This deteriorating prospect, combined with a three-year-long government credit squeeze on BSC, led directly to acceleration of plant closures and redundancies.[8]

During 1977 and 1978, all open-hearth furnace plants were demolished, on or ahead of the 1975 schedule. There was no justifiable case for retention of this outmoded and costly method of steelmaking, above all at Glengarnock, where the melting shop and majority of furnaces were 50 years old. The last open-hearth furnace to close in Scotland was at Glengarnock, on 22 December 1978, its final effort taking over 12 hours to reach tapping stage, a reminder of chronic failure to invest in modern plants.[9] With this set of major closures of melting shops went nearly 3,000 jobs, consigning most men to the dole queues, and some for redeployment.

Among the casualties of accelerated closure was Clyde Iron Works, closed in autumn 1977, despite attempts by the ISTC to persuade the men to take a stand against closure. However, according to ISTC leader Bill Sirs, the government 'allowed BSC to make much bigger redundancy payments to those workers who accepted early works closure. At Clyde Iron, BSC went over our heads direct to the workforce and the lure of a few thousand pounds' severance pay was enough to make the majority vote for acceptance.'[10] Similar

Glengarnock Steel
Works

terms were offered at Hallside and the Lanarkshire, and both works closed completely by early 1980. Hallside's production of billets for the car and other industries was transferred to the electric arc furnace and bar mills at Clyde Alloy, Craigneuk. BSC reckoned to save £3.5 million per year by closing the Lanarkshire's section mill and eliminating 400 remaining jobs there, reserving its main business – making pit arches for the coal industry – for Glengarnock and Teesside.[11] BSC had also intended to close the whole Glengarnock plant in 1978, but the section mill was retained, saving 200 jobs, while 700 open-hearth and melting shop workers had already accepted redundancy terms. The rolling mill jobs survived only after the ISTC had conceded a flexible work agreement. Nevertheless, the consequence of major job loss in Garnock Valley raised the male unemployment rate to 25 per cent.[12] On the wider scale, the entire total of job losses in steel in Scotland between 1974 and 1979 was around the 7,000 mark. Steel employment dropped from 25,700 to 18,800 between September 1974 and July 1979, nearly half the losses occurring in Motherwell District alone.

At this juncture, in 1979, the end of steelmaking in Scotland was by no means a foregone conclusion, although warning signs were beginning to appear. Already, the implications of cancelling direct reduction plant and planned production of steel at Hunterston was a major blow to Ravenscraig's future viability, as Hunterston steel was intended as low-cost supply for the Motherwell plant's high-capacity strip mill.[13] However, shorn of most ailing and outmoded parts, the steel industry in Scotland still had the appearance of viability. Its principal units were intact at Ravenscraig, Gartcosh, Dalzell and Clydebridge; also at Clydesdale Tube Works, and production of specialist alloy steels at Craigneuk.

In retrospect, the closures of the late 1970s, under a Labour government, were the first stage of rationalisation within an unprofitable steel industry. However painful those closures and job losses, no steel worker, trade union or labour movement activist could predict or prepare for the sheer scale and pace of cataclysmic destruction of plant and livelihoods within the next five years. In May 1979, a Conservative government, led by Margaret Thatcher, had come to power. Its mission would soon become clear: to break the power of trade unions; to strip and streamline nationalised industries such as coal and steel and transform them into a profitable core. By the mid 1980s it was also evident that government policy would include preparing a slimmed-down steel industry for sale into private ownership, against the wishes of the great majority of the public in Scotland.

GATHERING STORM: THE EARLY 1980s

Between January and March 1980, the government and BSC had to confront
a national steel strike, the first since steel workers were called out to support
the miners in the General Strike of May 1926.

    With inflation running at 17 per cent, the ISTC rejected a derisory offer
of a 2 per cent wage increase, other increases to come from locally negotiated
productivity deals. The steelmen believed they were being provoked into a
dispute, disunity and then quick defeat, preparing the ground for an end to
orderly national bargaining, scrapping the guaranteed working week and
forcing through large-scale closures and redundancies. At marches and rallies

Last tap of steel at
Glengarnock open-
hearth furnaces,
22 December 1978
(North Lanarkshire
Council)

Swinging a hot
steel billet to rolling
mill at Clyde Alloy
Works, Wishaw

in Motherwell and other centres, and on picket lines, steel workers voiced their anger and dismay. The ISTC could not afford to pay any strike benefits, and single men were ineligible for social security money. Despite the hardships, the strike stayed solid, and all works were at a standstill, except for the furnaces which were kept fired and safe for resumption of operations. After 13 weeks, the steel unions accepted what they regarded as a reasonable offer of 11 per cent across the board, plus a productivity element.[14]

BSC losses arising from the long stoppage was a colossal £1.8 billion, of which half was attributed to idle plants and lost output in Scotland. In the aftermath of the strike, around 20,000 jobs were cut within the steel industry, including no fewer than 2,000 in Scotland. The outlook for the Scottish division was already ominous before the appointment of Ian MacGregor as chairman of BSC in June 1980. He was to be demonised as Mrs Thatcher's hatchet man in steel and later in coal mining, held responsible for slashing tens of thousands of jobs in both industries during the early 1980s. In 1981–2, MacGregor's reappraisal of steel capacity in conditions of declining market demand, with no signs of recovery, raised obvious question marks over the future viability, not only of Ravenscraig and Gartcosh, but of all operations in

Scotland. In autumn 1981, government declarations that subsidies would no longer be available to prop up 'lame ducks' in nationalised industries was a further tightening of the policy screw on loss-making plants.

One consequence of this deteriorating situation was the negative climate of fear and disillusionment, but also of rage and resentment, among steel workers, especially in the Motherwell area, while jobs were threatened and destroyed at an unprecedented rate during the early 1980s. Between 1980 and 1983, no fewer than another 5,000 jobs were lost, including 2,000 at Ravenscraig; 1,300 with the closures of Clyde Alloy and Craigneuk Foundry and around 700 as a consequence of Clydebridge plate mill closure. A continuing and severe drop in orders at Dalzell plate mill and Clydesdale Tube works also led to considerable lay-offs. There were also feelings of relief and resignation, notably among older men, among managers and manual grades alike, who grasped the opportunities of early retirement or voluntary severance offers. A manager at Clyde Alloy remarked how, in 1983, 'redun-

Making a seamless steel tube, Clydesdale Steel Works, 1959. The operator makes a hole through the hot billet in the hydraulic press (North Lanarkshire Council)

dancies were grabbed – even £2,000 was like winning the pools. If you got another job for sixteen hours a week or more for six months, BSC made up your wages to 90 per cent, so workers took all sorts of jobs just to get this wage benefit'.[15] Many settlements were comparatively generous, in line with redundancy packages sanctioned by MacGregor and the Tory government. Such inducements and incentives continued to be part of a strategy to shed the expendable labour force, while quietening any potential resistance, and leaving work colleagues and their unions to argue over the issue of accepting or opposing redundancies.

From 1982 onwards, threatened closure of the linked Ravenscraig and Gartcosh complex was the primary focal point of concern. MacGregor's original intention was to shut down the entire complex and thereby reduce BSC expenditure by £100 million a year. Ravenscraig was singled out for closure as the smallest of the five integrated plants in the UK, and the least profitable of the hot strip mills. However, such a drastic proposal was rejected, not least by government ministers and wide swathes of Conservative opinion in Scotland. They were sensitive about the inevitable political revolt which would result from a proposed Ravenscraig closure, including defeats in Scottish constituencies in the forthcoming General Election (1983). Scottish Secretary George Younger supposedly made Ravenscraig a resignation issue but, in this battle of steel and politics, MacGregor's closure plan was thwarted by intense pressure from a broad-based Scottish lobby, representing a consensus for integrated steelmaking and finishing capacity north of the border. This coalition was led by the STUC, as the principal co-ordinating body for the affiliated trade union movement, in conjunction with the ISTC. In close support were other trade unions, local authorities and Labour MPs, but also cross-party political representation from Communists to concerned Conservatives. The Scottish Council (Development and Industry), local chambers of commerce and leading church figures, also lent supporting voices.[16]

The Ravenscraig complex was given a three-year lifeline, subject to review in 1985–6 but the short-term declaration to retain the whole plant was a hollow promise. The steel unions, backed by the broad-based coalition which had acted to win the reprieve in 1982, had to exert themselves again in 1983 to reject MacGregor's revised plan to close down the hot strip mill and Gartcosh finishing plant. Ravenscraig was to be downgraded to a bulk slab producer, utilising the newly installed continuous casting facility to supply slabs for rolling mills in the United States. The plan to ship slabs to

Pennsylvania was dismissed by Clive Lewis, ISTC officer in Scotland, as a
'madcap' scheme, and was opposed vociferously by steel unions and labour in
Scotland and in the United States when it became clear that the scheme was
conditional on the loss of vital plants and around 2,000 jobs at both locations.
The American link-up was also questioned at government level, and subsequently dropped.[17]

Maintaining a wider campaign profile, enlisting the support of influential
bodies within Scottish public life, was the chosen strategy to impress and
convince government ministers of the case for a viable steel industry, and it
appeared to be effective in 1982–3. However, within the workplace, the steel
trade unions and workforce had already adjusted to the pressures of co-
existence with the 'new realism' of a hard-line Tory government and BSC
demands for higher productivity. Since the end of the national strike in 1980,
leading shop stewards at Ravenscraig had come to accept the BSC argument
that lost custom could only be regained by the right quality, price and
guaranteed delivery of product, and agreed that the workforce should co-
operate in efforts to improve performance. They heeded dire warnings about

A finished coil of
strip steel, Gartcosh

unacceptable levels of absenteeism, unnecessary overtime and over-manning generated by restrictive working practices. Drastic changes in conditions and practices were drawn up and carried through by managers, with shop steward co-operation. A new bonus was introduced, rewarding productivity and quality effort.[18] Tightening of discipline and performance led to improved results as, in 1982–3, the first of many output and productivity records were achieved and surpassed.[19]

SURVIVING THE MINERS' STRIKE: 1984–85

The resolve of steel workers at the Ravenscraig complex was tested in 1984 during the national miners' strike, when they were caught in a dispute not of their making.[20] Among the controversial events of the miners' strike, the stance of steel union leaders and workers at Ravenscraig, and relationships with the National Union of Mineworkers, were contentious issues. As members of a triple alliance with miners and transport workers, the steel workers were obliged to assist fellow trade unionists in struggle and, at least, to avoid taking action likely to jeopardise solidarity and a favourable outcome. This relationship came under immediate pressure from the outset of the strike in March, as the NUM placed an embargo on movement of coal from ports and depots, and BSC commissioned road hauliers to deliver vital coal supplies from Hunterston. However, after strong ISTC representations to the NUM, a special case was allowed for Ravenscraig and other major steelmaking plants in the UK. In early April, the Triple Alliance members made local agreements for resumption of rail delivery of sufficient supplies of coal to keep coke ovens and blast furnaces in working order. At this stage, BSC agreed to the arrangement and cancelled further road deliveries.

The NUM concession of two train loads of coal a day was the overriding concern for Ravenscraig and its four thousand workers. They feared that failure to secure adequate supplies would have fatal consequences. Starving the coke ovens would lead to rapid shutdown of the plant's ageing blast furnaces, causing irreparable damage to lining and fabric, and thereby providing BSC with justification for permanent plant closure. The critical period of uncertainty and threat was from May until September, when the initial agreement on essential supplies was contested in a series of tortuous twists and turns. BSC intervened first, to secure larger deliveries by rail from Hunterston. The NUM retaliated, and railwaymen reduced the load to one a day. BSC then hired hauliers and non-union truckers, enraging the NUM and the Transport and General Workers' Union. In early May, the NUM organised mass picketing at Hunterston and Ravenscraig to stop road deliveries, and the gates of both sites became flashpoints of violent clashes involving pickets and police.

At Ravenscraig, it is clear that picketing was not directed at steelmen going into work, but at lorry drivers whose passage was protected by massive police presence. The NUM appealed to steel workers not to handle 'blackleg coal', but they refused. Steel union spokesmen stated that their priority was to keep the plant open, and to use any coal coming in. They had to deny accusations of strike-breaking and of collusion with BSC and plant managers in efforts to increase production as well as safeguarding ovens and furnaces. For Tommy Brennan, ISTC convenor at Ravenscraig, torn between his support for the miners' cause, and the interests of preserving plant, production and the jobs of his members, 'it was the most difficult time of my life.'[21] Some shamefaced steel union delegates attended Labour Party meetings in Motherwell, apologising for going past picket lines at Ravenscraig; but their view did not reflect the more single-minded position of the majority of steelmen in defence of plants and jobs against outside forces.[22]

An STUC deal brokered with Triple Alliance unions to deliver 18,000 tons of coal fell through when an inter-union dispute halted supplies at Hunterston, and in late June the NUM persuaded railwaymen to blockade delivery of iron ore. BSC acted quickly to increase coal and ore supplies but another dock dispute in August again placed Ravenscraig in a critical situation as supplies ran dangerously low, and the plant was allegedly a week away from closure. Some ISTC members at Hunterston incurred the wrath of the NUM when they helped unload supplies. However, work continued apace at Ravenscraig through the remaining months of the miners' strike after the crisis of supplies and production was finally resolved in September when, at an emergency steel meeting convened by Jeremy Bray, Motherwell South MP, the Transport and General Union agreed to deliver the desired BSC quotas of coal and ore.[23]

THE FINAL RECKONING: 1985–92

At Glengarnock, the remaining workforce accepted redundancy terms in February, 1985. Its final closure was lamented and resented in the Garnock

Valley, but did not raise a storm. Meanwhile, as workers at the Ravenscraig complex and Dalzell plate mill/Clydebridge finishing plant continued to break production and productivity records and satisfy the quality end of the market, BSC and the government determined their future. In the review of August 1985, Ravenscraig was granted another three-year reprieve, but the decision was accompanied by two hammer blows to its future viability: closure of Gartcosh finishing mill by March 1986, and no investment in new coke ovens. Clearly, the Ravenscraig–Gartcosh complex was confirmed as peripheral in the short term, with investment earmarked for South Wales, at

Some Gartcosh marchers outside Smelters Arms, Corby. Left to right: Jim Wright (SNP); John Reid (Labour candidate, Motherwell North); Willie Pettigrew (Gartcosh Works); Tommy Brennan (Ravenscraig shop stewards convenor); Jim Bannerman (Liberal councillor, Strathclyde Region) (courtesy of Mary McKenna, campaign organiser)

Port Talbot and Llanwern, where continuous casting facilities were planned. BSC calculated that Gartcosh was surplus to requirements, too costly and remote from alternative markets, especially since its principal customer – the motor-vehicle industry at Linwood and Bathgate – had collapsed. Moreover, the Gartcosh closure would mean that Ravenscraig was no longer an integrated plant, but was to become dependent on sending its hot-rolled coil product to the finishing mill at Shotton, in North Wales. Ravenscraig was to be relegated to a 'standby plant'.

Glengarnock's passing had not been unexpected, but the proposed closure of Gartcosh, with 1,000 direct jobs at stake, and threatened failure to refurbish Ravenscraig's worn-out coke ovens and ailing blast furnaces, were entirely shocking prospects, triggering an almighty uproar of protest. The grand coalition launched its most sustained campaign, effort yet to save Gartcosh and safeguard Ravenscraig as an integrated plant. For the next six months, a flurry of meetings, conferences, lobbying and media briefings dominated the political agenda in Scotland. In December, Gartcosh workers gave shop stewards a mandate to continue the campaign, and between 3 and 13 January steel workers and others representing a cross-section of political support marched in relay from Gartcosh to London, arriving to coincide with the parliamentary debate on the plant's fate. However, marchers were rebuffed at Downing Street, and after the Opposition motion was defeated, Gartcosh workers accepted the inevitable and voted for redundancy terms. Instead of succumbing to the lure of generous severance money after the closure announcement in August, they had been buoyed up by the enormous campaign effort mounted on their behalf, and had persevered until the bitter end.[24]

More than ever, it appeared that Ravenscraig was on borrowed time, but the particulars of the final process had to take their agonising course. In December 1987, the re-elected Tory government granted what was to be a final stay of execution for the giant plant. The strip mill was guaranteed until the end of 1989, but coke ovens were not to be replaced. With BSC already back in profit, the government announced its plans to sell off the industry by December 1988.

After privatisation, Ravenscraig and its workforce operated to the best of their abilities, continuing to break productivity records, outperforming Llanwern, but remaining starved of further investment. Now reduced to 3,200 workers, Ravenscraig was put on extended holiday shutdown in early 1990, as its order book was shifted to South Wales plants. This was the ominous prelude to BSC's announcement, in May, of closure of the strip mill, and of Clydesdale Tube works, by early 1991.

The Tories were reminded that their predecessors had brought the 'big mill' to Ravenscraig 30 years earlier, to boost the Lanarkshire economy and local employment; and now they were intent on its destruction. Again, the closure announcements provoked renewed mobilisation of the Scottish campaign lobby. The STUC and its allies, and the widely representative Standing Committee for Defence of the Steel Industry, worked tirelessly to present the economic case for retention and to extend resistance. In early 1990, Scottish Conservatives made a last effort to persuade BSC into a U-turn, but to no avail, and largely retreated from the fray. Robert Scholey, chairman of privatised British Steel, disdained and ignored the Scottish Office and the campaign lobby. However, the unity of the broad coalition was already fractured and weakened. After the failure to save Gartcosh, the SNP had increasingly run a different campaign agenda, to support the claims of Ravenscraig and other plants in Scotland over the case of plants south of the border. This standpoint was contrary to that of Labour and the STUC, who had consistently backed retention of all viable plants in the interests of industrial renewal across the UK. Unfortunately, steel workers were not immune from this divisive infighting over Scottish plants versus those of England and Wales. Also, in this final battle for survival, steel workers could count on support from the miners, but they were now few in number, and no longer a force in the land.

In any case, the die was already cast, as Scholey had the freedom to make vital decisions without even having to justify them. 'Once BSC had been cut loose from political control, Ravenscraig's fate was irrevocably sealed.'[25] Yet, as the distinguished historian of the steel industry in Scotland has pointed out, whatever the reasons for closure, 'they were not the consequence of an intransigent labour force'. The record-breaking efforts of that labour force had 'contributed to the profitability of British Steel and to the BSC in its final years.'[26] No fewer than 18 production records were broken in 1987 alone, and more than 90 per cent of delivery targets met, despite the threat of oblivion. 'They deserved better,' says Brennan simply.[27] Within three months in 1991, 3,000 jobs were axed (1,800 at Ravenscraig; 1,200 at Clydesdale), leaving Ravenscraig with a workforce of 1,200, and raising the local unemployment level to over 20 per cent. The cushion of redundancy payments was welcome, especially for long-serving workers, but there was little or no alternative employment for thousands of men who wanted to work.

In January 1992, the government announced the complete closure of Ravenscraig. It was the end of an era on 24 June, as bulk steelmaking ceased in Scotland, the last shift was worked and the final slab was cast. Only Dalzell and part of Clydesdale survived the onslaught. There was a final irony in the Ravenscraig closure, as workers were awarded medals for achieving daily, weekly and monthly production records during February and March. It is little wonder that many workers threw away their medals in gestures of disgust, as their pride and effort were rewarded with redundancy and the scrap heap.[28]

Blast Furnace,
Ravenscraig (North
Lanarkshire Council)

NOTES

CHAPTER 1

As an introductory guide the classic survey, W.K.V. Gale, *Iron and Steel* (1969), gives a clear description and analysis of technical detail and work processes. Also very useful is the modern study, R. Hayman, *Ironworking: the History and Archaeology of the Iron Industry* (2005), although both works have little on Scotland.

Key background studies on Scotland for this chapter are A. Slaven, *The Development of the West of Scotland 1750–1960* (London, 1975) and C.A.Whatley, *Scottish Society 1707–1830* (Manchester, 2000).

1. R.H. Campbell, *The Carron Company*, (Edinburgh, 1961) is the standard work; for origins, H. Hamilton, 'The Founding of Carron Iron Works', in *Scottish Historical Review* (1928). B. Watters, *Where Iron Runs Like Water: A New History of Carron Iron Works 1759–1982* (Edinburgh, 1998) is also useful for social history aspects.
2. J. Shaw, *Water Power in Scotland 1550–1870* (Edinburgh, 1984), chapters 7 and 25, for coverage of the early iron industry.
3. J.M. Lindsay, 'The Iron Industry in the Highlands: Charcoal Blast Furnaces', in *Scottish Historical Review* (1977); J.H. Lewis, 'The Charcoal-fired Blast Furnaces of Scotland: A Review' in *Proceedings of the Society of Antiquaries of Scotland* (1984); G.D. Hay and G.P. Stell, *Bonawe Iron Furnace*, (Edinburgh, HMSO, 1984).
4. According to I. Donnachie, 'A Tour of the Works: Early Scottish Industry Observed', in A.J.G. Cummings and T.M. Devine (eds), *Industry, Business, and Society in Scotland since 1700* (Edinburgh, 1994), p. 46.
5. C. Evans, 'A Skilled Workforce During the Transition to an Industrial Society: Forgemen in the British Iron Trade 1500–1850', in *Labour History Review*, vol. 36, No. 2 (summer 1998).
6. H. Hamilton, *An Economic History of Scotland in the Eighteenth Century* (Oxford, 1963), p. 190.
7. Shaw, *Water Power*, p. 90.
8. Quotations in Hay and Stell, *Bonawe*, pp. 11 and 14. Also subsequent quotes this section.
9. Shaw, *Water Power*, pp. 435–6, citing translated passages in *Scots Magazine* LXI, 1799 (pp 371–5); see also later translated edition of the original, Faujas de Saint Fond, *A Journey to England and Scotland in 1784*, 2 vols, Archibald Geikie (ed.) (Glasgow, 1907). Vol. 1, chapter 7, contains the account of Carron.
10. Quoted in Watters, *Carron*, p. 17.
11. Quoted in Watters pp. 75–76, from the journal of Jacob Pattison, National Library of Scotland, MS 6322, pp. 129, 131.
12. S. Pollard, *The Genesis of Modern Management* (Harmondsworth, 1968 Penguin edition) p. 197.
13. Evans, 'A Skilled Workforce' (1998) p. 146.

14. *The New Statistical Account of Scotland: Lanarkshire* (1845), pp. 79–80.

15. J.R. Hume and J. Butt, 'Muirkirk 1786–1802: The Creation of an Industrial Community', in *Scottish Historical Review*, vol. 45, 1966.

16. E.T. Svedenstierna, *Tour Through England and Scotland in 1802 and 1803* (Stockholm, 1804), English edition, introduction by M.W. Flinn (Newton Abbott, 1973), p. 151.

17. G. Thomson. 'The Dalnotter Iron Company', in *Scottish Historical Review*, vol. 35, 1956.

18. P. Cadell, *The Iron Mills at Cramond* (Edinburgh, 1973).

19. From 'SRO Carron MSS: letter to Benjamin Roebuck, Sheffield, 16 December, 1760' in R.H. Campbell and J.B.A. Dow, *Source Book of Scottish Economic and Social History* (1968), p. 150.

20. Cadell, *Cramond*, p. 5.

21. Campbell and Dow, *Source Book*, p. 151.

22. Watters, *Carron*, p. 91.

23. Cadell, *Cramond*, p. 8.

24. Campbell, *Carron*, p. 68

25. Ibid., *Carron*, p. 69

26. Hume and Butt, 'Muirkirk'; also H. Hamilton, *An Economic History*, p. 373.

27. *New Statistical Account of Scotland: Lanarkshire*, for Carnwath Parish (1845).

28. J. Butt, 'Glenbuck Iron Works', in *Ayrshire Collections*, vol. 8 (1967–9), p. 72.

29. J. Butt,' The Scottish Iron and Steel Industry Before the Hot Blast' in *West of Scotland Iron and Steel Institute Journal*, vol. 73, no.6 (1965–6).

CHAPTER 2

Neil Ballantyne, *Ironmasters and Steelmen: Authority and Independence in Lanarkshire's Iron and Steel Industries 1870–1900*, Strathclyde University PhD (2004), chapters 2–4, is an essential reference point for malleable iron workers. I have also drawn on C. Evans, *A Labyrinth of Flame: Work and Social Conflict in Early Industrial Merthyr Tydfil* (Cardiff, 1973), an inspiring study of smelting and furnace workers.

1. Children's Employment Commission, *Parliamentary Papers (1842)*, vol. XVI, Appendix to First Report, Part 1, p. 313.

2. R.H. Franks, in 1842 Report.

3. G. Thomson, 'The Iron Industry of the Monklands: An Introduction', in *Scottish Industrial History*, vol. 5, no. 2 (1982).

4. D. Bremner, *The Industries of Scotland* (1869), reprinted in new edition, with introduction by J. Butt and I. Donnachie (New York, 1969), pp. 38, 39.

5. Ibid., p. 39; A. Miller, *Coatbridge: Its Rise and Progress* (Glasgow, 1864), p. 171.

6. 1842 Report, XVI, p. 328.

7. *Colville's Magazine*, May–June 1920.

8. Bremner, p. 34.

9. 1842 Report, XVI, p. 336.

10. M. Moss and J.R. Hume, *Workshop of the British Empire: Engineering and Shipbuilding in the West of Scotland* (London, 1977), p. 13.

11. Bremner, pp. 44–45.

12. Moss and Hume, *Workshop*, pp. 14, 16.

13. 1842 Report, XVI, p. 329.

14. Svedenstierna, *A Tour of England and Scotland*, p. 152.

15. 1842 Report, XVI, pp. 481–483.

16. Children's Employment Commission, *Parliamentary Papers (1864)*, Third Report and Minutes of Evidence, 1862, F.D. Longe, 'Metal Trades in the Northern Districts', p. 44.

17. 1842 Report, XVI, pp. 329 and 345.

18. Campbell, *Carron Company*, p. 231.

19. H.J. Fyrth and H. Collins, *The Foundry Workers: A Trade Union History* (Manchester, 1959), p. 42.

20. Tom Bell, *Pioneering Days* (London, 1941), pp. 64–65.

21. J.R. Hume and M.S. Moss, *Beardmore: The Making of a Scottish Industrial Giant* (London, 1979).

22. N. Ballantyne, thesis, chapter 4; also his article, 'The Lanarkshire Puddlers: A Case Study of Work and Wages in the Malleable Iron Industry, 1870–1900', in *Scottish Labour History*, vol. 36 (2001).

23. Bremner, p. 51.

24. Ibid., pp. 51–53.

25. B. McAulay, *Colville's Magazine*, winter 1960.

26. David Willox, *Diary 1872–1886*. Typed ms., Mitchell Library, Glasgow Collection Archives, p. 72.

27. David Willox, *Reminiscences of Parkhead, its People, and Pastimes* (1920). Typed ms., Mitchell Library, Glasgow Collection Archives.

28. James Kerr, 'The Manufacture of Wrought Iron', *The Journal of the West of Scotland Iron and Steel Institute*, vol. 3 (Glasgow, 1896), pp. 206–209, 216.

29. W. Millsop, interview with the author, 1982.

30. Ballantyne, 'The Lanarkshire Puddlers' article, p. 13.

31. *Colville's Magazine*, January 1920, p. 4.

32. Willox, *Diary*, 2 December 1873.

33. Bremner, p. 53.

34. Children's Employment Commission, 1862 Report, Minutes of Evidence, p. 45.

35. Scottish Manufactured Iron Trade Conciliation and Arbitration Board, Minutes, 22 November, 1912.

36. 1842 Report, XVI, p. 329

37. 1862 Report, examples from Minutes of Evidence, p. 44.

38. Ibid., p. 45.

39. Millsop, interview.

40. *Colville's Magazine*, autumn 1958.

41. *Colville's Magazine*, autumn 1957.

42. Children's Employment Commission, *Appendix to Second Report, 1842*, 'Trades and Manufactures', Part 2. Nail-making is included in the Report and Minutes of Evidence for 'Manufactures in the East of Scotland', reporter R.H. Franks. p. k32.

43. R. Duncan, *The Mineworkers* (Edinburgh, 2005), Chapter 3.

44. 1842, Second Report, Appendix, pp. k3, 4, 5.

45. Ibid., p. k3.

46. Ibid., p. k31.

47. Ibid., p. k31.

48. Ibid., p. k32.

49. Ibid., p. k36.

CHAPTER 3

1. A. MacGeorge, *The Bairds of Gartsherrie* (Glasgow, 1875), p. 82.

2. Ibid., p. 58.

3. Ibid., p. 59.

4. N. Ballantyne, thesis, for case study of Bairds.

5. C.A. Whatley, *The Process of Industrialisation in Ayrshire*, PhD thesis, Strathclyde University (1976).

6. 1842 Report, XVI, p. 346.

7. Miller, *Coatbridge*, pp. 171–2.

8. R. Duncan, *Calderbank: An Industrial and Social History* (Airdrie, 1984); also Census Enumeration Books for 1841–61.

9. R. Duncan, *Wishaw: Life and Labour in a Lanarkshire Industrial Community 1790–1914* (Motherwell, 1986), chapter 2.

10. R. Duncan, *Steelopolis: The Making of Motherwell c.1750–1939* (Motherwell, 1991), chapter 2.
11. A.B. Campbell, *The Lanarkshire Miners* (Edinburgh, 1979), chapter 7, p. 170.
12. Miller, *Coatbridge*, p. 171.
13. Census Enumeration Books 1851, Auchinleck parish, for Lugar.
14. Census Enumeration Books 1851–71, for Dalmellington parish.
15. Census Enumeration Books 1851–61, Kilbirnie, for Glengarnock.
16. R.D. Corrins, 'Scottish Business Élites in the Nineteenth Century: the case of William Baird and Company', in A.J.G. Cummings and T.M. Devine (eds), *Industry, Business and Society in Scotland Since 1700* (1994).
17. Campbell, *Lanarkshire Miners*, pp. 215, 223 and chapter 8.
18. Duncan, *Wishaw*, pp. 76–7, 134, 135.
19. Ibid., pp. 128–9.
20. Duncan, *Steelopolis*, chapter 7.
21. Duncan, *Calderbank*, p. 17.
22. Report of Royal Commission on the Truck System, *Parliamentary Papers.1871*, vol. 1 of 23. Minutes of Evidence, from Lanarkshire.
23. Ballantyne, thesis, p. 156.
24. Campbell, *Lanarkshire Miners*, p. 221.
25. Glengarnock Oral History Project, transcript of interview with John Ramsay, 11 January, 1980.

CHAPTER 4

1. Fyrth and Collins, *Foundry Workers*, pp. 21–5.
2. Campbell, *Lanarkshire Miners*, p. 140.
3. R.D. Corrins, *William Baird and Company 1830–1914*, PhD thesis, Strathclyde University, 1974, p. 368.
4. Ballantyne, thesis, p. 52.
5. Duncan, *Wishaw*, p. 88.
6. W.W. Knox, *Industrial Nation: Work, Culture, and Society in Scotland, 1800–Present* (Edinburgh, 1999), chapter 16 discusses this point in relation to metal and other trades.
7. Royal Commission on Labour, *Parliamentary Papers, 1892*, Part 1, vol. 36, 'Evidence before Group A: Charles Vickers and William Snow, National Association of Blast-furnacemen', 12 February 1892.
8. Ballantyne, thesis, p. 376 ff; N. Ballantyne, 'The Lanarkshire Blast Furnacemen's Strike 1890–1891', in *The Raddle: Journal of the Monklands Heritage Society*, Vol. 11, September 2006; Royal Commission, 1892, 'Evidence of Charles Vickers'.
9. Board of Conciliation for the Pig Iron Trade in Scotland. Minutes 1900–1940 (Archives, Mitchell Library, Glasgow, TD 171/3); also Ballantyne, thesis, for coverage of the Board's work.
10. Board, 19 February 1913.
11. *Colville's Magazine*, winter 1956.
12. Board, 28 November 1919.
13. N.P. Howard, 'Strikes and Lockouts in the Iron Industry and Formation of Ironworkers' Unions 1862–69', in *International Review of Social History* (1973); Ballantyne, thesis; Ballantyne, 'Lanarkshire Puddlers' article (2001).
14. Ballantyne, thesis, p. 364 ff; Duncan, *Steelopolis*, pp. 101–3.
15. *Hamilton Advertiser*, 18 March 1871.
16. Duncan, *Wishaw*, p. 90.
17. *Wishaw Advertiser*, 13 December 1873–24 January 1874.
18. *Motherwell Times*, 22 May 1884.
19. Willox, Diary, 20 September 1873.
20. St John V. Day, *Notice of Principal Manufactures of West of Scotland* (British Association, Glasgow, 1876), pp. 51–2.
21. Willox, Diary, 7, 11 and 12 July 1873.

22. Ibid., 7 June 1873.
23. Ibid., 3, 5, 7 and 9 June 1873.
24. Ibid., 29 July 1872.
25. Ibid., 28 June 1873; 18 March 1874.
26. Ibid., 16 December 1877.
27. Day, *Principal Manufactures*, p. 55.
28. SMITCAB Minutes 1897–1940 (Archives, Mitchell Library, Glasgow, TD 171/4).
29. Ibid., 26 November 1897.
30. Ibid., 19 November 1897.
31. Ibid., 4 April and 16 October 1916, for roughers dispute; 19 October, 1917.
32. Ibid., 20 November 1914.
33. Ibid., 14 May 1915.
34. Ibid., 28 February 1919; 7 April 1919.
35. 1842 Report, Vol. XVI, p. 375.
36. Ibid., p. 374 .
37. Fyrth and Collins, *Foundry Workers*, pp. 60–1.
38. Ibid., p. 41.
39. Ibid., p. 61.
40. Ibid., p. 93.
41. Ibid., p. 106.
42. Ibid., p. 114.
43. Ibid., p. 129.
44. Ibid., p. 137.
45. T. Bell, *Pioneering Days* (London, 1941), p. 64.
46. Associated Ironmoulders of Scotland, Monthly Reports, February 1917–January 1918 (National Library of Scotland, Dep. 204).
47. Fyrth and Collins, p. 147.
48. Associated Ironmoulders of Scotland, Monthly Reports for 1919 (National Library of Scotland, Dep. 204).

CHAPTER 5

1. Patrick McGeown, *Heat the Furnace Seven Times More. An Autobiography* (London, 1967), pp. 22–3.
2. P.L. Payne, *Colvilles and the Scottish Steel Industry* (Oxford, 1979) has comprehensive coverage of the early steel industry; my own books on Motherwell and Wishaw provide a popular version.
3. J. Hodge, *Workman's Cottage to Windsor Castle* (London, 1931), pp. 40–1.
4. Ibid., p. 27.
5. Ibid., p. 40.
6. *Colville's Magazine*, February and July 1920.
7. D. Shepherd, *From Halfway to Hallside* (1996), p. 42.
8. R. Duncan, *Calderbank*.
9. R. Duncan, *Wishaw*, pp. 118–9; McGeown, *Heat the Furnace*, p. 41.
10. Payne, *Colvilles*, p. 106.
11. *Colville's Magazine*, autumn 1957.
12. Payne, *Colvilles*, p. 108.
13. Multiple quotes from McGeown, *Heat the Furnace*, pp. 70–81.
14. Patrick McGeown, 'Steelman', in Ronald Fraser (ed.), *Work*, Vol. 2 (Penguin, Harmondsworth, 1969), p. 62.
15. Ibid., p. 82.
16. Ibid., pp. 34–5.
17. Ibid., pp. 79–80.
18. Ibid., p. 80.

19. *Colville's Magazine*, April 1920.
20. *Colville's Magazine*, December 1921.
21. *Colville's Magazine*, July 1922.
22. McGeown, *Heat the Furnace*, p. 10.
23. Ibid., pp. 10–11.
24. Ibid., p. 90.
25. Ibid., pp. 63–4.
26. Ibid., p. 89.
27. Royal Commission on Labour, *Parliamentary Papers 1892*, Session vol. 36, Part 1, 'Evidence before Group A', vol. 2, Hodge at Q16,334–16,544.
28. Royal Commission on Labour, Cronin, at Q16,229.
29. *Motherwell Times*, various years 1899–1913, using index to reference items.
30. *Motherwell Times*, 21 March 1913.
31. Quoted in Lorna Lewis, 'Glengarnock Steel', in B. Kay (ed), *The Complete Odyssey*, p. 182.
32. McGeown, *Heat the Furnace*, pp. 40–41.

CHAPTER 6

1. J. Hodge, *Workman's Cottage to Windsor Castle*, p. 41.
2. *Motherwell Times*, 12 and 26 January; 2 February, 1884.
3. R. Duncan, *Steelopolis*, p. 103–7.
4. Hodge, *Workman's Cottage*, p. 33.
5. *Colville's Magazine*, April 1920.
6. *Workman's Cottage*, pp. 34–5.
7. Ibid., p. 36.
8. Ibid., p. 39.
9. *North British Daily Mail*, 29 September 1886.
10. *Workman's Cottage*, p. 33.
11. Royal Commission on Labour (1892), Q16,571.
12. *Workman's Cottage*, p. 52.
13. Ibid., pp. 52–3; *Motherwell Times*, 25 September 1886.
14. *Workman's Cottage*, p. 45.
15. Ibid., p. 53.
16. *Motherwell Times*, 29 January 1887.
17. *Motherwell Times*, 4 May 1889; *Workman's Cottage*, pp. 55–9.
18. *Workman's Cottage*, pp. 84–5.
19. A. Pugh, *Men of Steel* (1951), p. 214.
20. *Workman's Cottage*, p. 283.
21. Ibid., pp. 283–4; Pugh, *Men of Steel*, pp. 216–8.
22. Scottish Manufactured Steel Trades Conciliation and Arbitration Board, Minutes, 12 May 1893 (vol. 1, 1890–1905 only, in North Lanarkshire Council Archives).
23. Royal Commission on Labour 1892, Cronin at Q15,940.
24. Conciliation and Arbitration Board, Minutes, 12 May 1893; 11 January 1894.
25. Conciliation and Arbitration Board, Minutes, 18 February and 18 March 1895.
26. N. Ballantyne, thesis pp. 395–411, for case study of this dispute; Pugh, *Men of Steel*, pp. 114–16; *Hamilton Advertiser*, 21 October 1899.
27. *Bellshill Speaker*, 23 December 1899.
28. *Bellshill Speaker*, 10 March 1900; 25 August 1900.
29. *Bellshill Speaker*, 11 November 1899; *Hamilton Advertiser*, 4 and 11 November 1899.
30. *Hamilton Advertiser*, 17 March 1900.
31. Pugh, *Men of Steel*, pp. 115–16, for all quotes in this paragraph.
32. Pugh, *Men of Steel*, pp. 145–6; *Workman's Cottage*, pp. 287–8. (Also for quotes in previous paragraph.)
33. *Workman's Cottage*, pp. 285–6.

34. James Walker, entry in W.W. Knox (ed.), *Scottish Labour Leaders 1918–1939* (Edinburgh, 1984), pp. 262–6.

35. McGeown, *Heat the Furnace*, p. 61.

36. *Motherwell Times*, 18 March and 18 April 1910; *Wishaw Press*, 8 April 1910.

37. *Motherwell Times*, 7 October 1910.

38. J.C. Carr and W. Taplin, *History of the British Steel Industry* (Oxford, 1962), p. 140; F. Wilkinson, 'Collective Bargaining in the Steel Industry in the 1920s', in A. Briggs and J. Saville (eds), *Essays in Labour History 1918–1939* (1977).

39. *Motherwell Times*, 10–31 October 1919.

40. Pugh, *Men of Steel*, p. 299.

41. Ibid., p. 294.

42. *Motherwell Times*, 7 and 14 November 1919.

43. *Motherwell Times*, 12 March and 2 April 1919.

44. Pugh, *Men of Steel*, p. 377.

CHAPTER 7

I have made extensive use of personal testimony from former workers interviewed for the Glengarnock Oral History Project (1979–80); and the Salt of the Earth: WEA Oral History Project (1999). Original tapes and typescripts for the Glengarnock Project are held in the School of Scottish Studies, Edinburgh University; a copy of the typescripts is also available in North Ayrshire Council Libraries HQ. D. Charman (ed), *Glengarnock: An Open Hearth Steelworks – the Works, The People* (Manpower Services Commission, Netherlands, 1981), is a report of the project. Mini-discs and typescripts of 'Working Lives: Iron and Steel (Lanarkshire)', part of the Salt of the Earth Project, are deposited in the National Museum of Scotland, Edinburgh (reference file SOE 199–201). A copy of scripts and discs is in Summerlee Heritage Centre, Coatbridge.

1. *Colville's Magazine*, autumn 1957.

2. *Colville's Magazine*, summer 1958.

3. Quoted in Lorna Lewis, 'Glengarnock Steel'.

4. *Colville's Magazine*, spring 1957.

5. A. Slaven, *Development of the West of Scotland*, chapter 8, has useful coverage of heavy industry during the 1920s and 1930s.

6. A. Borthwick, *Hallside – A Hundred Years* (British Steel Corporation, 1973).

7. J.A. Henderson, *Autobiography*, unpublished typescript, no date, copy in Motherwell Heritage Centre, p. 151.

8. *Colville's Magazine*, summer 1958.

9. Joe McAulay, transcript of interview, 11 December 1979.

10. *Colville Group Technical Survey* (1957), p. 30 for Clyde Iron Works.

11. *Colville's Magazine*, summer 1958.

12. Ian Murray, interview, 27 April 1999. Discs 1 and 2.

13. *Motherwell Times*, 22 January 1981.

14. *Steel News: Scottish Edition*, October 1984.

15. Murray, interview.

16. Ibid.

17. *Housing the Heroes; the Struggles of a Small Town 1919–1939*, several authors (Barrhead Community Council, c. 1983), pp. 68–70.

18. Ibid., p. 71.

19. Jack Summers, interview, 10 February 1999.

20. Jim Gardner, *The Foundry and the Foundry Worker* (NUFW, 1944), p. 12.

21. Ibid., p. 14; the other pamphlet is Gardner, *Searchlight on the Foundry* (Stirlingshire Area Committee of the Communist Party, 1943).

22. *Colville's Magazine*, spring 1956.

23. *Colville's Magazine*, summer 1965, pp. 13–14, for Fullwood.

24. S. Morrison, 'The Factory Inspectorate and the Silica Dust Problem in UK Foundries 1930–1970', in *Scottish Labour History*, vol. 40, 2005.

25. John Ramsay, interview typescript, 11 January, 1980.

26. Harry McLean, interview typescript, 4 December, 1979.

27. McGeown, *Heat the Furnace*, p. 8.

28. Anon., interview, 10 July 1980, Glengarnock.

29. Alex Fraser, interview, 20 May 1999.

30. *Colville Technical Survey* (1957), pp. 63, 79.

31. Fraser, interview.

32. *Colville's Magazine*, March–April, 1954.

33. *Colville's Magazine*, spring 1962.

34. Anon, interview typescript, 25 January 1980, Glengarnock.

35. Harry McLean, interview typescript.

36. Fraser, interview.

37. Anon, interview typescript, 25 January 1980.

38. Murray, interview, 24 September 1999. Disc 2.

39. *Motherwell Times*, 'Craig News', 10 April, 1964; *Colville's Magazine*, autumn 1960 and spring 1964.

40. Fraser, interview. Also subsequent quotes this section.

41. Annual Report, 20 January 1956, reprinted in *Colville's Magazine*, winter 1956; Payne, *Colvilles*, for other information on Craig; also D. Murray, *Sir John Craig: Sixty-seven Years with Colvilles* (no date; privately printed).

42. *Colville's Magazine*, May–June 1948, for early notices.

43. D. Charman (ed), *Glengarnock* (1981), p. 76; also Anon, interview typescript, 10 July 1980.

44. Wilkinson, 'Collective Bargaining' article (1977); also C. Docherty, *Steel and Steelworkers* (London, 1983), chapter 3.

45. Lorna Lewis, 'Glengarnock Steel', for examples.

46. Payne, *Colvilles*, p. 392.

47. *Motherwell Times*, file for 1950s and 1960s, for strikes (using index in Motherwell Heritage Centre).

CHAPTER 8

1. C. Baur, 'The Future of Steel in Scotland' in *British Steel*, autumn 1974.

2. P. Payne, 'The Decline of the Scottish Heavy Industries 1945–83', in R. Saville (ed.), *The Economic Development of Modern Scotland* (Edinburgh, 1985).

3. *British Steel*, autumn 1975; also P. Payne, *Colvilles and the Scottish Steel Industry* (1979), pp. 415–27; and his 'The End of Steelmaking in Scotland c. 1967–1993', in *Scottish Economic and Social History*, 15 (1995).

4. *Motherwell Times*, 16 and 23 May 1975.

5. *Motherwell Times*, 23 May 1975.

6. *Motherwell Times*, 17 October 1975.

7. *Motherwell Times*, 24 October 1975.

8. A. Bell and D. Harrison, 'The Steel Industry in Scotland – The Fight for a Future', in *Scottish Trade Union Review*, summer 1978; and D. Stewart, 'Fighting for Survival: The 1980s Campaign to save Ravenscraig Steelworks', in *Journal of Scottish Historical Studies*, vol. 25, No. 1 (2005).

9. D. Charman (ed), *Glengarnock*.

10. B. Sirs, *Hard Labour* (1985), p. 68.

11. *Motherwell Times* 10, 31 August, 21 September and 7 December 1979.

12. Lorna Lewis, 'Glengarnock Steel'; also Anon. interview, 10 July 1980, Glengarnock project.

13. Payne, 'End of Steelmaking', p. 72.

14. Coverage in Sirs, *Hard Labour;* and *Motherwell Times,* January–April 1980.

15. Anon. interview, 29 July 1999, Salt of the Earth Project.

16. K. Aitken, *The Bairns o' Adam: The Story of the STUC* (1997); and Stewart, 'Fighting for Survival'.

17. STUC Annual Report, 1983, p. 349; STUC Annual Report, 1984, p. 427.

18. K. Aitken, interviewing Brennan, *Scotsman,* 25 June 1992.

19. The weekly *Steel News, Scottish Edition* reported production records from 1982 onwards.

20. D. Stewart, 'A Tragic Fiasco? The 1984/5 Miners' Strike in Scotland', in *Scottish Labour History*, vol. 41 (2006); also Stewart,' Fighting for Survival'; Sirs, *Hard Labour*; Aitken, *Bairns*; and *Morning Star*, for daily coverage, April–June 1984.

21. Quoted in Stewart, 'Fighting for Survival', p. 50.

22. From my own recollections of 1984.

23. Sirs, *Hard Labour*, p. 28.

24. D. Harrison, 'The Case for Ravenscraig and Gartcosh', in *Scottish Trade Union Review*, April-July,1985; also STUC Annual Report, 1986, pp. 50–57 for Gartcosh case and campaign.

25. Aitken, *Bairns*, p. 295.

26. Payne, 'The End of Steelmaking', p. 79.

27. Brennan, quoted in Aitken, *Scotsman* article, 25 June 1992.

28. *Wishaw Press*, 26 June 1992; Matthew Hume, introduction to his pictorial booklet, *Out of the Furnace: the Lanarkshire Steel Industry* (North Lanarkshire Council, 1992).

INDEX